高职高专
国际商务应用
系列教材

跨文化交际与沟通

许雷　吴石梅　杨易 主　编

钟欣　刘太伟　苏丹 副主编

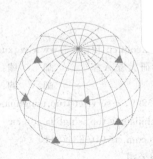

清华大学出版社
北京

内 容 简 介

  本书共8个单元，包括文化与跨文化交际、英国文化、美国文化、语言交际、非语言交际、跨文化商务交际礼仪、文化冲击、跨文化交际能力提升。本书先介绍跨文化交际基本概念、问题和理论基础，然后分析跨文化沟通的不同模式和礼仪，最后探讨如何克服跨文化商务沟通的障碍和提高交际能力。

  本书的每个单元都设有单元导读、课前活动、课内阅读、课堂练习及拓展知识，"基于技能培养，重视案例引导"是本书的主要特色。

  本书可用作高职高专院校商务英语、国际贸易、旅游管理、国际酒店管理、文秘等专业跨文化商务交际相关课程的教材，也可用作商务人员和外事人员提升跨文化交际能力的自学教材。

本书封面贴有清华大学出版社防伪标签，无标签者不得销售。
版权所有，侵权必究。举报：010-62782989，beiqinquan@tup.tsinghua.edu.cn。

图书在版编目(CIP)数据

跨文化交际与沟通：英文/许雷，吴石梅，杨易主编．—北京：清华大学出版社，2023.7
高职高专国际商务应用系列教材
ISBN 978-7-302-64300-5

Ⅰ.①跨… Ⅱ.①许… ②吴… ③杨… Ⅲ.①英语-文化交流-高等职业教育-教材 Ⅳ.①H31

中国国家版本馆 CIP 数据核字(2023)第 139162 号

责任编辑：吴梦佳
封面设计：傅瑞学
责任校对：袁　芳
责任印制：刘海龙

出版发行：清华大学出版社
网　　址：https://www.tup.com.cn，https://www.wqxuetang.com
地　　址：北京清华大学学研大厦A座　　邮　编：100084
社 总 机：010-83470000　　邮　购：010-62786544
投稿与读者服务：010-62776969，c-service@tup.tsinghua.edu.cn
质量反馈：010-62772015，zhiliang@tup.tsinghua.edu.cn
课件下载：http://www.tup.com.cn，010-83470410

印 装 者：三河市天利华印刷装订有限公司
经　　销：全国新华书店
开　　本：185mm×260mm　　印　张：10　　字　数：239千字
版　　次：2023年9月第1版　　印　次：2023年9月第1次印刷
定　　价：39.00元

产品编号：095520-01

前　言

党的二十大报告中指出，要推进文化自信自强，铸就社会主义文化新辉煌。跨文化交际课程围绕中外不同文化进行介绍，使学生在了解文化差异的同时，提升对中国文化的理解和认同，增强文化自信和自强。编者坚持"以提高跨文化交际能力为目标、以市场需求为导向、以学生为中心"的理念，注重能力培养，精心组织编写。

本书通过提供商务专题知识和文化背景展示，对部分国家文化进行描述、阐释和讨论，帮助学生在参与具体商务交际活动前，了解和熟悉相关背景知识，提高跨文化敏感度，培养跨文化交际意识；通过学习中西文化，提高批判思维意识，在增强国际商务竞争力的同时培养家国情怀，提升学生的文化自信。

本书主要面向高职学生，注重"分析问题、解决问题"能力的培养。本书遵循知识、技能、实践为一体的原则，力图让学生通过边做边学逐步熟悉行业相关的跨文化知识和技能，使学生能更好地适应和胜任未来的岗位工作。

本书注重务实与实践性，商务理念贯穿全书，主要特色如下。

（1）文化案例与实用技能并存。本书设计了企业跨文化交际案例，设置了实训课堂，重视理论教学的同时重视实务和课程实训。本书的编写本着培养学生思辨能力和自我学习能力两大原则，语言难度和知识范畴适合高职英语及其他专业二年级学生。具体而言，作为跨文化交际教学双语教材，本书基于西方主要跨文化交际理论，以国家文化为主线，将商务文化交际理论与文化相结合，以深入浅出的方式，通过任务学习、项目案例研究和关键术语解释，帮助学生领会跨文化交际中协商、对话的真谛。每单元末推荐中国传统文化及"一带一路"国家商务礼仪，帮助学生拓展视野、进行更为深入细致的研究。与此同时，本书注重结合中国"国际化"现实情况和学生的兴趣关注点组织编写内容，如介绍基于工作过程的中外企业工作模式比较、"一带一路"沿线就业地的国情特点等。

（2）突出跨文化交际能力的融通应用。本书内容分为"文化与跨文化交际""英美文化""语言与非语言交际""文化适应"四大主体模块，以选取某些国家文化为主线，将交际理论与文化相结合，使学生认识到跨文化关注的不仅仅是表面的文化特征，还要关注影响交际的各种文化因素。

其中，"文化与跨文化交际"部分（Unit 1）主要介绍跨文化交际原理，演练跨文化沟通技巧；"英美文化"（Unit 2、Unit 3）部分探讨、展示英美民族特征；"语言与非语言交际"部分（Unit 4、Unit 5）通过总结沟通方法，比较得出跨文化商务沟通的注意事项；"文化适应"部分（Unit 6、Unit 7、Unit 8）介绍不同类型语境下语言表达的特点，分析讨论商务谈判风格背后的缘由。

（3）基于工作过程，体现国际化视野。实践性已经成为跨文化交际最重要的特点之一，跨文化交际的魅力在于对现实问题的解释力。因此，本书立足双语教学，以文化教学、任务型教学等理论为指导，从跨文化交际视角剖析国际商务交流实例，以培养学生对目的语文化的兴趣及文化敏感度。

本书分为8个单元，涵盖跨文化交际各方面的主要内容。第1单元从文化的定义、重要性及文化与交际的关系入手，打开跨文化交际的大门。第2单元和第3单元分别以英国和美国为代表，分析英语国家的主要民族特征及文化属性。第4单元和第5单元从语言和非言语交际的角度探讨文化在商务沟通过程中的重要性。第6单元具体关注跨文化商务交际的礼仪，主要涉及电话、礼物、谈判、社会习俗等方面。第7单元和第8单元探讨跨文化交际过程中的经典文化价值，以此帮助学生进一步意识到风俗习惯对沟通交际的重要作用。本书拓展阅读部分主要通过对中国传统文化、"一带一路"国家的介绍，进一步拓宽学生的国际视野。

本书是广东科学技术职业学院校级金课建设研究成果，是一本理论与实践应用相结合的教材，配备多媒体课件资源，编写力求适用于高职院校各专业及其他学习跨文化沟通、交际和传播的读者。本书由许雷、吴石梅、杨易担任主编，由钟欣、刘太伟、苏丹担任副主编，前言、文化与跨文化交际部分由许雷编写，英国文化、美国文化部分由钟欣编写，语言交际和非语言交际部分由苏丹编写，跨文化商务交际礼仪部分由杨易编写，文化冲击和跨文化交际能力提升部分由刘太伟编写。全书由许雷设计大纲和体例，由许雷、吴石梅和杨易统稿。湖南环境生物职业技术学院杨帆、珠海横琴跨境说网络科技有限公司罗兴对本书进行了内容审核，特此致谢！

由于编者的水平和经验有限，书中难免会有疏漏和不足之处，恳请专家、师生和读者批评、指正。

编　者
2023年3月

目 录

Unit 1 Culture and Intercultural Communication
         文化与跨文化交际 ………………………………………………… 1

Unit 2 British Culture
         英国文化 ………………………………………………………… 17

Unit 3 American Culture
         美国文化 ………………………………………………………… 40

Unit 4 Verbal Communication
         语言交际 ………………………………………………………… 61

Unit 5 Nonverbal Communication
         非语言交际 ……………………………………………………… 78

Unit 6 Cross-cultural Business Communication Etiquette
         跨文化商务交际礼仪 …………………………………………… 94

Unit 7 Culture Shock
         文化冲击 ………………………………………………………… 114

Unit 8 Improving Intercultural Competence
         跨文化交际能力提升 …………………………………………… 133

参考文献 ……………………………………………………………… 151

Unit 1　Culture and Intercultural Communication

文化与跨文化交际

 Learning Objectives 学习目标

- 了解文化的内涵；能利用相关图示解析文化内涵、交际的模式与要素。
- 掌握交际的模式与要素。
- 掌握文化与跨文化交际及跨文化商务交际之间的关系。

 Lead-in 单元导读

　　在当今全球化商务环境中，我们需要和来自不同国家和文化背景的人进行交流。跨文化交际是人类交际的一种形式，而文化则是跨文化交际的一个核心问题。霍尔说："文化是交际，交际是文化。"①这个著名的定义把文化与交际紧密地联系在一起。但是文化与交际的侧重点又有区别：文化关注的是结构，而交际关注的是过程。虽然文化与交际相互作用，但是在跨文化交际领域，人们谈论更多的是文化对于交际的影响。因为文化决定人们如何感知和理解周围的世界，文化影响人们如何处理人际关系和日常琐事。文化和交际的关系十分密切，文化为交际提供了行为指南，也影响人们对其他人交际行为的解释。文化是什么？提到文化，有人想到文学艺术，有人想到风俗习惯，有人想到名胜古迹，有人想到宗教哲学……虽然人们常常谈论文化，但是每个人心中的文化却有不同的含义。因为，人总是生活在文化中，文化现象在人的世界中无所不在。文化在跨文化商务中表现得更为突出和重要，它是人们理念和价值观的直接体现，直接影响商务沟通效果。正如文化的定义一样，交际的定义也非常丰富和复杂。要找到一个统一而简洁的关于交际的定义并不是一件容易的事

---

① HALL T E. Silent Language [M]. New York: Anchor Books, 1959.

情。我们追求的不是所谓"正确"的交际定义,而是对于我们理解文化交际的特点有帮助的定义。

从跨文化交际的角度来看,若把communication一词译成汉语,不同的学科对它有不同的译法。如通信学把它译为"通信";心理学把它译为"交流";管理学把它译为"沟通";新闻学科把它译为"传播";语言学科把它译为"交际"。因此"交际"一词就容易被人理解为一般的语言交际,而intercultural communication也就被认为是文化背景不同的人们之间的语言交流。其实并非如此,对于"交际"一词的理解可以超越语言范畴。如非语言行为、情感交流等都是交际的范畴。同时,交际还是交际双方交流的双向过程。如果一方未参与交流或不发表任何意见,这就不是交际,当然也就达不到交际的目的,而仅仅是谈话(talk)。

交际就是属于不同文化圈的人进行的文化交际,包括语言交际和非语言交际。从信息传播的角度来看,在进行表达,尤其是第二语言的交际时,不是说仅仅用语言清楚地表达自己的思想观点或听懂对方语言的表层意义就算完成信息的输出与接收了。这是远远不够的。要使所传输的信息能被接收者准确地接收,除了熟练使用作为传输工具的语言外,还要理解语言背后所隐含的种种影响和制约语言理解的深层文化意义。这种深层文化意义常常决定着信息传输与接收的成败。

跨文化交际(intercultural communication)是指不同文化背景的人之间的交际,是一门跨多门学科的交叉学科。随着我国经济不断发展,综合国力不断提升,与世界各国在经济和科技领域的合作增多,跨文化交际日趋频繁,由此产生的文化冲突不断涌现。由于交际双方文化背景不同,社会环境各异,思维方式和交际方式有别,因此会对同一词、同一句话、非言语行为和事物产生不同的理解、不同的联想和不同的所指意义。在跨文化交际过程中由文化差异导致的误解在所难免。根据跨文化交际模式,有效交际是交际双方必须理解对方发出的信息,必须领悟非语言含义、言语含义和信息含义。换言之,meaning is in the person, not in the word。

跨国企业是当今经济全球化的主要载体。对跨文化企业来说,有效沟通是跨文化企业经营管理的出发点。这是因为在跨文化企业中,管理者和员工、消费者面对的是不同文化背景、语言、价值观念、民族心理和交际行为的合作者,经营与管理在异文化沟通和交流的基础上进行,如何克服不同文化的差异,并据以创造出企业独特的文化,进行卓有成效的管理沟通,从而最大限度地发掘企业的潜力和价值,值得讨论。2016年,世界教育创新峰会与北京师范大学中国教育创新研究院共同发布了《面向未来:21世纪核心素养教育的全球经验》研究报告。报告对比分析了5个国际组织和包括中国在内的24个经济体的21世纪核心素养框架。从全球范围来看,许多核心素养的选取都反映了社会、经济、科技、信息发展的最新要求,内容虽有所不同,但目标都是适应21世纪的挑战。结果表明,最受国际组织和各经济体重视的七大素养分别是沟通与合作、创造性与问题解决、信息素养、自我认识与自我调控、批判性思维、学会学习与终身学习,以及公民责任与社会参与。沟通与合作包含跨文化素养,是学生的基础素质,是指在一个文化异质化、多样化的世界中,个体能够与他人适恰地交际并且完成工作任务的各类品质的综合。

国家文化有其优秀、独特的一面,文化对跨文化商务交际的影响涉及营销、组织激励、人员选拔、团队管理与建设等各个方面。如何对待跨国文化,是决定企业在经营管理中能否取得成功的关键。通过本单元的学习,学生应了解文化的概念和特点,分析跨文化沟通技能和文化影响沟通的方式,并对文化有更深入的理解。

Pre-class Activity 课前活动

Understanding the cultural differences of any nation which we choose to do business with will require great efforts. To be successful in international business and to be good citizens of the international community, we should learn to honor and respect our own cultures and also to develop an appreciation, tolerance, and respect for others' cultures. All of us, no matter how hard we try, will commit some social blunders related to cultural differences. The important thing to remember is that if we create an environment of mutual understanding and respect through our attitude and actions, our blunders are usually met with understanding and forgiveness. Have you ever realized that your life is greatly affected by the culture and communication you're living in? What are culture and communication? How can we avoid culturally related business blunders in China? What's the relationship between them? Please have a discussion with your neighbor and air your view to your classmates.

Reading 课内阅读

Reading One: The Iceberg Model of Culture[①]

The Iceberg Model of Culture was proposed by Edward T. Hall (1976), who indicated that the smaller part of the iceberg above water represents those aspects of your own culture that you are aware of. The larger part of the iceberg represents deep culture which is hidden below the surface of conscious awareness (Figure 1.1). Deep culture consists of feelings, thoughts and behaviors which you may never have reflected on because they are so familiar that they are part of you. This model which is often used in seeking to understand cultural differences reflects a psychoanalytic（心理分析）frame of reference.

Becoming bicultural or multicultural（多文化的）is a process of becoming more accepting and tolerant of different ways. This is not easy but it may be possible to understand that the person you clashed with did not intend to upset you, but was simply doing what they were used to. In societies where relationships are hierarchical（分等级的）, and where communications are indirect, a breach of the cultural norms may be regarded as a serious matter. Many miscommunications are based on poor understanding of the other person's culture. If you are bilingual you can change to the language of the other person; if

---

① 改编自：周小微. 跨文化商务交际[M]. 北京：对外经济贸易大学出版社，2011.

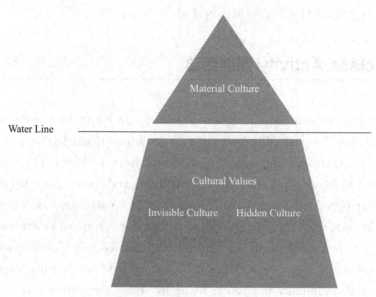

Figure 1.1　The Culture Iceberg

not, you are at a disadvantage. Similarly, if you are bicultural or multicultural you can choose to behave in ways that are expected and acceptable in a different culture. It becomes second nature to greet people by shaking their hands in Sweden, nodding in England, kissing in France and putting your hands together under your chin in India. If you are a man you will understand that it will probably be **taken amiss**((可能因误会)对……生气;因……而见怪).①

Not every difference is as easy to come to terms with as those of greeting. One problem we may face is what to tolerate and what not to tolerate. We may need to examine our legal, moral and ethical boundaries. Some share the value that customs and habits can be tolerated if they are not harmful to use or to another person, nor destructive to another person's property. In some parts of the world, some of us may find the law morally and ethically unacceptable and we have to decide where to draw our personal boundaries and how to protect ourselves in such situations.

Another challenge can be found around food. It is very helpful to educate ourselves on the food habits of different cultural and religious groups. It is embarrassing for roast pork to be served to a Muslim or a Jew. If you have grown up with dietary prohibition with accompanying beliefs, you may choose to stick to the food you are used to even if you no longer believe in the reasons. The philosopher Arthur Koestler writes about his grandfather insisting that his Jewish(犹太人的)grandson should not be confined to the same rules as he was. One young development worker made the decision to eat meat when she was working in remote areas of Ecuador(厄瓜多尔)although she was a confirmed vegetarian.

---

① 参考中华人民共和国中央人民政府网(http://www.gov.cn/govweb/fwxx/ly/2007-01/26/content_597607.htm)。

Reading Two: The Cultural Onion: Layers of Culture

Culture can be intepreted in different ways. We look at culture from a special perspective this time to compare culture with an onion. Similar to an onion, culture consists of many layers (Figure 1.2). Much like what has been described in the culture iceberg, the outer layer of culture consists of symbols, such as the way people are dressed, the language they speak, the cars they drive, the food they eat, the houses they live in, etc. It includes all the direct contents in the field of culture-language, food, housing, all the products of arts and so on. This is the level of explicit culture.

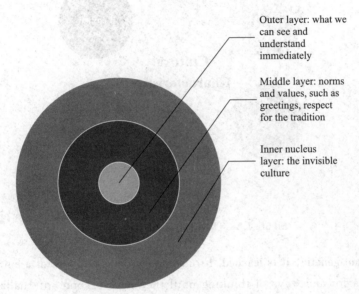

Figure 1.2 The Cultural Onion

Middle layer: criterion (标准) and sense of worth. Criterion and sense of worth lead to the recognition of being right and wrong. People's behaviors and ways of communication are affected by criterion and sense of worth. But they are not visible, despite their influence on what happens in the observable surface.

Deep layer: basic judgment. People have a basic judgment on the questions: What is life? How to deal with the problems appearing in life? What is beauty ... This is the deepest layer: the level of implicit culture. Understanding the core of the culture onion is the key to successfully working with other cultures. The core consists of basic assumptions, a series of rules and methods to deal with the regular problems that it faces. Every culture has developed its own set of basic assumptions. These assumptions are very difficult for an outsider to recognize, and can be measured by dimensoins. Each dimension is like a continuum. Cultures differ in how they deal with these dimensions, but they do not differ in needing to make some kind of response. These methods of problem-solving have become so basic that, like breathing, we no longer think about how we do it.

Reading Three: The Characteristics of Culture

Six characteristics of culture have special significance for intercultural communication: ①Culture is learned, ②culture is shared, ③culture is dynamic, ④culture is symbolic, ⑤the **facets**(一个方面)of culture are interrelated, and ⑥culture is ethnocentric (Figure 1.3).

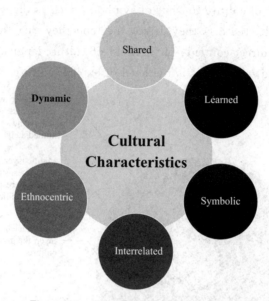

Figure 1.3　The Characteristics of Culture

Culture is not genetic; it is learned. From infancy on, members of a culture learn their patterns of behavior and ways of thinking until they have become internalized. The power and influences of these behaviors and perceptions can be seen in the ways in which we acquire culture. Our culture learning proceeds through interaction, observation, and imitation. A little boy in North America whose father tells him to shake hands when he is introduced to a friend of the family is learning culture.

All of this learning occurs as conscious or unconscious conditioning that leads one toward competence in a particular culture. This activity is frequently called acculturation, denoting the total activity of learning one's culture.

Culture is shared. Members of a culture share a set of ideas, values, and standards of behaviors, and this set is what gives meaning to their lives, and bonds them together as a culture. For example, almost all people living in China share the Chinese language, dress themselves in similar styles, eat similar food, and celebrate many of the same holidays or festivals. When Spring Festival comes, for example, Chinese people all over the world will celebrate it in the same way: wearing new clothes, setting off firecrackers, eating dumplings, extending good wishes for the New Year, having antithetical couplets on doors and hanging lanterns.

Culture is dynamic（动态的）. As with communication, culture is ongoing and subject to fluctuation; cultures seldom remain constant. As ideas and products evolve within a culture, they can produce change through the mechanisms of invention and diffusion.

Invention is usually defined as the discovery of new practices, tools or concepts that most members of the culture eventually accept. The invention of television is a good example of how products reshaped a culture.

Change also occurs through diffusion, or borrowing from another culture. The assimilation of what is borrowed accelerates as culturTheTes come into direct contact with each other. For example, as Japan and North America share more commerce, we can see Americans assimilating Japanese business management practices and the Japanese incorporating American marketing tactics.

Culture is symbolic. People have culture primarily because it enables them to communicate with symbols. Symbols allow people to develop complex thoughts and to exchange them with others. Language and other forms of symbolic communication, such as art, enable people to create, explain, and record new ideas and information. In China, children usually give senior parents a birthday cake with a large peach on it on their birthdays, wishing them a long life. The cake here is called Good-health Cake, a symbol of good health and longevity.

Facets of culture are interrelated. This characteristic serves to inform us that culture is like a complex system. As Hall clearly states, "You touch a culture in one place and everything else is affected." The women's movement in the US may serve as an example of this. Women's movement may be but two simple words but the phenomenon has been like a large stone cast into a pond. The movement has brought about change in gender roles, sexual practices, educational opportunities, the legal system, career opportunities, and even female-male interaction.

Culture is ethnocentric. The characteristic of ethnocentrism being centered on one's own group, might well relate most directly to intercultural communication. The important tie between ethnocentrism and communication can be seen in the definition of the word itself. Keesing notes (1974) that ethnocentrism is a "universal tendency for any people to put its own culture and society in a central position of priority and worth". Ethnocentrism, therefore, becomes the perceptual window through which a culture interprets and judges all other cultures. Ethnocentrism leads to a subjective evaluation of how another culture conducts its daily business. That this evaluation can only be negative is clear if you realize that a logical extension of ethnocentrism is the position that "our way is the right way". Most discussions of ethnocentrism even enlarge the concept to include feelings of superiority.

As we have seen, culture is extremely complex and influences every aspect of our lives. There are, however, specific aspects of culture that are of particular interest in the study of intercultural communication. For the sake of simplicity and to put some limitations on our discussion, we will examine three major elements: *perceptual processes, verbal processes, and nonverbal processes*.

These three interacting cultural elements are the constituent elements of intercultural communication. When we combine them, as we do when we communicate, they are like the components of a **quadraphonic**（四声道的，立体声的）stereo system — each one relates to and needs the others to function properly. In our discussion, we separate these elements to identify and discuss them. But in actuality they do not exist in isolation nor do they function alone.

Read to Learn More

Definitions of Culture and Intercultural Communication

Have you ever realized that your life is greatly affected by the culture and communication you're living in? You've probably heard about many different definitions of the word "communication". But what on earth are culture and communication? Let's take a look in this section.

Culture is such a pervasive（普遍的；扩大的）and evasive（含糊的；逃避的）concept that so many scholars have tried to convey it from different aspects and disciplines. Definitions of culture range from all-encompassing（包罗万象的）ones, such as "it is everything", to narrow ones, like "it is opera, art and ballet". The most widely accepted definition is created by Edward T. Hall(1959), "Culture is the total accumulation（积累）of beliefs, customs, values, behavior in situations and communication patterns that are shared, learned and passed down through the generations in an identifiable group of people".

Intercultural communication is a form of communication that aims to share information across different cultures and social groups. It seeks to understand how people from different countries and cultures act, communicate and perceive the world around them. Many people in intercultural business communication argue that culture determines how individuals encode（把……编译成）messages, what medium they choose for transmitting them, and the way messages are interpreted. As a separate notion, it studies situations where people from different cultural backgrounds interact.

Reducing Stereotypes and Prejudice in Intercultural Communication

To have effective intercultural communication, people need to ensure that messages are communicated accurately. As Gundykunst (1998) writes: "To communicate effectively, we must transmit our messages in a way that strangers (people of other cultural backgrounds) can understand what we mean, and we need to interpret strangers' messages in the way they meant them to be interpreted."

Stereotypes are a form of generalization about some group of people, or a means of organizing images into fixed and simple categories that are used to stand for the entire collection of people. This kind of generalization may be positive or negative. But most stereotypes tend to make us feel superior in some way to the person or group being stereotyped. Stereotypes ignore the uniqueness of individuals by painting all members of a group with the same brush.

Stereotypes can be found in the media because of the biases of writers, directors, producers, reporters and editors. But stereotypes can also be useful to the media because they provide a quick identity for a person or group that is easily recognized by an audience. When deadlines loom, it's sometimes faster and easier to use a stereotype to characterize a person or situation, than it is to provide a more complex explanation.

Prejudice refers to negative attitudes towards other people that are based on faculty and inflexible stereotypes. It is an unfair, biased, or intolerant attitude towards another group of people (Lusting & Koester, 2013).

Stereotypes and prejudice can lead to errors in interpretations of the behaviors of others. They can also lead to errors in interpretations about the future behaviors of others. Successful intercultural communication requires an ability to move beyond stereotypes and prejudice and to respond to the individual objectively.

Empathy

(1) Be open-minded in terms of information sharing.

(2) Be imaginative in correctly drawing the picture of other's situations.

(3) Show a commitment or strong willingness to understand our culturally different partners in any kind of situation.

Involve

(1) Involve others in your world and involve yourself in others'.

(2) Don't build walls between people and learn from one another.

Be Wise

(1) Be aware of how to interact with people with respect and knowledge.

(2) Show maturity of thought and action in dealing with people.

Cross-cultural Awareness

(1) Learn a new language and be exposed to a new culture.

(2) Get rid of our ethnocentric tendencies and accept another culture on its own terms.

(3) Become more aware of the influence of cultural values.

It is important to remember that although many moments of discomfort occur when we are interacting with people from other cultures, no one culture is inherently better or worse than any other. Each culture has its own set of values, norms and ways of doing things that are considered "right" for it. That one culture's way of doing things is right for its people does not necessarily mean it is "right" for everybody, and herein lies the potential conflict in cross-cultural encounters.

In-class Activity 课堂练习

Ⅰ. Comprehension questions.

Go over this unit and try to make an assessment on what you have learned with the following questions.

1. What do culture and intercultural communication mean? Please give some examples to support your points.
2. What are the two main images of culture?
3. In intercultural communication, what may become a barrier to a successful communication? Then how can you avoid it? Please give some detailed suggestions.

Ⅱ. Comparative analysis.

Insert the phrase "intercultural/cross-cultural communication" into a search engine on the Internet and report to your group what you can find out about the studies of intercultural communication both at home and abroad.

Ⅲ. Culture image exploration.

Think about the following similes and metaphors. How do you think about culture related to these references?

1. Culture is like an iceberg.
2. Culture is our software.
3. Culture is like the water a fish swims in.
4. Culture is the grammar of our behavior.

Ⅳ. Case study.

1. Is "龙" a dragon?

Huang Guangqin studies in America. One day she had a chat with her hostess Susan about family relationships and child-raising.

She said, "in China, the parent is more likely to make the decision for the child, and the children are not supposed to make their own decisions when they're young."

Susan said, "Really? But in America, every person is encouraged to act independently and be responsible for his actions, so children are encouraged at an early age to start making decisions. This allows them to learn to express their individual desires and make choices."

Guangqin said, "But whatever the parents do, they do it for the sake of their children since all the parents in China hope their children will be dragons."

After hearing that, Susan felt very surprised, "Dragons? Why do your Chinese parents hope their children will be *Monsters*?"

Questions

(1) What is the conflict of the case?

(2) Why does Susan think that Chinese parents hope their children will be *Monsters*?

2. What does wenhua/culture mean?

Dear tutor,

I have heard or read "wenhua" a lot which sounds a bit confusing to me. I remember you told me that "wenhua" means culture, but the other day I saw a notice in Chinese at our dorm and I asked the cleaning woman to read it and tell me what it was about. But she said,"对不起,我没文化,不识字。"

While yesterday, I asked Liu Ming, my Chinese Kungfu coach, to a gallery show but Mr. Liu declined by saying,"我没文化,欣赏不了。"

This evening I attended a lecture by Mr. Wang about tea. I enjoyed it very much. Wang started the lecture by saying,"茶文化也是我们的传统文化之一。"

Question

Could you tell me what wenhua/culture means in the above situations?

Ⅴ. Word match.

In Column A there are some key ideas in intercultural communication. Please match each item with its corresponding information in Column B.

A	B
1. communication	A. the communication between African Americans and European Americans
2. international communication	B. the process whereby one person transits a message through a channel to another, with some effect
3. interpersonal communication	C. the communication between culturally similar individuals
4. interracial communication	D. the communication between two people
5. intercultural communication	E. the comparison of cultural phenomena in different cultures
6. cross-cultural communication	F. interactions among people from different nations
7. intracultural communication	G. face-to-face interactions among people of diverse cultures
8. intrapersonal communication	H. communication we have with ourselves

Background Information 背景知识

1. Culture(文化)是一个非常广泛的概念,给它下一个严格和精确的定义是一件非常困难的事情。哲学家、社会学家、人类学家、历史学家和语言学家们一直试图从各自学科的角度来界定文化。根据 Edward T. Hall 的定义,文化是人在社会历史发展过程中所分享与传承下来的信仰、习俗、价值观和行为方式的总和。有比较宽泛的定义,如文化是无所不包的知识和行为的综合;有比较狭窄的定义,如文化是政治、经济、教育、文学、艺术、科技、语言等的总和;还有把文化定义为物质和精神的总和。物质文化就是人类所创造的物质;精神文化是指物质之外的一切,如价值观念、行为准则、思维方式、语言表达、信仰、世界观等。物质文化是精神文化的外在表现,是人类社会的表层现象,容易发现、容易理解;精神文化则是人类社会深层现象,经过人类社会代代相传,约定俗成。对于跨文化交际这门课的学习而言,与价值观念、行为准则、思维方式、语言表达、世界观等有关的文化范畴即精神文化更适合跨文化交际研究。

2. Intercultural communication(跨文化交际)是指在特定的交际情景中,具有不同文化背景的交际者为了共享信息而进行的口语交际。通俗来说,就是如果你和外国人打交道(由于存在语言和文化背景的差异),应该注意什么问题,应该如何得体地去交流。

3. Cultural onion(文化洋葱),我们把文化比喻成一个洋葱,有层次之分。文化由外而内分为四层——符号、英雄形象、礼仪和价值观。

4. Cultural iceberg(文化冰山)是指我们把文化比喻成冰山一样,具有双重性特征——显性与隐性。文化像冰山一样,露出水面的只是很少的部分,更多的是隐藏在水下的部分。我们不能禁止差异的存在,但是可以预防冲突,只要双方了解彼此的深层文化,增强文化差异意识,用宽容的态度对待由文化差异引发的误解,不要把与本国文化不同的行为、观点、观念、做事方式、思考方式、决策方式、沟通方式误认为是"错的""不可行的"或"不可取的",而应认为这是"不同",是"差异",同时再以换位的思维方式去思考:为什么这些方法在另一国是行之有效的呢? 认识到这些道理,不同文化背景的人在共事和合作时,就可以探索双方是否可以互相学习,双方的文化是否可以融合并产生互补效应。

5. Stereotypes(文化定势)最初由美国社会学家 Lippmann 提出的。人们用一个简化的认知方法将具有相同特征的一群人或民族种族塑造成一定形象。不同文化背景的人交流,就好比"瞎子摸象",在对对方文化不甚了解的情况下,其认识只能说是肤浅的、片面的,触摸到的仅仅是大象庞大身形的一个部分而已,但如果只是由此对对方文化得出单一甚至是扭曲的结论,那势必会阻碍两种文化之间积极有效的交流。跨文化交际的一个重要基础就是要有接受差异的意识,而不是武断设定对错的标准,否定差异的积极意义。如果在交际过程中,我们像摸象的瞎子一样,非但没有意识到自己的认识具有相当的局限性,反而还否定他人的看法,那就对跨文化交际起到了消极的作用。如何才是积极有效的跨文化交际呢? 首先要建立"差异"的意识,并以此取代固有的"对错"观念。在此前提下,了解对方文化在价值观念、思维模式、感知等方面的表现,并和自身文化的相应部分做出一定的比较和分析,在差异中寻求最佳的融合方式,从而使两种文化达到最和谐的共存。

6. Prejudice(文化偏见)是指基于错误的观点而对一群特定的人或民族具有的消极的不公平的看法。

Cultural Kaleidoscope 文化万花筒

联合国教科文组织 2001 年 11 月 2 日在其第三十一届会议上通过了《世界文化多样性宣言》。该宣言旨在将文化多样性作为一种生命力,把捍卫文化多样性作为与尊重人的尊严密不可分的一种应尽的义务。不同的民族之间会有文化差异。然而,差异不是差错。虽然差异是混乱的渊源,但差异也是能量的渊源和动力的来源。以水为例,要是没有水平的差异,水就不会流动,就会变成死水。只有差异才能使水流动。既然我们不能也不应该使每个人和每种文化都变得一样,既然我们应该保持文化之间的差异,让我们的世界更为多姿多彩和更加美丽,我们就需要更进一步了解不同文化和文化差异的意义。通过比较,我们能更进一步地了解不同的人,并更进一步减少不同文化之间的误解。本部分将提供多种跨文化视角和观点,融知识性、趣味性于一体,拓展跨文化视野。

30 Ways to Know If You Are a Chinese

If you are a Chinese...

1. You prefer your shrimp with the heads and legs still attached.

2. You like congee with thousand-year-old eggs.

3. You tap the table when someone pours tea for you.

4. You carry a stash of your own food whenever you travel (travel means any car-ride longer than 15 minutes). These snacks are always dried and include dried plums, mango, ginger, and squid(鱿鱼).

5. You wash your rice at least 2-3 times before cooking it.

6. You keep a thermos of hot water available at all times.

7. Your house is covered with tiles instead of carpets.

8. You sing Karaoke and play mahjong in your spare time.

9. You leave the plastic cover on your remote control.

10. You use the dishwasher as the dish rack.

11. You take showers at night and your hair sticks up when you wake up.

12. You drive around looking for the cheapest petrol.

13. You unwrap Christmas gifts very carefully, so you can reuse the paper.

14. You also use the jam jars as drinking glasses.

15. Your toothpaste tubes are all squeezed paper-thin.

16. When there is a sale on toilet paper, you buy 100 rolls and store them in your closet or in the bedroom.

17. You don't use measuring cups.

18. You stir eggs with chopsticks instead of a whisk.

19. You twirl your pen around your fingers.

20. If you are a male, you clap at something funny and if you are a female, you giggle whilst placing a hand over your mouth.

21. When you are sick, your parents tell you not to eat fried foods or baked goods due to yeet hay(上火).

22. You know someone who can get you a good deal on jewelry or electronics.

23. You own your own meat cleaver and sharpen it.

24. You bring oranges (or other products) with you as a gift when you visit people's

homes.

25. You fight over who pays the diner bill.

26. You live with your parents when you are 30 years old and they prefer it that way. Or you're married and 30 years old; you live in the apartment next door to your parents, or at least in the same neighborhood.

27. You like the number 8 or 6.

28. You hold an umbrella even if it is a sunny day.

29. You have a Chinese knick-knack(小玩意)hanging around your cell phone or your bag.

30. You see the truth in this and then send it to all your Chinese friends.

中国传统文化 1

Business Etiquette in Belt and Road Countries
"一带一路"国家的商务礼仪

丝绸之路的开辟和兴盛,体现了中华民族"厚德载物"的精神和气度。"厚德载物",就是说要对天下万物采取友善的态度。对于人类自己,不仅对待本民族的人要友好相处,而且对待其他民族也要友好相处。古书《中庸》说"怀柔远人",特别强调大国对周围小国的态度要友好,要学习他们好的东西,对于他们还做不到的事情,则要给予帮助。大国不要用武力欺负小国。汉唐等朝代的君王对西域各族人民就是这么做的。

丝绸之路的畅通,不但使中国的物产、文化传到西方,也使西方的物产、文化(如西域的蔬菜、药材、花卉、乐器和印度佛教等)不断传入中国,从而促进了中国古代文明的发展。中国灿烂的古代文明和善于吸收国外文明精华是分不开的。由此,丝绸之路是通商之路,更是文化交流之路。在新时代推进"一带一路"经济合作倡议过程中,我们会与更多的文化相遇,它们各自不同的文化和传统都会在企业的日常经营中时时刻刻地、淋漓尽致地表现出来。下面我们将分章节进行商务文化简介和梳理,希望能够提供一些可资借鉴的启示。

印 度

印度宗教盛行,跟印度人进行商务贸易往来,需了解其民族文化特点、礼仪礼节和商务特点。

(1) 语言的准备:英语是印度的商业语言,与印度人相见应递英文名片。资料的翻译要准确,公司和产品的介绍资料必须是英文的。

(2) 生意报价要留有较大余地:印度人有砍价的习惯。在生意商谈中,物美价廉的产品肯定是首选。

(3) 学会赞美和恭维:印度人喜欢谈论他们的文化业绩、印度的传统、其他民族的情况。不要谈及个人私事、政治情况。

(4) 不要迟到:印度人的时间观念虽不是很强,但跟他们做生意千万不要在见面时迟到。即使等一两个小时也要按约定时间提前到达,这样会在谈生意过程中占主导优势地位。

India is a country where religion is prevalent. To conduct business and trade with

Indians, it is necessary to understand its national cultural characteristics, etiquette and business characteristics:

(1) Language preparation: English is the business language of India. When meeting with Indians, English business cards should be presented. The translation of the materials should be accurate, and the introduction materials of the company and products must be in English.

(2) There must be a lot of room for business quotations: India is a nation of bargaining, and in business negotiations, high-quality and low-cost products are definitely the first choice.

(3) Learn to praise and compliment: Indians like to talk about their cultural achievements, Indian traditions, the foreign situation about other people, but do not talk about personal affairs, or political situations.

(4) Don't be late: Indians are not very time-conscious, but when doing business with them, don't be late for the meeting because of their weak sense of time. Arrive early at the agreed time, even if you wait an hour or two, and this will dominate the business negotiation process.

Intercultural Tips 跨文化拓展知识

习语和典故的文化渊源

文化包括内隐的文化和外显的文化,其中大部分都是内隐的,这就好比一座冰山,我们只能看到其中的一部分,而大部分的冰山存在于海平面下。外显的文化包括服饰、食物、建筑、文物古迹、艺术文学作品、科学技术成果等。而内隐的文化则以价值观为核心,是一系列观念和信仰的集合。价值观是看不见、摸不着的,但却对人们的行动起着规定性的作用。人们在社会化的过程中不自觉地通过交际的方式习得所处文化的价值体系,将其融入自己的潜意识当中,并在实际的生活当中践行该体系。可见,了解一个国家的文化,有必要深层次地了解该文化的价值体系。而英语文化中有大量的习语和典故,承载着丰富的文化内容。

(1) 英语习语和典故反映出宗教对语言的影响。汉语中的很多表达受到佛教影响,如"醍醐灌顶""回头是岸""七级浮屠"等。英语中的很多习语和典故源自《圣经》,其中很多还包含圣经中的人物,如 the apple of one's eye 掌上明珠;an eye for an eye 以眼还眼;as greedy as Ahab 像亚哈一样贪婪;as devout as Abraham 像亚伯拉罕一样虔诚;as forceful as Samson 像参孙一样力大无穷;as poor as Job 像乔伯一样穷等。再次,英语中的格言也不例外,如 God helps those who help themselves. 天助自助者;Do as you would be done by. 己所不欲,勿施于人;Man proposes, but God disposes. 谋事在人,成事在天等。

(2) 不同文化中动、植物的词汇往往会承载不同的文化意蕴。horse(马)代表辛苦劳作;serpent(蛇)代表邪恶;sheep(绵羊)、goat(山羊)、lamb(羔羊)也是《圣经》中经常出现的动物,sheep 和 lamb 代表温顺和柔弱,而 goat 则有贬义,英语中有这样的说法 separate the

sheep from goats，意为区分好人和坏人。dove(鸽)和 olive branch(橄榄枝)象征和平和希望，是源于洪水和诺亚方舟的故事。而 fig-leaf(无花果树叶)代表遮羞布，是源于亚当和夏娃以无花果树叶遮体的故事。

(3) 英语习语和典故是生产、生活实践的结晶。如人类早期的活动与 bush 关系非常紧密，于是有了这样的表达：beat about/around the bush 拐弯抹角地讲话，绕圈子；A bird in the hand is worth than two in the bush.—鸟在手胜过双鸟在林。在同大海的接触中，人类将对大自然的敬畏做了如下表达：all at sea 茫然不知所措。

由此可见，语言是文化的载体，习语和典故已经渗透到英语文化的方方面面，发挥着深远而微妙的作用，因此要了解英语文化，必须充分理解并感受这种影响。

Movie to See 观影学文化

Please watch the movie *Lost in Thailand*（《泰囧》）with your classmates and discuss what intercultural elements are involved in it.

Unit 2　British Culture

英 国 文 化

 Learning Objectives 学习目标

- 了解英国文化背景知识、英国社会与生活。
- 熟悉英国人文景观和宗教习俗。
- 熟悉英国人的民族特征和性格特点。
- 掌握应对中英文化差异的正确态度和得体方式。

 Lead-in 单元导读

所谓文化,是指一个社会的整个生活方式或一个民族的全部活动方式。一般来说,文化分为两类。一类称为"正式文化",包含文学、艺术、哲学等社会科学及各种自然科学的成果,集中反映了人类的精神文明和物质文明;另一类称为"普通文化",即人类生活中一系列不同的特征,如风俗习惯、价值观念、礼仪禁忌、庆典节日、衣食住行,等等。两种文化在人们的交往中所起的作用不同,一个国家的正式文化对每个人固然有影响,但最有影响的还是普通文化。普通文化不仅影响着跨文化交际中的信息传递、交流和沟通,而且对人们能否迅捷有效地学习语言、提高外语能力也起着至关重要的作用。

英国文化具有浓厚的宗教色彩。英国人具有强烈的民族自豪感、幽默感及宽容心,自由和自律的文化精神是英国文化特性中极具闪光点的部分。英国人是具有阶级意识的民族,对于出身的贵贱和等级较许多其他西方国家更为敏感。在谈及英国文化特性时,不能不考虑到英国文化的复杂多样性。

英国位于西北欧,南隔英吉利海峡与法国为邻,东对荷兰、丹麦等国,西邻爱尔兰共和国。全国总面积为 243 610 平方千米。英国是一个岛国,全称为大不列颠及北爱尔兰联合王国,由大不列颠岛、爱尔兰岛东北部及许多的小岛屿构成。英国全境可分为苏格兰的高原区、英格兰东南部平原区、威尔士山地及北爱尔兰区。英国属海洋性气候,由于受到大西洋湾流的影响,比其他国家同一维度的地方要更加温润且温和。英国常年降雨,由于一系列低气压潮的影响,每天的天气变化无常。

英国人口由英格兰人、苏格兰人、威尔士人和爱尔兰人组成。英国民族包括最早从地中海来的伊比利亚人、凯尔特人、罗马人、盎格鲁-撒克逊人、丹麦人和诺曼人。英国主要民族为英格兰人,只有盎格鲁-撒克逊才是英格兰人的真正始祖。英国人传统上喜欢被人称为英格兰人、苏格兰人、威尔士人或者爱尔兰人,不愿意被通称为英格兰人(English),否则可能引起其他民族的反感。这不只是个感情问题,苏格兰有自己的国会和宗教,威尔士有自己的语言和文化,爱尔兰在宗教和民族所属问题上分为两大派。

英国人具有自己独特的思维和行动方式,有着区别于其他国家的品质和特点。例如:英国人具有与他人不同的孤傲特质;不愿接受新生事物的保守思想;讲究文明用语和礼貌的良好习气;酷爱独居和个人自由的天性;感情不外露的冷淡与缄默的性格;自我嘲笑的英式幽默;等等。此外,英国人具有特殊的风俗习惯,尤其是与皇家有关的风俗习惯更为独特。比如:英国人比较矜持庄重、生活刻板,外貌有崇尚"绅士"和"淑女"之风。英国绰号"约翰牛"就是个头戴礼帽、足蹬长靴的矮胖绅士形象。由于天气变化无常,英国人衣着不分年龄,但是他们喜欢通过打扮和化妆进行形象管理。此外,英国人比较守规矩,忌讳插队,忌问女士年龄,以及不喜欢在市场上讨价还价,但他们有喝酒和给小费的社会习气。

英国虽小,但历史悠久,有着许多著名的古迹。本章着重介绍伦敦的名胜古迹,包括圣保罗大教堂、大不列颠博物馆、海德公园、伦敦塔、白厅、白金汉宫、格林尼治天文台和杜莎夫人蜡像馆等,分别描述这些名胜古迹的地理位置、历史背景、建筑特色、艺术特点和使用价值。英国文化深受基督教的影响,特别是基督教新教在英国被赋予了特殊的地位。宗教在英国社会生活中起着重要的作用,如结婚到教堂举行仪式等。宗教对英国文学作品也具有深远的影响。

伴随着经济全球化和互联网的普及,不同国家和不同民族之间的文化交流和商务往来变得越来越频繁,文化多元与文化杂糅的现实使得跨文化交际与沟通能力更显重要。因此,熟知所学语言国家的文化背景知识是培养跨文化交际能力的重要组成部分。通过本单元的学习,你将了解英国的自然地理轮廓、人口构成、性格特征、风俗习惯、名胜古迹,并对英国的宗教文化有进一步的理解。

Pre-class Activity 课前活动

England is the first home of many of the modern world's most popular sports. English people are great lovers of competitive sports. It is so natural for them to begin talking with a sports discussion even when they are neither playing nor watching games. They still have an admiration for sportsmanship, for playing with respect for the rules and the opponents and for winning with modesty and losing with good temper. Can you figure out which sport is the most popular one in the UK? And which sport is regarded as the most English of all games and reflects the English character?

Reading 课内阅读

Reading One: A Brief Introduction to the UK

The UK is located in Western Europe between the North Atlantic Ocean and the North Sea, lying to the northwest of France, from which it is separated by the English Channel, and to the west of the Netherlands and Denmark. Its official name is the UK of Great Britain and Northern Ireland. Great Britain includes England, Scotland, and Wales.

The capital of the UK is London which is also the largest city of this country. Other large cities include Glasgow, Birmingham, Liverpool, and Edinburgh. The UK has a total area of 94,058 square miles (243,610 sq km). Much of the topography of the UK consists of rugged, undeveloped hills and low mountains but there are flat and gently rolling plains in the eastern and southeastern areas of the country. The highest point in the UK is Ben Nevis at 4,406 feet (1,343 m) and it is located in the northern UK in Scotland.

The climate of the UK is considered temperate despite its latitude. Its climate is moderated by its maritime location and the Gulf Stream. However, the UK is known for being very cloudy and rainy throughout much of the year. The western parts of the country are the wettest and also windy, while the eastern portions are drier and less windy. London, located in England in the south of the UK, has an average January low temperature of 36℉ (2.4℃) and a July average temperature of 73℉ (23℃).

The Union Jack, or the Union Flag, is the flag of the UK. As a symbol of unity, the Union Jack is a transnational flag full of historical significance. The Union Jack has been in existence since 1606, when England and Scotland merged, but changed to its current form in 1801 when Ireland joined the UK. The crosses on the flag relate to the patron saints of each entity—St. George is the patron saint of England, St. Andrew is the patron saint of Scotland, and St. Patrick is the patron saint of Ireland. In 1606, when England and Scotland were both ruled by one monarch (James Ⅰ), the first Union Jack flag was created by merging the English flag (the red cross of Saint George on a white background) with the Scottish flag (the diagonal white cross of Saint Andrew on a blue background). Then, in 1801, the addition of Ireland to the UK added the Irish flag (the red Saint Patrick's cross) to the Union Jack.

The National Anthem is God Save the King. The British National Anthem originated as a patriotic song first performed in 1745. It became known as the National Anthem from the beginning of the nineteenth century. On official occasions, the first verse is sung, and the second verse is occasionally sung as well. The National Anthem is played whenever the

Queen or the King makes a public appearance and is played by the British Broadcasting Corporation every night before closedown. It is also sung at the end of all Remembrance Day services, medal ceremonies for Team GB (representing all countries), and England and Northern Ireland football matches (the Scottish using Flower of Scotland and the Welsh using Land of my Fathers).

The Queens or the Kings of Britain are representatives of the "constitutional monarch". This means that although she or he is officially the head of the state, the country is actually run by the government, led by the Prime Minister. The English Bill of Rights Act of 1689 curtailed the power of the sovereign and confirmed the Parliament's place at the heart of the English constitution. From this date English Monarchs (now British Monarchs) would rule in partnership with Parliament. The official of the late Queen (1926—2022) is "Elizabeth the Second, by the Grace of God of the UK of Great Britain and Northern Ireland". The Queen has ruled longer than any other Monarchs in British history. Her reign has seen her travel more widely than any other monarchs, undertaking many historic overseas visits. She has been an important figurehead for the UK and the Commonwealth during times of enormous social change. Queen Elizabeth II (Elizabeth Alexandra Mary) was born on April 21, 1926 at 17 Bruton Street, London. Her birthday is officially celebrated in Britain on the second Saturday of June each year. The day is referred to as "the Trooping of the Colour", and the official name is "the Queen's Birthday Parade". Queen Elizabeth II ascended the throne on February 6, 1952 upon the death of her father, King George VI. Her Coronation, at Westminster Abbey followed on June 2, 1953. The Queen used to live at Buckingham Palace in London.

The British Pound is the currency of the UK. The currency code for Pounds is GBP, and the currency symbol is £. The British Pound is the oldest currency still in use today, as well as one of the most commonly converted currencies. As the fourth most traded currency, the British Pound is the third most held reserve currency in the world. The UK's central bank is the Bank of England.

In speaking of John Bull, an image immediately appears in our mind. He is short and fat, with a tall hat on his head and a pair of boots on his feet. It is the nickname for Britain. Originally, John Bull denoted generally Britain or any Englishman in the seventeenth century, just as Uncle Sam referred to the US in the nineteenth century and became the symbol of America in 1961. In the eighteenth century, a Scottish writer named John Arbuthnot (1667—1735), who wrote five political satire pamphlets, collected them in 1721, in a book called *The History of John Bull*, in which he bitterly and vividly depicted the frankness, uneasiness and funniness of a gentleman called John Bull, in order to exemplify the Englishmen in the Spanish War over the succession to the throne. He described him so vividly and with such remarkable truth to life that the nickname spread far and wide, and has become a synonym for Britain which everybody knows.

Much of the UK's history is known for the British Empire, its continuous worldwide trade and expansion that began as early as the end of the 14th century, and the Industrial Revolution of the 18th and 19th centuries. The formation of the British race is long and complicated. Actually, the UK has a long history that consists of several different invasions, including a brief entry by the Romans in 55 B.C.E. In 1066 the UK area was part of the Norman Conquest, which aided in its cultural and political development. In 1282 the UK took over the independent Kingdom of Wales under Edward I and in 1301, his son, Edward II, was made the Prince of Wales in an effort to appease the Welsh people. The oldest son of the British monarch is still given this title today. In 1536 England and Wales became an official union. In 1603, England and Scotland also came under the same rule when James VI succeeded Elizabeth I, his cousin, to become James I of England. A little over 100 years later in 1707, England and Scotland became unified as Great Britain. In the early 17th century Ireland became increasingly settled by people from Scotland and England and England sought control of the area (as it had for many centuries before). On January 1, 1801, a legislative union between Great Britain and Ireland took place and the region became known as the UK. However, throughout the 19th and 20th centuries, Ireland continuously fought for its independence. As a result, in 1921, the Anglo-Irish Treaty established the Irish Free State which later became an independent republic. Northern Ireland, however, remained a part of the UK which is today made up of that region as well as England, Scotland, and Wales. Since the 19th century, the population growth has been increasingly slow. The limitations of immigration are the principal stabilization factors. There are of course other factors, for example, the fall of the birth rate.

Today the UK is considered a constitutional monarchy and a Commonwealth realm. The executive branch of the UK's government consists of a Chief of State (King Charles III) and a head of government (a position filled by the Prime Minister). The legislative branch is made up of a bicameral Parliament consisting of the House of Lords and the House of Commons, while the UK's judicial branch includes the Supreme Court of the UK, the Senior Courts of England and Wales, Northern Ireland's Court of Judicature and Scotland's Court of Session and High Court of the Justiciary.

Reading Two: Character and Manners of British People

Different people have different qualities and attitudes, and the British people have their own ways of thinking and acting. It is difficult to generalize about the British. The characteristics of the people living in different regions of different social classes vary enormously. Some of the descriptions below are limited to the upper and upper-middle classes, particularly in the south of England.

Exclusiveness

The British people, especially the English people, is best-known for their exclusiveness. This means, "I am English. You stay away from me. I am exclusive. I am quite happy to be myself. I do not need you. Leave me alone." It is very difficult to know such a man who does not talk much, never says anything about himself, does not show much emotion and hardly ever gets excited. Why do English people have this characteristic? Perhaps there are many reasons, two of which are quite important. One is the special geographical location of Britain; the other is its distinct historcal development.

Britain is an island country which is cut off, separated and isolated from the rest of the world. First it is cut off by the English Channel from the rest of Europe, and then it is separated from the rest of the civilized world. So the special geographical location isolates Britain and its people as well. When the British are in Britain, they do not even regard themselves as Europeans for the Europeans are foreigners to them. And within the country, if you say "English" instead of "British", you sometimes annoy the Scots and the Welsh who are very proud of their separate nationality.

Another reason is perhaps a matter of history. English people take enormous pride in their history. If you ask English people why they are so exclusive, standoffish and thinks themselves better than most people in the world, they will say, "why, we've been educated in that way." They will tell you a lot of things they are proud of. They might tell you that the King James Bible and Shakespeare's plays have had an incalculable influence on Western culture and culture in the world; the British Parliament has a long history; as early as 1215 when the rest of the world was suffering under arbitrary kings and royal power, in England they were able to develop a certain amount of parliamentarism; there was an Industrial Revolution as early as the 18th century and other things.

Conservativeness

Conservativeness is taken as another feature of the English people. The Americans say that the English people always need 20 or 40 years to do things that they do today because the English people are so conservative that they have to wait a long time before they are prepared to try something new. Perhaps this is an exaggeration, but there may be some truth in it. Englishmen think their way of doing things is always the best, and always the most normal. So an Englishman is not very interested if somebody in America has a new idea. He is very careful. He will say, "Be careful. It might be dangerous."

There are many examples to show this. One is that the British people have been slow in adopting rational reforms, such as the metric system. They suffered inconvenience from adhering to the old ways, yet they did not want the trouble of adopting new ones. In 1966, it was decided that decimal money would become the regular form in 1971; in the 1960s the twenty-four clock was at last adopted for railway timetables. Furthermore, the public attitude to the monarchy illustrates conservativeness, too. The majority of the English people hold an affection and reverence for it. You seldom hear them complaining about the high cost of the trappings of the monarchy, and in particular of the royal yacht. In fact, you can perceive many voices and reasonable arguments in favour of the monarchy. For the majority of the British people, they accept it and take it for granted. However, there is a growing disillusionment with the Royal Family and the cost of maintaining it in these days of rising unemployment. The marital problems of three out of the four children of the Queen have also caused concern. The Queen volunteered to pay taxes for the first time in 1993. Another example is that the British people do not accept change because they are told so. They favour the old ways. In Britain, all the houses, even in big cities like London, Liverpool, Manchester and Birmingham, had fireplaces in the past. When central heating was developed in the US, the English people thought this was a horrible thing. They said that this was going to ruin the health of the people. Until 1960 they continued to have the fireplace in most towns. And then in 1960, a law was passed saying that you could no longer have open fires in the house. Then they installed electric stoves which looked much like fireplaces. This is what some British people consider "a long-established tradition" that they would be most unwilling to lose. Even today, some people build a house with an open fireplace.

Politeness

For the British people, being polite means showing consideration for others. The British people do not readily ask you to do anything inconvenient for them. They prefer to wait for such service to be offered, rather than ask for it. If they do want to ask, you would hear them say so with an implied apology like, "I know the trouble I am causing you, but would you mind..." or "I don't really like asking you, but...". Sometimes the British people make offers simply out of politeness, not really expecting them to be accepted, so you reject the offers with the same politeness. Similarly, it is often polite to refuse an offer of service by replying "Oh, please don't bother". In the everyday life of the British, "Excuse me" is heard as an apology for troubling somebody. "Sorry" expresses regret for an unconscious disturbance; "Sorry" also replaces "no" when you cannot accede to a request. And "Pardon?" or "Sorry?" rather than "What?" is the more polite way of asking somebody to repeat what he has said. A bare "Yes" or "No" is considered very rude when you reply to an offer. "Please" and "Thank you" are quite common words for the British people who are particular about saying these. The British people are also quite particular about table manners. When you are invited to dinner in a person's home, you should not arrive early since the hostess is preparing for your visit. Being ten minutes late is excellent. At table, it is advisable to sit up straight, copy others, gaily ask what to do if you are not sure and keep the conversation going. As to when to leave, there is no rule, but it is most impolite to stay too late. The British people usually do not cry and shout in public. They do not cry in public even if they are very unhappy. If they can't help crying, they must cover their faces with their hands or handkerchiefs to restrain their feelings.

Love of Privacy

The right to privacy and personal freedom is unquestioned by the British. Perhaps it is the lack of space that has fostered and maintained their fierce individualism. There is a common saying among the British people, "My home is my castle. The wind can come in, but the Kings and Queens and human beings can never come in without my permission." When an Englishman moves into a new house, he often builds a fence around the house to separate himself from his neighbours. So deeply does the British man immerse himself in his private interest that he can sometimes quite ignore the fact that the world is rocking precariously. Everything is fleeing just as long as nothing disturbs his favorite "castle".

Stiff Upper Lip

There is another quality of the British people showing their mentality which is called "phlegm". It means calm and undemonstrative behavior. The British do not show their feelings very much. They do not show their emotion if they are very happy and nor if they are sad. Rigid formality is familiar to the upper classes. So some people say that the upper-class English man is like a cold fish that has just come out of the ice. When you travel by underground in London between seven o'clock and nine o'clock every morning, there are six million people in the underground in London, but you cannot hear a sound because everybody is sitting in silence behind his or her newspaper. And the only word they speak to each other is "sorry" when they get up and walk out fast. So when you walk through the underground station in the morning and there are millions of people moving about, you only hear their feet and you don't hear them talking much. This reluctance to communicate with others is demonstrated in another case. When you work at a factory, the guy you work with may not tell you anything about himself. You may work for years with him, yet you don't even know where he lives, how many children he has and what his interests are. Some English people tend to be like that. Therefore, you may feel that the English people are very cold towards others.

Sense of Humor

"He has no sense of humor" is often heard in the UK, where humor is highly valued. The English sense of humor is self-deprecating, that is the act of laughing at oneself. An Englishman laughs at his own faults, his own shortcomings, his own failures and his own embarrassment. He even laughs at his own ideals. This is an attitude towards life rather than the mere ability to laugh at jokes. This attitude is never cruel or disrespectful or even malicious. There is a story connected with this. When someone laughs at a woman who is well over thirty and does not get married, an English person would express disapproval by saying, "Why does he laugh at her misfortune?" So the quality is observable in the individual and the criticism. Englishmen do not laugh at a misfortune, a failure or a tragedy. They do not laugh at a cripple or a madman, either. Sympathy is felt to be much stronger than laughter in this case.

Reading Three: British Customs and Habits in the UK

The British people have their own customs, particularly the customs associated with the Royal Family. Their traditions and habits are quite different from those of the Chinese. Here are some important ones.

Unit 2 British Culture
英国文化

Talking About the Weather

What do the Englishmen usually talk about in their daily life? The first thing they usually talk about is the weather. There are probably two reasons why the English people love this subject. One is the uncertainty of the weather. In Britain the weather is constantly changing. Some people even say, "One can experience four seasons in the course of a single day!" So you may laugh when you see in London that the Englishmen are wearing raincoats or carrying umbrellas on a bright sunny day. Another reason is that talking about the weather, unlike discussing politics, seems a way of being friendly, without getting heated. The weather is a subject which is quite safe to talk about.

"Ladies First"

"Ladies First" is also a British custom, though it is less observed today than it used to be. The reason seems to be the fact that women are the equals of men in having the vote, taking paid employment and receiving higher education, but there is still the feeling that they need protection. It is still considered polite to let a woman go first, to protect her from traffic, to help her get on and get off the bus and to do many other things for her.

Gardening

The British always love gardens. Walk down the street on a summer evening and everybody's out watering or weeding. In fact, until television arrived, gardening used to be the most popular hobby in Britain. Nearly two out of three Britons thought of gardening as "outside housework".

Driving on the Left

Until the early 19th century, traffic used to drive on the left in most European countries. But nowadays they have all changed over to the right, all except Britain. Fortunately, visitors to Britain soon get used to looking right instead of left when they cross the road.

Fish and Chips

Former British Prime Minister Winston Churchill called fish and chips "the good companions". In Britain, over 382 million servings of fish and chips are consumed per year. Fish and chip shops used to be the only take-away food shops in Britain. The food was wrapped in newspaper and eaten with your fingers. Today there are a lot more choices. People have been used to eating Indian, Chinese, Italian and American "fast" food.

Three "Don'ts"

The British have the habit of queuing—lining up one after another, such as getting on the bus, getting on the train or buying something. There is seldom any jumping in the queue. If somebody jumps the queue, the British people look down upon him or her. They think that he or she is ill-bred, and take a remarkably dim view of such behavior. In England, you should never ask a woman her age. Women do not like others to know their ages. They think it is very impolite of you to ask their ages. Don't try to bargain in Britain when you do the shopping. The British do not expect or welcome bargaining. Sometimes they consider it losing face. The British people seldom bargain, they just buy what they want at what they think a reasonable price, and take such a practice for granted.

Three "INGS"

Three "INGS" refer to betting, drinking and tipping, the ending for each of which is ING. The British people are great lovers of betting. They bet mainly on horse racing and bingo. Drinking is a habit of the British people. Most men have the habit of drinking beer, wine and so on. There is another type of drinking, the drinking of tea. British drinking habits are severely regulated. The British have also become accustomed to tea-drinking. It is said that the British are the biggest tea consumers, and use up a quarter of the world total of tea production. Tipping is a custom which the British have. As elsewhere in the West, the tip depends on the type and extent of the service you have received. In some hotels, a service charge of 10 to 15 percent will be added to your bill.

Three Royal Traditions

Playing the flute is one of the royal traditions. Every morning after breakfast, the King listens to the playing of a flute by the royal flutist who does so outside the dining-hall for a quarter of an hour. This is a tradition inherited from Queen Victoria.

The changing of the King's guard is another of the royal traditions. There are two places in which the ceremonies take place. One ceremony is in front of Buckingham Palace. The other is at Whitehall. Both take place at eleven a.m. on weekdays and at ten on Sundays. The King's guards, dressed in red coats and black trousers, a white belt, in white gloves, with a glittering sword at the waist and a tall black fur hat on the head, hold this colorful military ceremony in front of Buckingham Palace. The daily ceremony of changing the household cavalry guard occurs in front of the Horse Guard building.

The third is a royal ceremony involving only the monarch. Annually, the British King makes a parliamentary speech, the ceremony for which is rather solemn. He starts out from Buckingham Palace in a brilliant carriage and arrives at the Palace of Westminster by the side of the Thames. When he is seated on the throne in the House of Lords, he sends a messenger with a black walking stick in his hand to the House of Commons at the other end of the Palace to inform them of the King's speech. But the gate of Commons is always closed. When he gets there, he knocks at the door three times with his stick. After the approval of the Speaker, the guard opens the gate and lets him in, and he conveys the King's words and bows to the Speaker. Then the Speaker leads all the members of the House of Commons to the House of Lords and attends the speech.

Lavatory

The word "lavatory" literally means a place for washing the hands and face, but it is really a genteel name for the water closet, i.e. the "W.C.", a place where you relieve yourself. And the English have some very strange habits connected with this. The English have evolved the words "the Ladies' Room" or "the Ladies", "the Gentlemen's Room", or simply "the Gents", or the "Men's Room". If you want to go to the lavatory, you may say, "I want to go to the 'Men's Room', or 'Ladies' Room'." Sometimes you might say "I want to wash my hands". When children want to go to the lavatory, they simply say, "I want to go somewhere."

Read to Learn More

Scenic Spots and Historical Sites

Britain is a small, ancient collection of countries which are plentifully stocked with the artistic and historical legacy of a particularly interesting past. The landscape in Britain varies greatly not only from region to region, but from country to country. There are also many historical sites and scenic spots, especially in London such as Westminster, the British Museum, Hyde Park, the Tower of London and others. Dr. Johnson once said of London that "when a man is tired of London he is tired of life; for there is in London all that life can afford". London is not as perfect as that but it can offer us something to see.

Westminster

Parliament Square at the end of Whitehall is bounded by Westminster Palace on the east and Westminster Abbey on the south. Westminster Palace is the seat of the British Houses of Parliament, which is the largest Gothic edifice in England, covering eight acres and located in the heart of London. The hall has witnessed many dramatic events, such as the condemnation of Charles I. The remainder was burnt down in the Great Fire in 1834. The present perpendicular structure was erected in 1840—1867 under the direction of Sir Charles Barry. The most popularly symbolic part of the House of Parliament is the 315 foot Clock Tower, famous for housing the largest and most "authoritative" clock in the world and for its 13-ton bell, called "Big Ben". It was named after Sir Benjamin Hall, Commissioner of Works when it was erected and its resonant chimes can be heard all over London.

Across the Parliament Square stands St. Margaret's, a small but not-to-be-missed 15th-century church with the finest stained-glass window in the country and more importantly, Westminster Abbey. This is where sightseeing in London begins for most travellers. Westminster Abbey is a veritable national shrine. Many of the country's greatest literary and scientific figures are buried in the abbey such as Geoffrey Chaucer, Edmund Spencer, Robert Browning, Isaac Newton, and Charles Robert Darwin, among others. There are also monuments to well-known statesmen and many of England's monarchs are buried here. Therefore, the abbey enshrines many of the traditions and commemorates many of the achievements of the British people.

The British Museum

The British Museum is in London's Great Russel Street; it consists of the British National Museum of Antiquities and Ethnography and the British National Library. It was founded in 1753 when Sir Hans Sloane, a physician and naturalist, gave his library and collection of coins, antiquities and paintings to the country. Originally it was housed in Montague House, Bloomsbury, but it was moved to the present building between 1826 and 1850. The museum is financed by Government funds and is managed by a board of 25 trustees. Services to the public include lectures, guided tours, portable taped tours, photographic and photocopying facilities and the sale of publications and replicas. There is a restaurant and a lecture theatre.

The museum's collection of antiquities is organised into three main departments. One comprises Greek and Roman, Egyptian, Western Asian, Oriental, British and Medieval antiquities; the other two are the departments of coins and metals and of ethnography. Much of the collection is magnificent, but much of it can be merely exhausting, depending on your interest. The Print Room exhibits one of the world's greatest collections of drawings and prints, including works by Leonardo and Michelangelo. The British Museum Library is one of the largest and richest in the world. There are many treasures and, in particular, many unique manuscripts, including an autograph of Shakespeare. It is especially strong in English books of all kinds and of all times, particularly in the world's earliest printed books including the Guttenberg Bible. Karl Marx once came to study and work in the museum library regularly and completed most of his famous book *Das Kapital* (*Capital*) there.

Hyde Park

Hyde Park, in the centre of London, is one of the world's most famous city parks. It covers 341 acres (140 hectares) extending westward from Park Lane to Kensington Gardens. There are roads through the park, but pedestrians can walk freely over the beautifully landscaped grounds. At the northeast end is Marble Arch which is famous for its lovely plants and the world-famous Speakers' Corner, where outdoor orators make their eloquent free speeches on wooden soap boxes. It is the symbol of the bourgeois democracy. Forming an arc from the northern centre of Hyde Park toward the southeast is the Serpentine, a 41-acre (16-hectare) lake. It is a favorite spot with Londoners who come out during the fair weather months to sit for hours in the sun or to row or bathe in it. There are some swans on the clear lake. South of the lake is Rotten Row, a fashionable bridle path where you can go for a long stroll or ride on horseback.

The Tower of London

The Tower of London is an ancient fortress occupying nearly 13 acres. It is situated on the east side of the city and on the northern side of the Thames. The Tower is surrounded by a ditch, formerly fed by the Thames but now dry. Gardens surround it on the north and west, and an embankment borders the river on the south. Two lines of fortifications enclose the inner bail, in which can be found the magnificent White Tower, flanked by four turrets. There are two chapels within the Tower walls; the Norman St. John's Chapel, London's oldest church which is situated in the White Tower, and St. Peter and Vincula, which was burned and rebuilt in 1512. Executions took place both within the tower and on

Tower hill. Many of those executed were buried in the chapel of St. Peter and Vincula. The tower was not only a state prison from Norman times until now, but was a royal residence at intervals from the reign of Stephen until the reign of James. Inside you can see a collection of old armour and instruments of torture.

St. Paul's Cathedral

St. Paul's Cathedral, the biggest and most well-known church in London, is a typical example of the architecture of the Renaissance. The original St. Paul's, of which John Donne was made dean in 1621, was severely damaged during the Great Fire of 1666. Sir Christopher designed and personally supervised every stage of the building operation of St. Paul's Cathedral. He had great mathematical and engineering skill and used the classical style with great imagination. It took thirty-five years to complete it. The dome was a brilliant feat of engineering in its time and the church is noted for its beautiful Baroque proportions. Wall paintings, stone and bronze carvings inside the cathedral are masterpieces of the eighteenth-century art, especially the delicate carvings. The pleasant chimes of the 17-ton bronze bell perform, as it were, a most splendid church music. You can ascend not only to the Whispering Gallery to test its mysterious acoustics, but also to the ball on top of the spire above the dome, from which there is an extraordinary panorama of London. It survived German bombing of the Second World War, even though the neighborhood all around it was almost completely ruined.

Whitehall

Whitehall, the most important street in London, is named after the ancient sprawling Whitehall Palace that had successive monarchs until it was destroyed by fire in the 18th century. The only survival from the old palace was luckily the Banqueting Hall, which was designed by Inigo Jones in about 1620 and which is one of the most beautiful buildings in London. Whitehall is a short wide thoroughfare, where some of the most important offices, such as the Home Office, the Treasury, and War Office, are located, each in its own mansion. Pigeons fly here and there on the pavement and around the column and walk to and fro. Two fountains cast plumes of water into the air, and through the spray we can see the National Gallery, which contains one of the most valuable collections of paintings in the world. The square is also famous for political demonstrations. Two 18th-century buildings, Nelson's Old Admiralty and the Horse Guards, are especially notable. Sightseers may gaze at a magnificently uniformed soldier who sits motionless on a beautiful horse, guarding the gateway to the Horse Guards, a well-known military building with a huge parade ground where once a year the King watches the ceremony of Trooping the Colour. Opening into Whitehall is the narrow unimposing cul-de-sac of Downing Street and across from it are the offices of New Scotland Yard, the headquarters of the London police.

Buckingham Palace

Buckingham Palace is the monarch's present London home, facing St. James's park. It was built for the 1st Duke of Buckingham and Normandy, on John Sheffield, the site of

Arlington House after its demolition in 1703. As is known to all, Buckingham House was bought by George III for his wife in 1761 and the royal family moved there from St. James's Palace. It was rebuilt in the Palladian style by John Nash in the reign of George IV and then the building became known as Buckingham Palace. When Victoria came to the throne, she made it the royal palace. In the palace can be found the Marble Hall, Sculpture Gallery, the Picture Gallery, the Throne Room, the Drawing Room, the Library, the Royal Stamp-Collecting Room, the Grand Staircase and Vestibule, well over 600 rooms and halls in all. The grounds cover 40 acres, there are collections of famous paintings and of furniture, most of which are works dating from George IV's time. Since 1993, Buckingham Palace has been open to the public during the summer months only.

The Royal Greenwich Observatory

The Royal Greenwich Observatory is about five miles down the river from central London. The old buildings of the Observatory are on the highest hill in Greenwich Park, but now the Royal Observatory has moved to Herstmonceux Castle in Sussex on account of the London pollution. But the prime meridian of longitude and official mean time is still reckoned from Greenwich for the purposes of geography and navigation. The terrace beside the Observatory gives a splendid view over London. Tourists like to watch the time-ball descent precisely at 1 p.m. Planetarium shows are given at stated hours.

Madame Tussaud's

Madame Tussaud's, a famous exhibition of about 300 life-size wax figures in London, was founded by Marie Tussaud (1761—1850). She modelled from life such noted men as Rousseau and Benjamin Franklin after she had learned her art of wax modelling from her uncle. She exhibited these and added other figures. Madame Tussaud's Exhibition was opened on the present site in Marylebone Road in 1884. It was damaged by fire in 1925, but the original moulds were saved, and it reopened in 1928. Portrait sculpture was carried on by her descendants until the death of her great-great grandson Bernard Tussaud in 1967. Wax portraits continue to be made in the exhibition's studios.

Religion in Britain

There are many religious denominations in the UK. Few English people actually belong to a denomination, but most of them are normally Christian. Religion is not now, as it was in the 19th century, an important factor in the national life; less than 1% of English people regularly attend church. There are five main features of the British worship: unity among the churches, social responsibility, the keeping-up with the time, no "Christian" political party and a widespread interest in religion. Religion is playing an increasingly less important role in the social life of Britain. It is of much significance in literature and art, in social life and in Western civilization.

The Church of England

The most important denomination is the Church of England. It is the established church of the English nation, though perhaps a quarter of the people belong nominally to other religious denominations and many others can be said to have no religious attachment. The Church of England is also called the "Anglican Church". The Church of England today is all-inclusive, having the ability to be both Protestant and Catholic. This is one of its important features. There is the "high church" and the "low church". A high church looks rather like a Roman Catholic Church. In a high church, candles may be lit. Incense may be used. The priest may wear various kinds of robes. The church is highly decorated. By contrast, a "low church" service is as simple as confessions and the church may be rather bare. It seems to have more in common with the nonconformist churches.

The Free or Nonconformist Churches

The main nonconformist denominations in England are the Methodist, the Congregational, the Baptist, the Quakers (the Society of Friends), the Presbyterian Church, the Pentecostal Church, the Salvation Army, and the Puritans.

Methodism sprang from the revival of the Church of England by John and Charles Wesley at Oxford. Now the Methodist Church is the main religion of the people in many northern mining and industrial areas, and also in Wales. English Methodists have a regular form of church service. They also make much use of the lay preachers.

Puritanism arose in the late 16th century. The Puritans were dissatisfied with the condition of the established Church. They wished the ceremonies to be simplified, the organization under archbishops and bishops to be abolished and the moral rule to be strict. They insisted that man should purify life and thus the name, Puritan. At the end of the 16th century and the beginning of the 17th century, many Puritans suffered from persecution, and some of them went to America as immigrants. They denounced many common pleasures as sinful and corrupting.

The Quaker religion (or the Society of Friends) was founded in the 17th century. They have no ministers and no organized services. They meet on Sundays and speak only when they have something important to say. They frequently worship in silence. They believe strongly in peace and helping people in trouble.

The Congregational Church was founded in the late 16th century and the Baptist Church in the 17th century. The Baptists insisted that each church should be independent, free from any interference from outside. The Presbyterian Church was founded in the 16th century. It adheres to the Calvinist doctrine. Both carry on and put into practice the ideas of the Puritan Church.

Other Religious Denominations

There are many other religious denominations in Britain besides the Church of England and the Nonconformist Churches.

There are about 450,000 Jews in Europe. More than half of them live in London. Jews still tend to marry Jews, for both racial and religious reasons. But among the young generation this is happening less and less.

The leader of the Roman Catholic Church in Britain is the Cardinal Archbishop of

Westminster. The UK is divided into eight Catholic provinces, four in England, two in Scotland, and one each in Wales and Northern Ireland. Each province is controlled by an archbishop and is divided into dioceses, each of which is headed by a bishop.

The Churches in Scotland are almost in every respect similar to the Low Church section of the Anglican Church. They have a similar kind of service and share the same apostolic succession (the passing on through bishops and priests of the powers and mission that was handed by Christ to his apostles).

The Churches in Wales are Calvinist or Presbyterian. This type of church is of purely Welsh origin, drawing its members from a large section of the Welsh-speaking population. It is not an established church, but it is a member of the British Council of Churches. The Calvinist Church is the Sunday school; adults as well as children go to the church to study the Bible. In England and Scotland only children attend such schools.

In-class Activity 课堂练习

Ⅰ. **Comprehension questions.**

Go over this chapter and try to make an assessment on what you have learned with the following questions.

1. Where is the UK? And what is it made up of?
2. What are the major characteristics of the British? Please give one example of each characteristic and talk with your partner.
3. Why do the British like to talk about the weather?
4. Where does sightseeing in London begin for most travelers?
5. What is the most important religious denomination in Britain?

Ⅱ. **Comparative analysis.**

Insert the phrase "English Characters and Manners" into a search engine on the Internet and report to your group what you have found out about the studies of intercultural communication both at home and abroad.

Ⅲ. **True or false questions.**

Alice has met Ms. Merrick, a Western English teacher, several times on campus and chatted with her. At the end of conversations, Ms. Merrick often says, "Come over and visit me sometime." So, one evening Alice decided to go and pay a visit. Alice knocked on the door of Ms. Merrick's apartment and after a moment, Ms. Merrick opened the door. But she didn't look very happy to see Alice. Instead of inviting Alice in, she said, "Can I do something for you?"

( ) 1. In this case, Ms. Merrick just makes polite invitations instead of real invitations when she converses with Alice.

(   ) 2. Alice's dropping by or casual visiting was regarded as impolite.

(   ) 3. Making an appointment in advance is the basic politeness rule in Western countries.

Ⅳ. Case analysis.

1. Why did the GM have difficulty in getting a Suzuki or Mini?

A British general manager upon arrival in Thailand refused to take his predecessor's car. The Thai finance manager asked the new GM what type of Mercedes he would like, then. The GM asked for a Suzuki or a Mini, anything that could be handled easily in the congested traffic in Bangkok. Three weeks later, the GM called the finance manager and asked about prospects for the delivery of his car. The Thai finance manager lost his reserve for a moment and exclaimed: "We can get you a new Mercedes by tomorrow, but a Suzuki takes much, much longer." The GM asked him to see what he could do to speed up the process. After four weeks the GM asked to see the purchase order for the car. The purchasing department replied that, because it would take so long to get a small car, they had decided to order a Mercedes. The GM's patience had run out. At the first management meeting he brought the issue up and asked for an explanation. Somewhat shyly, the predominant Thai management team explained that they could hardly come to work on a bicycle.

2. Rudeness or discrimination?

In London's Heathrow Airport, airport staff who ate in the employees' cafeteria complained about rudeness by cafeteria employees from India and Pakistan who had been hired for jobs traditionally held by British women. And the Asian women complained of discrimination. A communication expert was asked to tape talk on the job to see what was going on, and then he had Asian and British employees listen to the tape together. When a customer coming through the cafeteria line requested meat, the server had to find out if he wanted gravy on it. The British women asked, "Gravy?" The Asian women also said: "Gravy." But instead of rising, their intonation fell at the end. During the workshop session, the Asian women said they couldn't see why they were getting negative reactions, since they were saying the same thing as the British women. But the British women pointed out that although they were saying the same word, they weren't saying the same thing. "Gravy?"—with question intonation—means "Would you like gravy?" The same word spoken with falling intonation seems to mean, "This is gravy. Take it or leave it."

Background Information 背景知识

1. English Channel(英吉利海峡)是连接英、法两国的海底隧道,由一条直径为 7.6 米的火车隧道和一条直径为 4.8 米的服务隧道组成,全长 38 千米。1964 年,英、法政府宣布在两国同时施工。由于工程浩大,造价极高,一度停建,后于 1990 年 10 月底凿通服务隧道。

1993年6月,海底隧道正式运营。穿越英吉利海峡只需35分钟,大大方便了两国的交通运输。

2. Union Jack(英国国旗)俗称为"米"字旗,呈横长方形,长与宽之比为2∶1,由深蓝底色和红、白色"米"字组成。旗中带白边的红色正十字代表英格兰守护神圣乔治,白色交叉十字代表苏格兰守护神圣安德鲁,红色交叉十字代表爱尔兰守护神圣帕特里克。此旗诞生于1801年,是由原英格兰的白底红色正十旗、苏格兰的蓝底白色交叉十字旗和爱尔兰的白底红色交叉十字旗重叠而成的。

3. John Bull(约翰牛)为英国的别称。约翰原是18世纪英国作家兼宫廷御医约翰·阿布什诺特(John Arbuthnot,1667—1735)在《约翰·布尔的历史》(*The History of John Bull*)一书中的一个人物形象——头戴礼帽、足蹬长筒靴、手持雨伞、满脸横肉的矮胖绅士,身边跟着条牛头犬(Bulldog),用来讽刺当时辉格党(the Whig Party)当局参与西班牙王位继承战争的好战政策。由于人物刻画逼真,形象生动,因而很快传播开来以致家喻户晓。约翰·布尔的英语是"John Bull",而"Bull"在英语中是"牛"的意思,后来"约翰牛"的形象也被赋予能够代表英国人坚忍顽强精神风貌的性格色彩,使英国人为维护个人和国家的荣誉不惜一切的大名不胫而走,举世闻名。

4. Monarchy of the UK(英国国王)是大不列颠及北爱尔兰联合王国的国家元首、三军总司令、不列颠法院的首脑和英国国教最高领袖。英国许多重大国家事项法案形式上都需国王亲自审批,许多重要荣誉名衔也由国王亲授。按照传统,英国国王邀请大选中获胜的政党首脑组成政府,处理国家具体事务。在国际上,国王有权对外宣战和媾和,正式承认外国国家和政府,对外缔结条约以及吞并或割让领土等,但实权仍在内阁。

5. The House of Lords(上议院)又称贵族院或上院,现有议员1 200人,由772个世袭贵族(hereditary peers)、380个非世袭贵族(life peers)、22个上诉法院的法官(loads spiritual)和教会的两个大主教(archbishop,来自the Church of Canterbury 和 the Church of York)、24个主教(bishop,来自the Church of England)组成。上议院是英国最高司法机关(the Supreme Court of Judicature)。

6. The House of Commons(下议院)又称"众议院"(the House of Commons),共有659个议员(members of parliament),议员由普选产生。议员享有在议会中的言论自由权。议员根据其主张又分属不同的党派,下议院的职责主要是立法、监督政府和财政。大选中获得多数席位的政党成为执政党,英王任命执政党领袖为首相。

7. Palace of Westminster(威斯敏斯特宫)是世界上最大的哥特式(Gothic)建筑群,坐落于泰晤士河北岸,历史悠久。"Westminster"意为"西教堂",因为它最早是由撒克逊人在这里建立的一座教堂。1065年,英格兰国王忏悔者爱德华(Edward, the Confessor 1042—1066)重建了教堂并在附近建了一座宫殿,称为威斯敏斯特宫,并将其设为王宫。1840年,英国政府在原地上重建此宫,用作议会大厦,成为世界上最大的议会大厦。在议会大厦前的议会广场(Parliament Square)上建有英国首相丘吉尔的高大雕像,以纪念他在第二次世界大战中作出的巨大贡献。一个圆形中央大厅将议会大厦分为两院:南院为上议院(贵族院),北院为下议院(平民院)。威斯敏斯特宫的西南角有一高塔维多利亚塔(Victoria Tower),此塔为砖石结构,专门存放议会的重要档案文件。东北角则是一座方塔,塔上有一钟楼,挂着著名的"大本钟(Big Ben)"。

8. Hyde Park(海德公园)是伦敦最知名的公园。18世纪前这里是英王的狩鹿场。海德公园从东南方进入有三条路线:泰晤士河及伦敦眼(Thames & London Eye)左边是比较宽广的 Rotton Row,许多社交名流喜欢在此游乐骑马;另一条延伸到东北的 Park Lane,这里高级大饭店和住宅林立;北端有著名的演讲角(Speakers' Corner),演讲角是一个可以公开发表自己言论的地方,经常可见有人在此即兴演讲。在海德公园的南端有骑兵营,清晨最先看到的一定是驯马。海德公园西边即为肯辛顿公园,有一个蛇形湖泊,其旁的同名艺廊(Serpentine Gallery)颇受欢迎。

9. The Tower of London(伦敦塔)是不列颠群岛最受欢迎的历史景点,每年接待250万参观者。伦敦塔的官方名称是"女王陛下的宫殿与城堡,伦敦塔"(Her Majesty's Palace and Fortress, The Tower of London)。其中白塔是伦敦塔最重要、最古老的建筑,位于要塞中心的塔楼是整个建筑群的主体,因其用乳白色石块建成,故又称"白塔"。白塔原是守备人员进驻之所,因此最为坚固。塔楼高27.4米,东西长35.9米,南北长32.6米,底部墙厚4.6米,顶部厚3.3米,为双层墙壁,窗户很小,用坚硬粗糙的毛石砌成。塔楼四角外凸,耸出四座高塔。高塔三方一圆,在角隅设有螺旋楼梯,通达顶层。白塔西北角还有一座12世纪建的小礼拜堂。伦敦塔1988年被列为世界文化遗产。

10. The Thames(泰晤士河)发源于英格兰的科茨沃尔德山,沿途汇集了许多溪流,最后经诺尔岛流入北海,全长340千米,是英国境内最长的河流,可航行的河道有309千米。它造就了大英帝国,繁荣了英国伦敦。泰晤士河两岸有许多名胜古迹,也有许多美丽的故事,在泰晤士河边你可以看到举世闻名的大本钟、格林尼治天文台、温莎堡、伦敦塔、威斯特敏斯特教堂、塔桥,等等。

11. Downing Street(唐宁街)是英国伦敦白厅街旁一条长50米、宽10米的短而窄的横街。它是以英国17世纪的一位叫乔治·唐宁的外交官的名字命名的。此街实际只有两个门牌,10号是首相的官邸,已有二百多年历史,是一幢三层楼的建筑物,普通的铁栅门和灰砖墙,外表非常平常,而内部陈设精致考究。首相在这里召开内阁会议,会见来访的外国贵宾,有时还在这里接见民众。每当新的首相上任后,前首相就立刻迁出官邸,并在官邸内留下一张油画肖像。11号是财政大臣的官邸。所以说,这条街是英国权力机构的象征。

12. Scotland Yard(苏格兰场)英语正式名称为"New Scotland Yard",又称"The Yard",指英国首都伦敦警务处总部,位于伦敦的威斯敏斯特区(Westminster),离上议院约200码,负责包括整个大伦敦地区的治安及维持交通等职务(伦敦城除外)。所以,苏格兰场本身既不位于苏格兰,更不负责苏格兰的警备。苏格兰场这个名字源自1829年,当时首都警务处位于旧苏格兰王室宫殿的遗迹,并因此而得名。1890年曾迁至维多利亚堤区,1967年迁至现址。这两个新地址也被称为"新苏格兰场"。最老的苏格兰场后来被英国陆军占用,成为陆军的征募所和皇家军警的总部。1890年,新苏格兰场原址的一部分也依然是警察站。苏格兰场的犯罪数据库被称为"Home Office Large Major Enquiry System",其缩写是"HOLMES",以此来纪念小说中的大侦探夏洛克·福尔摩斯。

13. Buckingham Palace(白金汉宫)是英国的现代王宫,坐落在伦敦西区中心,东接圣詹姆斯公园(St. James's Park),西临海德公园(Hyde Park),起初是白金公爵于1703年建造的一座公馆。1761年,英王乔治三世将其买下作为他的妻子的私人宫殿。1825年,乔治四世花了10年时间加以重建,并把它作为王宫。1837年,维多利亚女王(Queen Victoria)接替王位后,白金汉宫正式成为王宫。现在的白金汉宫是一个三层楼的建筑群。整个建筑群富丽堂皇,精雅别致。宫内有宴会厅、音乐厅、画廊、图书馆、皇家集邮室等600多个厅室,陈列着历代皇室收藏的许多艺术珍品,还有一个占地约18万平方米的幽静而秀丽的御花园。国王查尔斯三世(King Charles Ⅲ)在伦敦时就住在这里。国王召见首相和大臣,接待和宴请外国元首,接受外国使节递交国书等重大活动都在宫内举行。不过,只有少数进行正式访问的外国元首才能下榻白金汉宫。

14. The Royal Greenwich Observatory(格林尼治天文台)位于泰晤士河畔的皇家格林尼治花园中,建于1675年。1884年,在华盛顿召开国际经度会议,会议决定以通过当时格林尼治天文台埃里中星仪所在的经线,作为全球时间和经度计量的标准参考经线,称为0°经线或本初子午线,以格林尼治天文台作为"世界时区"的起点。"二战"后,格林尼治地区人口剧增,工厂增加,空气污染日趋严重,尤其是夜间灯光的干扰,对星空观测极为不利。天文台于1948年迁往英国东南沿海的苏塞克斯郡的赫斯特蒙苏堡。格林尼治天文台旧址后来成为英国航海部和全国海洋博物馆天文站,到这里的游人都喜欢双脚跨在0°经线的两侧摄影留念,象征着自己同时脚踏东经和西经两种经度。

Cultural Kaleidoscope 文化万花筒

英美文化历史悠久,林林总总。学习者面对浩繁的内容,需要主动建构意义,获取新知识,而不是被动地接受、记忆事实。阅读英语文本是对书面信息进行理解的复杂过程,也是训练发展思维的过程。同时,在阅读英美文化文本时需要培养基本的认读能力、归纳总结能力、分析能力、批判鉴赏能力及应用创造能力。

Why Do the British Wear Paper Hats at Christmas Lunch?

On Christmas Day, British families enjoy sitting around their dining tables and have a traditional lunch of roast turkey with all the trimming. All family members, regardless of age, wear coloured paper hats. It is rumoured that even the Queen used to wear her paper hat over lunch!

So why this quaint tradition? Where do these paper hats come from? The answer is the Christmas Cracker.

A Christmas Cracker is a cardboard paper tube, wrapped in brightly coloured paper and twisted at both ends. There is a banger inside the cracker, two strips of chemically impregnated paper that react with friction so that when the cracker is pulled apart by two people, the cracker makes a bang. Inside the cracker there is a paper crown made from tissue paper, a motto or joke on a slip of paper and a little gift. Christmas crackers are a British tradition dating back to Victorian times when in the early 1850s, London confectioner Tom Smith started adding a motto to his sugared almond bon-bons which he sold wrapped in a twisted

中国传统文化2

paper package. The paper hat was added to the cracker in the early 1900s. The cracker was soon adopted as a traditional festive custom and today virtually every household has at least one box of crackers to pull over Christmas.

Business Etiquette in Belt and Road Countries
"一带一路"国家的商务礼仪

丝绸之路不仅是一条古代通商道路,更是连接古代中华文明、印度文明、埃及文明、希腊文明和美索不达米亚文明的纽带,是东西方文化和科学技术交流的桥梁,是横贯欧亚大陆的历史文化大动脉。丝绸之路促使人类文明在不同地域之间交流。不同文明传来的新鲜养分,孕育着新的文化。它是古老中国走向世界、接受世界其他地方文明营养的主要通道。

波兰的商务礼仪

波兰人高度重视诚信,因为信任是建立和培养商业关系的基石。建立良好的人际关系有助于成功地达成交易,尤其有助于建立长期的商业伙伴关系。波兰人以直率爽快闻名,他们说话不绕圈子,往往直接表达真实想法。而人际关系的亲疏远近决定了波兰人直截了当的程度。在正式场合,对于刚认识的商业伙伴,他们会小心翼翼地选择措辞。一旦过了初识阶段,当波兰人在相处中感到舒服安心时,会更加活跃坦率地交谈。商务问候时,确保在到达和离开时与每个人握手,握手有力并保持眼神交流。商务名片交换没有固定的仪式要求,但建议把名片的一面翻译成波兰文。商务会晤由最高级别的人致开场词,但会谈前经常进行一些闲聊,这时不要催促波兰人商谈正事,因为闲谈有助于培养人际关系。

Honesty is highly valued in Poland since trust is the cornerstone of business relationships. Building personal relationships is essential for successful business dealings, especially if you are looking for a long-term business relationship. Poles are known for being direct communicators, i.e. they say what they are thinking and the level of the relationship mostly determines how direct someone can be. For newly established and more formal relationships, a great deal of emphasis is placed on diplomacy. Once a relationship has passed through the initial phases, people feel more comfortable speaking frankly with each other and animated exchanges become more common. In greeting, it is recommended to shake hands with everyone upon arriving and leaving, and your handshakes should be firm and eye contact is appreciated. Business cards are exchanged without formal rituals, and it is preferable to translate one side of your card into Polish. The most senior Pole generally opens the meeting, but small talk is the norm at the start of meetings. Do not rush proceedings as this is part of the relationship building process.

Intercultural Tips 跨文化拓展知识

咖啡文化（Coffee Culture）

咖啡是用经过烘焙磨粉的咖啡豆制作出来的饮料，就像中国的茶一样具有丰富的滋味，可以细细品尝，慢慢感受。它作为世界三大饮料之一，全球贸易量仅次于石油。咖啡是一种全球化的产品，全世界有许多人会日常饮用咖啡。如今，咖啡以各种形式渗透到人们的生活中，让我们一起追溯咖啡风靡全世界的历史，一起了解有关咖啡的小知识，一起感知因环境变化而发展的多样咖啡文化。

（1）咖啡的发展历史。咖啡树原产于非洲埃塞俄比亚西南部地区，在咖啡起源的诸多传说中，有两个最为有名：一是牧羊人卡尔第的故事，据说牧羊人卡尔第发现山羊吃了一种红色果子后，变得非常兴奋活泼，进而发现了咖啡；二是奥尔玛僧侣的传说，奥尔玛僧侣被流放到街上，饥寒交迫，偶然用树上的红色果实煮水喝后顿时疲劳感消除。但是当时并没有留下文字记载，因此具体情况无从考据。10世纪左右，咖啡传播到了对岸的也门，因"药"效显著而备受瞩目。大概到了15世纪，咖啡渐渐成为嗜好品。大约在16世纪，咖啡的饮用文化在穆斯林地区开始传播开来。在16世纪末至17世纪，咖啡传入欧洲，并开发出"滴滤式咖啡"和"意式浓缩咖啡"这两种现在的主流饮用方式。此后，咖啡传入美洲大陆。以波士顿倾茶事件为导火索，咖啡替代茶成为当地百姓喜欢的饮品，咖啡文化也在美国这一世界咖啡第一消费大国扎根。19世纪，咖啡传入日本。

（2）咖啡树的生长环境。咖啡树的原种大致分为阿拉比卡种和罗布斯塔种，其中产量最多的是阿拉比卡种。咖啡树通常生长在南北回归线之间的地区，一般介于北纬25度到南纬30度，涵盖了中非、东非、中东、印度、南亚、太平洋地区、拉丁美洲、加勒比海地区的多数国家，统称为"咖啡生长带"。咖啡生长带之所以主要集中在该地区，是因为咖啡极易受到霜冻的伤害，热带地区的温度和湿度最为适合咖啡生长。在中国，适合咖啡种植的地方有云南、海南和台湾。其中，云南省引进咖啡种植已有一百多年历史，由法国传教士带来的咖啡树苗引入种植。云南小粒咖啡主要分布在云南省普洱市、临沧市、德宏州、保山市等地。小粒咖啡原产埃塞俄比亚或阿拉伯半岛，优越的地理条件使得云南的咖啡产业发展迅速。现在，云南小粒咖啡作为东方高品质精品豆也销往欧洲、美国、日本、韩国等二十多个国家和地区。

（3）咖啡的文化知识。风靡全世界的咖啡融合了各国丰富多彩的文化，有着独特的进化过程。非洲是咖啡的发祥地，拥有以埃塞俄比亚为首的诸多咖啡生产地。大洋洲现在被视为新的咖啡前线。亚洲的印度尼西亚种植着世界最珍贵且昂贵的咖啡豆。对于咖啡达人来说，印度尼西亚产的"猫屎咖啡"被认为是最珍贵的咖啡豆。麝香猫在吃完咖啡果后把咖啡豆原封不动地排出，人们把它粪便中的咖啡豆取出来，经过烘焙后，每磅售价超过300美元。中南美洲是包含巴西在内的世界最大的咖啡产地，咖啡豆产量和出口量均位列世界前三的国家依次为巴西、越南和哥伦比亚，其中位列第一和第三的国家都在中南美洲。欧洲对咖啡有着深厚的感情，在构筑现代咖啡文化基础的欧洲人的生活中，咖啡已经成为不可或缺的一部分。意大利人发明了意式浓缩咖啡,法国人创造了牛奶咖啡。英国的咖啡店里有一种"白咖啡",不是因为颜色是白色的,而是因为添加了牛奶;红茶在英国也分为加牛奶和不加牛奶两种。就咖啡的年销量和人均消费量而言,以北欧为首的欧洲地区远远领先于其他地区。在2013年世界咖啡消费量排名中,前5名有3个是北欧国家,分别是芬兰、挪威和丹麦。咖啡的消费第一大国是美国,有着不同于欧洲各国的根深蒂固的咖啡文化,其生产契机可以追溯到独立战争年代。第二次世界大战时,咖啡优先供应给军队,所以美国国内供不应求。充分利用少量咖啡豆等各种节约的方式十分常见,人们养成了薄泡的习惯,因此也有美式咖啡就是"味道淡的咖啡"这一说法。与欧美各国相比,日本在咖啡文化领域起步较晚,但发明了罐装咖啡和冰咖啡,普及的咖啡店等独特的咖啡文化在日本也很发达。

(4)饮用咖啡的餐桌礼仪。在餐后饮用的咖啡,一般都是用袖珍型杯子盛出。咖啡杯的正确拿法,应是拇指和食指捏住杯把儿再将杯子端起。咖啡匙是专门用来搅拌咖啡的,饮用咖啡时应当把它取出来,不要用咖啡匙舀着咖啡一匙一匙地慢慢喝,也不要用咖啡匙来捣碎杯中的糖。盛放咖啡的杯碟都是特制的,应当放在饮用者的正面或者右侧,杯耳应指向右方。饮咖啡时,可以用右手拿着咖啡的杯耳,左手轻轻托着咖啡碟,慢慢地移向嘴边轻啜,不要发出声响,不宜满把握杯、大口吞咽,也不宜俯首去就咖啡杯。添加咖啡时,不要把咖啡杯从咖啡碟中拿起来。刚刚煮好的咖啡太烫,可以用咖啡匙在杯中轻轻搅拌使之冷却,或者等待其自然冷却,然后饮用。

 Movie to See 观影学文化

Please watch the movies *The King's Speech*(《国王的演讲》)with your classmates and discuss what intercultural elements are involved in it.

Unit 3　American Culture

美国文化

 Learning Objectives 学习目标

- 了解美国文化背景知识及美国的主流价值观。
- 了解美国的影视音乐和宗教习俗。
- 熟悉美国商务人士的处事特点和原则。
- 掌握应对中美文化差异的正确态度和得体方式。

 Lead-in 单元导读

美国文化属于多元文化类型，其文化源自盎格鲁-撒克逊传统，但又不同于盎格鲁-撒克逊文化。在其两百年来的演变中，美国吸收了世界诸多文明的精华，成为一个独立的、具有自己鲜明特点的开放性文化体系。

地理位置上，美国位于西半球，北部与加拿大相邻，南接墨西哥和墨西哥湾，西濒太平洋，东临大西洋，海岸线长 22 680 千米。地势东西高、中央低，主要山脉为南北走向。境内地形从东到西大致分为大西洋沿岸平原、阿巴拉契亚山脉、内地平原、西部山系、西部山间高原五个自然地理区域。美国地形复杂，各地气候差异较大，主要分为五个气候区，即东北部沿海的温带气候区、东南部亚热带气候区、中央平原的大陆性气候区、西部高原的干燥气候区和太平洋沿岸的海洋性气候区。美国主要包括美国本土、阿拉斯加州及夏威夷州三个部分。美国本土划分为六大地区，包括新英格兰地区、大西洋中部地区、南部地区、中西部地区、西南地区和西部地区。美国包括 50 个州和首都所在地华盛顿哥伦比亚特区。

美国是多民族和多文化的国家，截至 2022 年 7 月 6 日，人口总量超过 3 亿人，居世界第三,其中白人占 80.5%,黑人占 13.1%,墨西哥人占 6.4%,印第安人 187.8 万人,华人 165.3 万人。根据美国文化的心理趋向,按照美国文化构成的方式及其稳定的特征,基督传统、自由主义和个人主义构成了美国文化的三大要素。这是在美国特定的历史发展过程中形成的,具有其特有的历史个性和价值取向。美国社会较开放,国民热切期望实现个人奋斗目标,即"美国梦"的文化特性非常显著。美国人尤其是美国商务人士的时间观念很强,各种活动都按预定的时间开始,迟到被视作不礼貌的行为。此外,美国也是一个权力距离指数较低的国家,其社会成员行为独立,彼此平等相待。

美国最早的音乐是教堂音乐。美国独立后,大批移民带来了欧洲音乐。20 世纪初,代表美国音乐特色的爵士乐出现了,它是一种即兴的艺术。布鲁斯作为爵士乐的一种,由黑人早期的宗教和世俗音乐相互影响而形成。美国流行音乐的另一个源泉是"乡村—西部音乐",一般称之为乡村音乐。20 世纪 50 年代后,受到节奏布鲁斯音乐、乡村音乐和打击音乐影响发展而来的摇滚乐开始风靡美国,爵士乐退居次要位置。摇滚乐分支众多,形态复杂,主要风格有民谣、乡村、重金属、朋克等。从文学艺术发展的脉络来看,每个世纪都有一个领域脱颖而出:18 世纪和 19 世纪是诗歌与小说交叉领衔的世纪;20 世纪则是影视的天下;21 世纪却是互联网与数字思维的时代。电影是大多数美国人推崇的娱乐活动,美国人不仅支持电影,而且热爱电影。电影是在美、法及欧洲其他各国发明家的竞争之中应运而生的。早在 1911 年,加利福尼亚州的好莱坞就已成为美国电影制片中心,它不仅是一个地域概念,还体现了美国电影的主要特色,就是美国商业电影在制片、发行和播映方面的一整套独特运营方略。宗教是美国文化中显著的一部分,目前美国有超过 60% 的人口信仰宗教。美国的宗教非常多元,基督教新教是美国具有极大影响力的文化要素。

在世界近现代史上,美国的立国和发展堪称独特。在中国文化"走出去"和"一带一路"倡议的宏大背景下,我们不仅要向世界各民族大力推广中国的优秀传统文化,也需要对他国文化有更全面的了解。通过本单元的学习,你将了解美国的自然地理轮廓、人口构成、主要价值观、音乐及电影,并对美国的宗教有进一步的理解。

Pre-class Activity 课前活动

The US is a sports-loving nation. Sports in America take a variety of forms and most sports are seasonal. Some sports are called spectator sports as the number of spectators greatly exceeds the number of those playing in the game. Other sports are called participant sports, drawing a crowd of onlookers only on special occasions, such as the tournament. Some sports are commercial and professional, with players who are paid for their participation, and with audiences who pay admission to watch. Can you figure out which sport is the most popular one boasting the overwhelmingly large number of audience in the US? And why is it regarded as an indication of the qualities and characters of American people?

Reading 课内阅读

Reading One: A Brief Introduction to the US

The US is located in North America with the Pacific Ocean on the west and the Atlantic Ocean on the east. The country is bordered by Canada on the north and along the southern border are Mexico and the Gulf of Mexico. The whole country includes 50 states and the District of Columbia.

More than twice the size of the European Union, the US has high mountains in the West and a vast central plain. The landscape varies across the large country from tropical beaches in Florida to peaks in the Rocky Mountains, from rolling prairie lands and barren deserts in the West to dense wilderness areas in the Northeast and Northwest. Interspersed throughout are the Great Lakes, the Grand Canyon, the majestic Yosemite Valley, and the mighty Mississippi River.

These conditions help create all sorts of weather: mild, moderate and extreme. In summer, some areas get very hot and the air is very wet. But others have dry air, so the heat does not feel so bad. In winter, parts of the country get cold and snowy while others stay warm and sunny. This is the difference between, for example, the East Coast and the West Coast. The oceans affect weather along the coasts. The Pacific coast has the smallest temperature changes and calmer conditions than along the Atlantic. Hurricanes are ocean storms that strike mainly in the Southeast. The hurricane season is, officially, June through November. Tornadoes are a risk across the country. These are locally severe windstorms in spring and summer.

The Fifty States

The country is divided into six regions: New England, the mid-Atlantic, the South, the Midwest, the Southwest, and the West.

European settlers came to New England in search of religious freedom. These states are Connecticut, Maine, Massachusetts, New Hampshire, Rhode Island, and Vermont. The mid-Atlantic region includes Delaware, Maryland, New Jersey, New York, Pennsylvania, and the city of Washington, D.C. These industrial areas attracted millions of European immigrants and gave rise to some of the East Coast's largest cities: New York, Baltimore, and Philadelphia. The south includes Alabama, Arkansas, Florida, Georgia, Kentucky, Louisiana, Mississippi, North Carolina, South Carolina, Tennessee, Virginia, and West Virginia, all of which struggled after the Civil War, which lasted during 1860—1865. The Midwest is home to the country's agricultural base and is called the "nation's breadbasket". The region comprises the states of Illinois, Indiana, Iowa, Kansas, Michigan, Minnesota, Missouri, Nebraska, North Dakota, Ohio, South Dakota, and

Wisconsin. The Southwest is a beautiful stark landscape of prairie and desert. The states of Arizona, New Mexico, Oklahoma, and Texas are considered the Southwest and are home to some of the world's great natural marvels, including the Grand Canyon and Carlsbad Caverns. The American West, home of rolling plains and the cowboy, is a symbol of the pioneering spirit of the US. The West is diverse, ranging from endless wilderness to barren desert, coral reefs to Arctic tundra, Hollywood to Yellowstone. The states of the West include Alaska, Colorado, California, Hawaii, Idaho, Montana, Nevada, Oregon, Utah, Washington, and Wyoming.

Symbols

For many immigrants who flocked from Europe to New York, the Statue of Liberty was the first image they saw of the US. Recognized as a universal symbol of freedom and democracy, "The statue of Liberty Enlightening the World" was a gift from the French government for the 100th anniversary of America's Independence.

Another great symbol is the American flag, 13 red and white stripes corresponding to the number of original states on a rectangular piece of cloth, one corner blue with 50 white stars for 50 states. The Star-Spangled Banner is also the national anthem of the US, with music adapted from the anthem of a singing club and words by Francis Scott Key. After a century of general use, the four-stanza song was officially adopted as the national anthem by an act of Congress in 1931.

The US Dollar is the single most popular currency in the world, and is the dominant reserve currency in use around the globe. The US Dollar is often called "The Greenback" in reference to its green coloring and can often be a favorite vehicle of traders looking to buy assets from or in the US.

Uncle Sam, a figure symbolizing the US, is pictured as a tall, white-haired man with a beard. He is often dressed in red, white, and blue, and wears a top hat. The exact origins of Uncle Sam as a symbol for the US are unknown, but most people accepted the idea that Uncle Sam was named after Samuel Wilson. During the War of 1812, Samuel Wilson was a businessman from Troy, NY, which supplied the US Army with beef in the barrel. The barrels were labeled "US" which stood for Uncle Sam Wilson. The suggestion that the meat shipments came from "Uncle Sam" led to the idea that Uncle Sam symbolized the Federal Government and the association stuck. In 1961, Congress approved Uncle Sam as an official representation of the US.

Although English is the most commonly spoken language used in the US and is the language used by the government, the country has no official language.

Population

For centuries native peoples lived across the vast expanse that would become the US. In the early 17th century, settlers moved from Europe to the New World, established colonies, and displaced the native peoples. The settlers fought for their independence from Britain in the late 18th century and formed a union of states based on a new constitution.

The nation continued to expand westward and although the country is a relatively young nation, it has become a global power since declaring independence from Britain on July 4, 1776.

Throughout its history, the US has been a nation of immigrants. The population is diverse with people from all over the world seeking refuge and a better way of life. The total population of the US is about 329,256 million (2018). Most of the inhabitants are of European origin, holding over eighty percent of the total. However, there are also many black people, Mexicans, Indians, Puerto Ricans, Chinese, Japanese and Philippines, etc. Although the country is honourably called "melting pot", a phrase commonly used to signify the mixture and assimilation of different races that have immigrated into the US, many immigrants, staying true to their cultures and keeping all their customs, believe in the "salad bowl" theory. The unique characteristics of each culture are still identifiable, yet contribute to the overall make-up of the salad bowl. This idea proposes a society of many individuals, "pure" cultures in addition to the mixed culture constituting modern American culture.

Government

Citizens over the age of 18 years old vote to elect the President and Vice President of the US every four years. The president lives in the White House in the capital city of Washington, D.C. There are two houses of Congress: the Senate and the House of Representatives. There are 100 senators, two from each of the 50 states and each serves a six-year term. There are 435 representatives who must be elected every two years. The Supreme Court is made up of nine justices who are picked by the president and must be approved by Congress. For the first time in the nation's history an African American, Barack Obama, was elected President of the US in 2008. He was reelected for a second term in 2012.

Reading Two: Dominant US Cultural Patterns

Listing American values is a difficult task since the US has its diverse multiracial and ethnic cultures. On a general level, however, American people do share a value system (Charon, 1999). As E.Y. Kim (2001) writes, "There are similar characteristics that all Americans share, regardless of their age, race, gender, or ethnicity."

Individualism

The single most important cultural pattern in the US is individualism. The interests of the individual are or ought to be paramount, and all values, rights, and duties originate in individuals. The value of individualism is so commanding that many other imperative American values such as equality of opportunity, independence, initiative and self-reliance spring from individualism. This emphasis on the individual has emerged as the cornerstone of American culture. The origin of this value has had a long history and a variety of champions. Whether it is literature, art or American history, the message is the same:

individual achievement, sovereignty, and freedom are the virtues most praised and glorified. For instance, Benjamin Franklin told Americans that "God helps those who help themselves". American role models, be they cowboys or action heroes in movies, videos, or computer games, are all portrayed as independent agents who accomplish their goals with little or no assistance. The result of these and countless other messages is that most Americans believe that each person has his or her own separate identity, which should be recognized and reinforced. As Kim points out, "In America, what counts is who you are, not who others around you are. A person tends to be judged on his or her own merit."

Equality

Closely related to individualism is the American value of equality. "The US was founded on the principle that 'all men are created equal'." (Hanson, 1998) You can see examples of equality being emphasized in everything from government (everyone has the right to vote) to social relationships ("Just call me by my first name"). Americans believe that all people have a right to succeed in life and that the state, through laws and educational opportunities, should ensure that right. The value of equality is prevalent in both primary and secondary social relationships. For instance, most of the primary social relationships within a family tend to advance equality rather than hierarchy. Formality is not important, and children are often treated as adults. In secondary relationships, you find that most friendships and coworkers are also treated as equals. People from cultures that have rigid, hierarchical social structures often find it disconcerting to work with Americans, who they believe negate the value of hierarchical structures within a society. We do not mean to imply that Americans completely ignore hierarchy. According to Althen (2003), Americans rely on more subtle ways to mark status, such as "tone of voice, order of speaking, choice of words, and seating arrangements". We would be remiss, when describing the dominant culture in the US, if we did not once again remind you of some of the contradictions that often exist when we speak of individualism and equality. Despite prevailing ideas about individualism and freedom, many people in the US still evaluate others according to their race, gender, ethnicity and social class. While granting that many Americans have experienced periods of inequality, Hanson (1998) is correct when stating, "Not all citizens have had equal rights throughout the course of the country's history, but Americans nevertheless value the notion highly and strive toward this ideal."

Materialism

Materialism has always been an integral part of life for most Americans. As Stewart and Bennett (1991) note, "Americans consider it almost a right to be materially well off and physically comfortable." This ideal is even displayed on a popular bumper sticker which proclaims, "The person who dies with the most toys wins." Americans expect to have swift and convenient transportation (preferably controlled by themselves), a large variety of foods at their disposal, clothes for every occasion, and comfortable homes equipped with environmental controls and countless labor-saving devices.

Science and Technology

For most Americans, science and technology take on the qualities often associated with a god. The following inscription, found in the National Museum of American History in Washington, D.C., expresses the same idea: "Modern civilization depends on science." Americans think that scientific and technical knowledge is linked to their very survival. This strong belief gives rise to the notion among most Americans that nothing is impossible when scientists, engineers, and inventors put their minds to a task. From fixing interpersonal relationships to walking on the moon, science has the answer. The American respect for science is based on the assumptions that reality can be rationally ordered by humans and that such an ordering, using the scientific method, enables people to predict and control much of life. Very broadly, this emphasis on science reflects the values of the rationalistic-individualistic tradition that is so deeply embedded in Western civilization. From John Locke to Francis Bacon, Rene Descartes, Bertrand Russell, and Albert Einstein, Western cultures have long believed that all problems can be solved by science. While Westerners tend to prize rationality, objectivity, empirical evidence, and the scientific method, these views often clash with cultures that value and believe in fatalism, subjectivity, mysticism, and intuition.

Progress and Change

In the US, as Hanson(1998) reminds you, "Change, newness, and progress are all highly valued". From altering their personalities with the assistance of self-help gurus, to changing where they live at a faster rate than any other people in the world, Americans do not value the status quo, nor have they ever. "Early Americans cleared forests, drained swamps, and altered the course of rivers in order to 'build' the country. Contemporary Americans have gone to the moon in part to prove they could do so (Althen, 2003)." Various aspects of this orientation are optimism, receptivity to change, emphasis on the future rather than the past or present, faith in the ability to control all phases of life, and confidence in the perceptual ability of the common person. You can observe this strong conviction in change and progress in how Americans view the environment. Hanson (1998) offers a summary of this point by stating, "This belief also has fostered a use of force in interactions with the environment and other people that is evident in phrases such as 'taming the wilderness', 'winning the West', and 'conquering space'." A passion for progress cultivates not only the acceptance of change but also the conviction that changes move in a definite direction and that the direction is good. Each new generation in the US wants the opportunity to be part of that change. So strong is the belief in progress and change that Americans seldom fear taking chances. Many older and more traditional cultures, which have witnessed civilizations rise and fall and believe in fatalism, do not easily embrace change, progress, and daring and often have difficulty understanding the way Americans behave.

Work and Leisure

Work, like all major cultural patterns, has a long history in the US. The value associated with work is so important in the US that people who meet each other for the first time often ask the common question "What do you do?" Embedded in this simple query is the belief that working (doing something) is important. For most Americans, work represents a cluster of moral and affective conditions of great attractiveness, while at the same time voluntary idleness often constitutes a severely threatening and damaging social condition. A major reward for hard work, and an important American value, is leisure. Most Americans seem to have embraced the words of the poet and philosopher George Santayana: "To the art of working well a civilized race would add the art of playing well." For Americans, play is something they have earned. It is relief from the regularity of work; it is in play that they find real joy. This emphasis on recreation and relaxation takes a variety of forms. Each weekend people rush to get away in their recreational vehicles, play golf or tennis, go skiing, ride their mountain bikes, or "relax" at a gambling casino or race track.

Competition

The late professional football coach Vince Lombard once said, "Winning isn't everything; it's the only thing." This attitude toward competition is part of an American's life that is taught from early childhood on. Whether it be through the games they play or their striving to receive a higher grade than the person they are sitting next to in class, a competitive nature is encouraged in the US. People are ranked, graded, classified, and evaluated so that everyone will know if they are the best. Young people are even advised that if they lose and it does not bother them, there is something wrong with them. As Kim (2001) points out, "For competitive Americans, who hate losing, everything in life is a game to win." Competition is yet another pattern that often causes problems for Americans when they interact with people who do not espouse this value. For instance, "Asians believe that it is neither necessary nor beneficial to be obsessed with winning (Kim, 2001)." Harris and Moran (1996) offer yet another example of differing perceptions of competition as it applies to the French: when confronted with individuals with a competitive drive, the French may interpret them as being antagonistic, ruthless, and power-hungry. They may feel threatened and overreact or withdraw from the discussion.

Reading Three: Understanding Values behind Business People

Hard Work

Americans generally work hard. They may devote long hours—as many as 16 or 18 a day—to their jobs. They may consider their work more important to them than family matters and social relations. Americans use the term "workaholic" to describe a person addicted to work, one who spends as much time as possible on the job and seems to think of little else. Workaholics are by no means rare in the American business world. American executives often embarrass their foreign counterparts by doing manual work or by doing tasks that elsewhere would be done by lower-status people—tasks such as serving coffee, rearranging the furniture in a meeting room, or taking out a calculator to figure out a problem that came up during a meeting.

Punctuality

Promptness and schedules are important. Meetings and appointments ideally begin and end on schedule. The topic that is supposed to be treated during the meeting or appointment is generally expected to be covered by the scheduled ending time. Delays cause frustration. Getting behind schedule is likely to be considered an example of bad management. In keeping with their notions about the importance of using time wisely and getting the job done, American executives generally want to get right down to business. They do not want to waste time with formalities or with long, preliminary discussions. In fact, they are usually quite uncomfortable with purely social interactions while they are working.

Impersonal Dealings

Americans generally have no particular interest in getting personally acquainted with the clients or customers with whom they deal. As long as they believe the other party is trustworthy in business dealing and has the ability to deliver whatever product or service being discussed, the Americans will proceed in an impersonal manner. They value decisiveness and efficiency. Concerns about human relations are lowered down in their scale of priorities. Western Europeans are likely to carry on in about the same way, but people from most other parts of the world are likely to find the American approach cold or otherwise uncomfortable. Even when they seem to be socializing, as at a diner or reception with business colleagues, their main purpose is more likely to be discussing business than becoming personally acquainted with other people.

Quantitative Reasoning

American business people, probably even more noticeably than Americans in general, prefer to think and analyze in quantitative terms. They want hard data and facts and figures when they are analyzing a business situation and trying to make a decision. The assumption is that wise decisions are made on the basis of "objective" information uncontaminated by considerations of personal feelings, social relations, or political advantage. American executives frequently use the term "bottom line", which refers to the final entry in an accounting statement. They want the statement to show a profit. Little else is as important. The purpose of a business is to make a profit, and executives are evaluated by stockholders with reference to their contribution to the company's financial standing.

Writing It Down

The written word is supremely important to American business people. They make notes about conversations, keep files on their various projects, and record the minutes of meetings. A contract or agreement must be written down in order to be taken seriously, and every written word in it is important. It must be the correct word, the one that makes clearest what each party's rights and obligations are. To Americans in business, then, it seems perfectly natural to consult lawyers about contracts and agreements. Lawyers are trained to select proper words for important documents and to correctly interpret them. Americans have difficulty understanding that people from elsewhere might consider oral agreements adequate. Businesspeople from abroad might feel insulted by the Americans' insistence on having written agreements, viewing the Americans' attitude as an indication of distrust.

Behavior in Meetings

Meetings are a common phenomenon in the business world, but what actually happens in meetings varies greatly, not just from country to country but from organization to organization. Meeting can have a variety of purposes—sharing information, giving instructions, heightening enthusiasm and dedication, discussing issues and problems, suggesting solutions, making decisions, and no doubt others. Americans like to know explicitly what the purpose of any given meeting is. "What's the point of this meeting?" they may ask. The leader's role in meeting varies. The leader might be the one who opens the meeting, does all the talking, and then dismisses those who have attended. Or the leader may play the role of a moderator, opening the meeting and then allowing others to discuss matters and make decisions. The role of those attending the meeting differs too. They may be expected to sit quietly and listen, to offer suggestions or comments, or even to challenge ideas others put forth. In the ideal American meeting, the leader encourages active participation from all those who might have ideas to contribute. The people at the meeting offer ideas and information intended to help illuminate the subject under discussion. They may openly and bluntly disagree with each other. Witnessing such meetings can shock foreigners who are accustomed to more formal, hierarchical arrangements, where the leader firmly controls what takes place and participants either remain silent or mask any disagreement they might have with what others say. In American meetings, issues are often resolved by means of a vote. "The majority rules." Americans often say—not just in this context but in others, too. The practice of voting in meetings might disconcert foreigners who are accustomed to a system in which decisions must be unanimous or one in which the people in authority are the ones who make the decisions.

Equality

American notions about equality strongly influence what happens throughout business organizations. Although people at various levels are quite aware of the status differences among them, they may not display superiority or inferiority in open ways. Rank-conscious foreigners may feel uneasy about the relatively relaxed and informal interactions they will see between lower status employees and those with higher status. Another manifestation of the equality assumption is the prevalence of written rules and procedures. If people are considered equal, then they must be treated fairly or impartially, that is, without reference to their own particular personalities. Fairness is best assured, in the typical American view, if there are written rules and procedures that apply to everyone equally. So there are written procedures for hiring, training, evaluating, rewarding, disciplining, and terminating employees. There are written procedures for handling employee complaints. There are job descriptions, safety rules, and rules for taking "breaks" (rest periods) from work. Great stress is placed on carrying out the written procedures completely and correctly. Foreign visitors are likely to think the constraints Americans impose on themselves by means of their rules are excessive, especially if labor-union rules are added to those of a company.

Staff Turnover

Foreign visitors may see more employee turnover than they are accustomed to. America is still a more mobile society than most (The rate of mobility may have slowed recently.), so people change jobs relatively readily. It is unusual to find a strong sense of company loyalty at the lower ranks of a business. People have their jobs to earn a living, and in many ways it does not matter to them just where that living comes from. They do what they are supposed to do (according to a written job description, usually), collect their pay, and go home. Supervisors are often seeking ways to enhance employee allegiance to the company, in the belief that employees who are more loyal will be more productive.

Read to Learn More

American Music and Film

American Music

The music of the US reflects the country's multi-ethnic population through a diverse array of styles. Rock and roll, country, rhythm and blues, jazz, and hip hop are among the country's most internationally renowned genres. BBC Radio DJ Andy Kershaw, for example, has noted that country music is popular across virtually the entire world. Since the beginning of the 20th century, popular recorded music from the US has become increasingly known across the world, to the point where some forms of American popular music are listened to almost everywhere. Indeed, out of "all the contributions made by Americans to world culture... (American popular music) has been taken (most) to heart by the entire world".

The earliest inhabitants of the US were Native American tribes, who played the first music in the area. Beginning in the 17th century, immigrants from the British Isles, Spain, and France began arriving in large numbers, bringing with them new styles and instruments. African slaves brought musical traditions, and each subsequent wave of immigrants contributed to the melting pot.

Much of modern popular music can trace its roots to the emergence in the late 1800s of African American blues and the growth in the 1920s of gospel music. African American music formed a basis for popular music, which used elements derived from European and indigenous music. The US has also seen documented folk music and recorded popular music produced in the ethnic styles of Ukraine, Irish, Scottish, Polish, Mexican and Jewish communities, among others. Distinctive styles of American popular music began to emerge early in the 19th century, and in the 20th century the American music industry developed a series of new forms of music, using elements of blues and other genres of American folk music. These popular styles included country, R&B, jazz and rock, having fans across the globe. The 1960s and 1970s saw a number of important changes in American popular music, including the development of a number of new styles, such as heavy metal, punk, soul, and hip hop. Though these styles were not popular in the sense of mainstream, they were commercially recorded and are thus examples of popular music as opposed to folk or classical music.

American Film

The US was the first country to turn film into a popular form of entertainment and important industry. Since the early 1900s, Hollywood, in California, has been the center of the US film industry. Even the name itself is synonymous with the American film industry. There are many film studios in America today, and the Hollywood "Big Five" refers to Universal Pictures, Paramount, Warner Bros, Walt Disney and Columbia.

The American film industry witnesses the booming of American blockbusters, which are a kind of specific and definite appellation of American commercial movies featuring huge investment, powerful producer lineups, high technology, positive publicity and admirable box-office income. As the typical indication of American movies, they are at the vanguard of the global movie market, and play a vital role in selling American values, lifestyles and national images.

In 1915, the first major feature film *Birth of a Nation* was made, and at the same time, the famous film star Charles Chaplin made his first silent comedy. In 1928, sound was introduced, and it brought in new styles of film acting and new types of film in particular. It made possible the development of Hollywood musicals during the 1930s. The 1930s also saw the rise of gangster and thriller films. But a large proportion of Hollywood films have always been "romance". The leading romantic star of the silent film was Mary Pickford. The best known of all romantic films was *Gone with the Wind* (1939). Another world famous film star was Marilyn Monroe. Since 1960 the main traditions of the American film industry have been kept up by such films as *Cleopatra* (1963) and *The Sound of Music* (1965) and spy thrillers. For the development of American movies from 1980s until 1999, we have to mention one important person—Steve Spielberg, who had dominated the movie industry at that time. The American motion-picture director and producer whose diverse films, which ranged from science-fiction fare, including such classics as *Close Encounters of the Third Kind* (1977) and *E.T.: The Extra-Terrestrial* (1982), to historical dramas, notably *Schindler's List* (1993) and *Saving Private Ryan*

(1998), enjoyed both unprecedented popularity and critical success.

Although the increasing popularity of TV has meant that the cinema is no longer the most popular form of entertainment, the quality of the films and techniques in making films have greatly improved. Many films are produced by independent producers with new ideas and approaches. New faces constantly appear on the American screen including foreign film stars such as those from Britain, Australia and Brazil.

Religion in the US

The US is a highly developed country with modern science, yet it is also a country of religion, in which people have religious fervency. Among the current population (up to July, 2022), there are over 3,000 religious denominations or groups, and sixty out of a hundred have religious beliefs. There are all sorts of the religious groups. Among the American people, 36% are Protestants, 24% Roman Catholics, 3% Jews and 2% Orthodists. There are also some other religious groups such as Buddhists, Muslims and Hindus, but they are found in much smaller numbers.

Here are some findings from the recent research (Adapted from the facts released by Pew Research Center).

(1) Protestants no longer make up a majority of US adults. Closely tied to the rise of the religious "nones" is the decline of Christians, including Protestants. The US has a long history as a majority Protestant nation, and, as recently as the 2007 Pew Research Center Religious Landscape Studies showed that, more than half of US adults (51.3%) identified themselves as Protestants. But that figure has fallen, and our 2014 study found that 46.5% of Americans were then Protestants.

(2) Religious switching is a common occurrence in the US. Depending on how "religious switching" is defined, as many as 42% of US adults have switched religions.

(3) There is a wide range of racial and ethnic diversity among US religious groups and denominations. Seventh-day Adventists, Muslims and Jehovah's Witnesses are among the most racially and ethnically diverse US religious groups.

(4) US Catholics' views of climate change mirrored those of Americans overall, including major partisan divisions. While six-in-ten Catholic Democrats say global warming is caused by humans and that it is a very serious problem, only about a quarter of Catholic Republicans feel the same way.

(5) In a typical week, about one-in-five Americans share their faith online. This is about the same as the number who tune in to religious talk radio, watch religious TV programs or listen to Christian rock music.

(6) Christians continue to make up an overwhelming majority of members of Congress (92%), compared with 71% of the general public (as of 2014).

 **In-class Activity 课堂练习**

Ⅰ. **Comprehension questions.**

Go over this chapter and try to make an assessment on what you have learned with the following self-assessment questions.

1. How is American territory on the continent divided?
2. What American values do you value most? Please give reasons and talk with your partner.
3. Can you say something about Hollywood?
4. How many religious groups exist in America?

Ⅱ. **Comparative analysis.**

Insert the phrase "Chinese dream" into a search engine on the Internet and report to your group what you have found out about the studies of intercultural communication both at home and abroad.

Ⅲ. **True or false questions.**

American: Mr. Sugimoto, I have noticed that you are doing an excellent job on the assembly line. I hope that the other workers notice how it should be done.

Japanese: (He is uneasy) Praise is not necessary. I am only doing my job. (He hopes other Japanese workers do not hear)

American: You are the finest, most excellent and dedicated worker we have ever had at the Jones Corporation.

Japanese: (He blushes and nods his head several times, and keeps working)

American: Well, are you going to say "thank you, Mr. Sugimoto", or just remain silent?

Japanese: Excuse me, Mr. Jones... May I take leave for five minutes?

American: Sure. (He is annoyed and watches Sugimoto exit) I can't believe how rude some Japanese workers are. They seem to be disturbed by praise and don't answer you... just silent.

(　　) 1. In this case, the American manager could have praised Mr. Sugimoto in private or could have given credit to Mr. Sugimoto's team effort because the Japanese people tend to be collectivists.

(　　) 2. The Japanese employee Mr. Sugimoto should have known that the American culture ranks high on individualism and he could have embraced the American manager's praise and recognition.

(　　) 3. It is advisable for the Japanese staff to communicate with the American superiors or his co-workers in a direct way instead of keeping silent.

Ⅳ. **Case analysis.**

1. Listening or participating?

In an office, an American department manager discussed something with his Chinese subordinate. Much to his surprise, he noticed that his Chinese colleague just listened and kept nodding and saying "Yes", "OK" and "En". But he never offered any verbal message as feedback. Then the manager wondered if his Chinese colleague understood him or would cooperate with him on their work project. Finally, he couldn't refrain from asking "Do you understand me?" "Yes, I see what you mean," replied his colleague. But the American manager still doubted his Chinese colleague's understanding, and thought that it was so hard to communicate with Chinese.

2. The tea price, to cut or not to cut?

David Evenson, manager of a supermarket chain based in the US, was eager to establish trade ties with the People's Republic of China. Through a Chinese employee, Wu Xin, David reached an agreement to import 2,400 two-ounce packages of Chinese green tea from Xin Cheng, an agricultural and animal products importing and exporting corporation in China's Zhejiang Province. The shipment came in just in time for the Thanksgiving Day sales peak. David, a tea lover himself, was impressed by the quality of tea, and the packaging was better than he had expected. He anticipated good sales of the tea in his stores. He even took the trouble to have Wu Xin write some bilingual ads for the tea, which ran in major local papers and on radio stations. However, because of the small size of the transaction, the transportation per unit was quite high. In order to profit from this transaction, David's accounting department suggested that the Chinese green tea be priced a little higher than the domestic and imported brands of tea they already sold. Mr. Sheng Jiaoru, a representative from Xin Cheng, disagreed, suggesting that David cut the price to match other brands first; once the Chinese brand was established and recognized by the consumers, both sides could profit from economy of sale, selling a larger amount of tea at a lower price per unit. David, who was unwilling to start out selling at a loss, decided to go with his accounting department's price proposal. Three weeks later, Sheng called David from China and learned that the green tea had not sold well at all and had been returned to the warehouse. Sheng again suggested that David try lowering the price, but David seemed to have lost interest in the project. Over the next several months, Sheng was unable to interest David in further deals, and he finally let things rest for a time.

Background Information 背景知识

1. Statue of Liberty(自由女神像)全名为"自由女神铜像国家纪念碑",正式名称是"自由照耀世界(Liberty Enlightening the World)",位于美国纽约海港内自由岛的哈德逊河口附近。它是法国于1876年为纪念美国独立战争胜利一百周年而建造的,1886年10月28日铜像落成。自由女神像是美国的象征,是美利坚民族和美法人民友谊的象征,表达美国人民争取民主、自由的崇高理想。

2. Uncle Sam(山姆大叔)缩写是"U.S."。1812年,英美战争期间,美国特罗城有一个专门供应军用牛肉的商人(也有说法称是军事订货的官员)名叫山姆尔·威尔逊(Samuel Wilson,1776—1854),人们平时都叫他山姆大叔(Uncle Sam)。战争期间,他担任纽约和新泽西州的军需检验员,负责在供应军队的牛肉桶和酒桶上打戳。他在那些被美国政府收购的牛肉箱上都盖上"U.S."字样。人们于是开玩笑说这些盖有"U.S."字样的箱子都是山姆大叔的。后来"山姆大叔"便成了美国的绰号。美国人还把"山姆大叔"诚实可靠、吃苦耐劳及爱国主义精神视为自己民族的骄傲和共有的品质。

3. Star-Spangled Banner(星条旗)是美国的国旗。1777年7月14日,为了代表这个新生国家的团结和独立精神,美国国会通过法案确定国旗。由于当时参加合众国的有十三个州,因此美国国旗由十三条红白相间的横条和十三颗衬以蓝底的白色五角星组成。同时决议还解释了国旗上白、红、蓝三色的意义:白色代表廉洁公正;红色代表勇敢无畏;蓝色代表警惕、坚韧和正义。美国自独立以后,各州陆续加入联邦。1818年4月4日,国会又通过一项决议案:每当合众国接受一个州,一颗新星将于下一年的7月4日添入国旗。现在美国国旗上仍是十三条红白相间的横条,五角星却已增加到五十颗,代表美国的五十个州。

4. *The Star-Spangled Banner*(《星条旗之歌》)为美国国歌,由美国律师弗朗西斯·斯科特·基(Francis Scott Key)作词,美国作曲家约翰·斯塔福德·史密斯(John Stafford Smith)作曲。1931年,美国国会正式将《星条旗之歌》定为美国的国歌。美国国歌共包括四节,绝大多数场合只唱第一节。

5. Melting pot(熔炉)即指美国,这是因为美国是一个由来自世界各地不同民族的移民融合组成的国度。这些移民说的英语不像英国人的英语那样具有较强的阶层性与地域多样性。他们形成了相似的生活习惯与礼节;城乡居民的差别也不像其他国家那样明显。美国社会竞争性强,且存在着种族歧视,但它在同化来自不同民族的移民方面表现出相当大的弹性和包容性。因而,形成了全新的基于个人奋斗、自我管束与竞争精神之上的整体文化与共同的民族意识,成为一个"多民族组成的国家"。

6. Salad bowl(沙拉碗)用来比喻美国文化多样性。20世纪60年代,美国出现了103个民族集团和173个土著民的单位,加起来有200多个民族单位,美国已不是"民族大熔炉",而似乎变成了"民族博物馆"。来自几大洲、几大洋的移民人群,几代人还依然保持着他们自己的语言和文化。在从所谓"主流文化"的概念出发考虑对这些人群的接纳或者拒绝问题时,1976年,穆瑞提出,"文化熔炉"(cultural melting pot)的概念似乎不适用于他们,美国已经是一个巨大的"沙拉碗"。这样一个定义主要是针对以前的"大熔炉"政策提出来的,综合学者的概括,意指美国多元文化背景的移民群体联合在一起,像一个大的沙拉碗,不同文化各自保持特色,根本没有合并融合为某种单一均质的文化。加拿大一般用"马赛克"(Mosaic)来概括其多元文化特征。随着美国多元文化现实状况的加剧,"沙拉碗"的文化比喻被越来越多的人接受,甚至还具有了某种"政治上正确"的色彩,进而取代"文化熔炉"政策和文化寓言进入了公共表述领域。

7. Individualism(个人主义)是美国文化的核心要素之一,是美国民众认可并遵从的重要行为价值原则。美国人信奉个人主义,并且乐于遵循建立在个人主义基础之上的理想化模式去生活。在一定意义上讲,美国国家和社会的建构也是以个人主义为逻辑起点实现的。

8. Punctuality(准时),美国公司主管对他人的个人生活不感兴趣,习惯开门见山,直接谈生意。他们不喜欢在隐私打听、社交寒暄上花时间,注重工作的效率。这种"脾性"常常让不同文化背景的人觉得冷漠、难相处。

9. Equality(平等),美国是一个权力距离指数较低的国家,其社会成员行为独立,彼此平等相待。即便是上级和下级之间,关系也依旧平等自在,并不紧张。

10. Country music(乡村音乐)是名副其实的美国"特产",是土生土长的美国音乐,体现了浓郁的美国南方民间音乐风格。传统的乡村音乐从19世纪的弦乐曲和传统叙事歌中发展而来。乡村音乐的一个显著特点就是:不受性别和年龄限制,也不受时间和地点的限制。一把吉他,外加班卓琴和口琴乐器的伴奏,歌手便可以抒发他们心中的快乐和忧愁。在一个多世纪的发展历程中,美国乡村音乐虽然在音乐风格上多种多样,但是几乎都有着共同的主题思想,即歌曲都毫无例外地反映了普通美国人,特别是生活在社会最底层的普通工人和农民的爱情婚姻生活、宗教信仰、对乡土的热爱和眷恋,以及他们生活中最普通也最感人的经历,其中不少歌曲都以工作场面为主题。

11. Steven Allan Spielberg(史蒂文·艾伦·斯皮尔伯格)(1946年12月18日—),生于美国辛辛那提市,犹太人,美国著名电影导演、编剧、电影制作人、慈善家,主要导演作品包括《头号玩家》《侏罗纪公园》《辛德勒的名单》和《拯救大兵瑞恩》等多部影史经典。在四十年的电影生涯中,斯皮尔伯格曾触及多种主题与类型。斯皮尔伯格早期以拍摄科幻小说与冒险电影为主,有时聚焦于儿童,被视为现代好莱坞大成本(Blockbuster)电影制作的典型。此时代表作有《大白鲨》(1975)、《E.T.外星人》(1982)与《侏罗纪公园》(1993)。斯皮尔伯格后来的作品则开始将触角延伸至犹太人大屠杀、奴隶制度、战争与恐怖主义等题材,比较突出的有《辛德勒的名单》《拯救大兵瑞恩》。前者是关于"二战"时犹太人大屠杀事件;后者则是关于"二战"时的战场事迹。斯皮尔伯格凭着上述两片进军奥斯卡,先于1993年凭《辛德勒的名单》荣获奥斯卡最佳导演奖;1998年凭《拯救大兵瑞恩》获同一奖项。《时代》杂志将他列入世纪百大最重要人物一员。《生活》杂志将斯皮尔伯格评为同时代中最有影响力的人物。

Cultural Kaleidoscope 文化万花筒

Comparison of North American and Chinese Cultural Characteristics

There are culturally conditioned differences between people, but differences do not automatically imply right or wrong. Although differences may be a source of chaos, it is also the source of energy and the source of dynamism. Differences should be celebrated rather than regarded as objects of ridicule or obstacles to understanding. Consider water: without a difference in levels, water will stand still and become stagnant. It is only with difference that water can flow. Life and human interaction would be easier to understand if we could make everybody the same again, would it not? But since it is neither possible nor desirable that everybody and all cultures be made the same, and since it is desirable to keep a certain difference between cultures so that our world can be more colorful and beautiful, we need to understand different cultures and meanings of cultural difference. Through making comparisons we can understand different people better and thus reduce intercultural and cross-cultural misunderstandings.

中国传统文化 3

North Americans	Chinese
Stress independence	Stress interdependence
Individual is seen as very important	Individual is seen as part of group
Understanding oneself is seen as the most important	Interpersonal harmony is more important
Equality is seen as important	Hierarchy is accepted as necessary
Arguments are seen as paths to truth	Open argument is seen as a divergence
Success is seen as a personal achievement	Success is attributed to group efforts
Privacy is seen as rather important	Privacy is seen as less important
Have a monochronic view of time	Have a moderate monochronic view of time
Have no tolerance for ambiguity	Have high tolerance for ambiguity
Seldom borrow and lend	Borrow and lend things often and easily
Are accustomed to a short-term relationship	Have a strong tendency to build life-time relationships

Business Etiquette in Belt and Road Countries
"一带一路"国家的商务礼仪

　　丝绸之路对中国人的精神生活产生了难以估量的影响。中国人的技术和文化通过这条道路传入西线诸国,如纸张、印刷术的传播,直接影响了这些国家文明的发展。而中国人通过这条文化大动脉,输入了异域的艺术、哲学和宗教,高昌、龟兹、敦煌等地的石窟艺术就是中外文化交流的见证。丝绸之路上这些当年的绿洲城邦,留下了令人惊叹的艺术遗迹,记载着中国与西方交流的灿烂历史。陆上丝绸之路促进了中国自汉代至唐代文化开放政策的形成。这条丝绸之路也带来了中亚、西亚和欧洲的文明,这个更广泛的"西方",也影响着中国文化后来的发展。通过丝绸之路,印度、东南亚、西亚、非洲和欧洲之间的贸易交流也迅速活跃起来,无数新奇的商品得以交换,新技术得以推广,从而推进了各自文明的发展。

土耳其的商务礼仪

　　大多数土耳其公司是家族企业。与土耳其商人打交道需要知道交易的成功不仅取决于精心准备的商业策划案,更取决于建立良好人际关系的能力。这是因为土耳其人更喜欢和他们认识并尊重的人做生意,而且在交流中极为注重礼貌。土耳其人不像其他国家那样需要保持个人空间,因此在交谈时他们会站在你身边。

商务会晤通常需要提前一至两周预约,最好通过电话安排会面,不要在七月和八月土耳其人度假时安排会面,也避免在斋月期间安排会议。和土耳其公司谈判时要有耐心,不要使用最后期限或高压战术。通常土耳其人只有确信双方愿意建立商业关系时才会交换他们的名片。商务着装要求穿着较为保守的正装。例如:男士应该穿西服和打领带,女士应该穿职业服装。

Many companies in Türkiye are still family-owned businesses. Two tips are provided for anyone who desires to close a deal with Turks. Your success is defined by your ability to build effective personal relationships combined with a clearly outlined and well-presented proposal. It would be advisable to spend time establishing a personal relationship since Turks prefer to do business with those they know and respect. Besides, courtesy is crucial in all business dealings. Unlike other countries, Turks do not require as much personal space and they would stand close to you while conversing.

Business appointments are necessary and should be made 1 to 2 weeks in advance, preferably by telephone. Many Turks take a vacation during July or August, so it is better to avoid scheduling appointments at that time. It is also not a good idea to arrange meetings during Ramadan. When negotiating, the negotiator should be patient and abandon the idea of using deadlines or pressure tactics. Often Turks do not give their business cards unless they are certain that they wish to establish a business relationship. Business dress is conservative. For instance, men will be expected to wear a suit and tie. Similarly, women should wear professional outfits.

沙特阿拉伯的商务礼仪

在沙特阿拉伯,宗教无处不在,完全渗透进沙特的商业文化和商业环境之中。与沙特企业达成交易的速度一般较慢,这是因为沙特人注重培养人际关系,非常看重人脉,遵守沙特当地的商业习惯和模式。

商务问候时,最好在沙特人的姓名前加上博士、教授、主席、殿下等头衔。商务会晤通常需要提前几周甚至一个月预约,会谈非常讲究守时,会谈前经常是一些闲聊。比如,沙特人会长时间地询问对方的健康或者家庭状况,并以此作为培养人际关系和建立信任的方式。沙特公司的决策速度慢,因为他们的大多数决定都需要经过多个层面的审批。沙特人是强硬的谈判者,需要谈判者极具耐心,不要使用高压战术。

商务着装礼仪要求穿着保守和传统的颜色。例如:男士应该穿西装、打领带;女士应该穿正式保守的商务服装,最好选择中性色彩的衣物,穿短跟鞋,也可带上一条轻便的羊绒披肩。除手和脸外,不要露出皮肤,不要穿传统的阿拉伯服装参加商务会议。

Religion pervades everything in Saudi Arabia including business culture and commercial environment. Business happens at a much slower pace with a huge emphasis on relationships, connections and local business practices.

In greeting, it is better to address Saudis with an honorific prefix such as "Dr.",

"Professor", "Chairman", "Your Highness", etc. Business appointments should be made several weeks or even a month in advance. Punctuality is regarded as essential even though meetings always start after prolonged inquiries about health and family, etc. Indulgence in conversations as this is all part of the relationship and trust building process. When they conduct negotiations, decisions are made slowly as most of them require several layers of approval. So do not try to rush the process. In addition, Saudis are tough negotiators and demand patience. Therefore, it is advisable to abandon the idea of using high-pressure tactics.

Business dress and colours should be kept conservative and traditional. For example, men should wear suits and ties. Women should wear conservative business attire, again in neutral colours, with short-heeled shoes and preferably a light pashmina scarf at hand. Other than hands and face, the skin should not be visible. Foreigners should not wear any local dress to business meetings.

Intercultural Tips 跨文化拓展知识

英汉动物词汇的文化意蕴及翻译

人类有许多共同的生活经验和感受，所以不同文化有不少重合之处，这也反映在英汉两种语言成语中动物的比喻义上。这时可采用直译法，在一定程度上能够保留原语的民族色彩和文化特色。英语中很多比喻性词语在汉语中已被广泛使用，如"as sly as a fox"（像狐狸一样狡猾）、"as hungry as a wolf"（饿狼般的）、"dark horse"（黑马——竞争中出人意料的获胜者）。汉语中被移植到英语中的比喻性词语也不少，如纸老虎（a paper tiger）、癞蛤蟆想吃天鹅肉（a toad hankering for a taste of swan）。

此外，可借助归化的手法使喻体入乡随俗，这是因为东西方语言文化存在着巨大的差异。尽管喻体形式不一，但译文读者与原文读者对所接受的信息反应基本一致，如胆小如鼠（as timid as a rabbit）、落汤鸡（a drowned rat）、养虎为患（cherish a snake in one's bosom）、瓮中捉鳖（like a rat in the hole）、热锅上的蚂蚁（like a hen on a hot girdle）、如鱼得水（like a duck to water）。

在英美人的传统文化观念里，"magpie"（喜鹊）并非是快活的形象，而是给人喋喋不休、令人生厌的感觉。在西方文化里，蝙蝠给人以坏的联想，人们提到蝙蝠就会想到丑陋、凶恶的吸血动物，与蝙蝠相关的词语大多带贬义，如"as blind as a bat"（鼠目寸光），等等。而在汉族文化中，蝙蝠是吉祥、健康、幸福的象征，这些意象很可能来自于"蝠""福"同音。由此可知，英汉语言中也存在明显的文化意象的错位或者文化冲突，这是因为英汉两种语言在动物词汇联想意义上的差异，造成了语义表述上的差别。在翻译中要尽量避免文化意象的流失或破坏，不仅要译出原作的语义信息，还要译出原作的内在文化信息。我们列举几个主要的动物词汇的联想意义来谈一谈英汉文化的差异及翻译。

（1）鱼（fish）　英语文化中鱼文化丰富多样、短小精悍，表意明确清晰，比喻搭配生动传神又耐人寻味。例如："The great fish eat up the small"（大鱼吃小鱼）；"Fish begins to stink at the head"（上梁不正下梁歪）；"Never offer to teach fish to swim"（不要班门弄斧），等等。汉语文化中的鱼文化，人们更容易联想到"姜太公钓鱼""城门失火，殃及池鱼""鱼与熊掌不可兼得""鱼跃龙门"等许多富于哲理的历史典故和生活故事。

（2）龙（**dragon**）　在英语文化中，"dragon"是一种会吐火伤人的怪物，是凶险邪恶的象征。但在汉语文化中，"龙"是古代传说中的神异动物，象征帝王，龙的传人赋予"龙"以深厚的感情意义、丰富的联想和深远的社会意义。因为西方谈"dragon"色变，我们在翻译时候要注意适当地转换形象，例如："亚洲四小龙"常被译为"the Four Tigers of Asia"或者"Four Asian Tigers"。

（3）狗（**dog**）　英国人把狗看成是人类朝夕相伴的忠实朋友，狗的比喻基本上也用于褒义，大多数用来形容和描述事物好的一面。例如："a lucky dog"（幸运儿），"Dog does not eat dog"（同类不相残），"Love me, love my dog"（爱屋及乌），等等。在汉语文化中，狗常用于比喻坏人做事，如"狗仗人势""鸡鸣狗盗""狗急跳墙"，等等。

（4）牛与马（**bull and horse**）　在英语中，"bull""ox"（牛）有愚笨、鲁莽的意思，如"a bull in a China shop"（瓷器店里的牛，意为动辄闯祸的人）；在商业上，"牛"有股票价格上涨的意思，汉语也借用了英语的"bull market"（牛市）一词。而汉语中与"牛"相关的表达相当于英语中的"horse"，例如："身壮如牛"（as strong as a horse）。所以，"他有一股子牛劲"译为"He is as strong as a horse"。"他真是一个老黄牛"译为"He is really a willing horse"。在英国历史上，马是农耕文化的代表，所以有关马的表述较多。例如："eat like a horse"（吃得很多）、"ride the high horse"（耀武扬威、趾高气扬）。

Movie to See 观影学文化

Please watch the movie *Forrest Gump*（《阿甘正传》）with your classmates and discuss what intercultural elements are involved in it.

Unit 4　Verbal Communication

语言交际

 Learning Objectives 学习目标

- 了解与跨文化交际有关的语义学和语用学的一些基本知识。
- 熟悉文化和语言之间的关系。
- 掌握基于语用学的文化差异。
- 了解语言中的禁忌和委婉语。

 Lead-in 单元导读

语言与文化

语言交际是跨文化交际的最主要方式。正是语言的产生和发展，人类文化才得以传承。不存在没有语言的文化，也不存在没有文化的语言。

语言是思维的物质外壳，它体现的是精神、涵养、气质、底蕴、态度、性格。从如何给自己的孩子起名，到如何称呼自己的亲戚长辈，再到饮食文化和语言词汇之间的关系，涉及社会文化生活的方方面面。

语言与文化的关系最直接的表现是语言表达了人们对世界的看法、态度和价值取向。每种语言都存在着大量的格言、警句、俗语。这些语句往往是这种文化价值取向的直接表达。以个体主义和集体主义两种不同的价值取向为例，我们从以下世界各地的谚语中，就可以看到不同文化的人们是如何看待个人与集体的关系的。

(1) 在团体中当傻瓜也比一个人有智慧好。（墨西哥）
(2) 离开羊群的羊会被狼吃掉。（土耳其）

(3) 当蜘蛛网连在一起的时候可以困住一头狮子。(非洲)
(4) 三个臭皮匠,顶个诸葛亮。(中国)
(5) 即使是在天堂,一个人独处也不好。(以色列)
(6) 出头的钉子被砸下。(日本)

在跨文化交际的过程中,语言与文化密不可分。词语和表示词语的声音因文化而异,词语的意义也受到文化的影响。

此外,语言的多样性不仅有助于人们洞悉社会现实,而且有利于表达其独特的文化价值观。为顺利完成交际,交际者必须考虑双方的民族特点、文化差异,以及语言的语义层面和语用层面。

语义与文化

在语言的诸要素中,词汇与文化关系最为密切,因此通过词汇来研究文化是必不可少的路径。有的学者将词汇分为一般词汇与文化词汇。文化词汇是指特定的文化范畴的词汇,它是民族文化在语言词汇中直接或间接的反映。文化词汇与其他一般词汇的界定有以下两点:一是文化词汇本身载有明确的民族文化信息,并且隐含着深层的民族文化的含义。文化词汇的另一特点是它与民族文化,包括上面所说的物质文化、制度文化和心理文化有各种关系。有的是该文化的直接反映,如龙、凤、华表等;有的是该文化的间接反映,如汉语中的红、黄、白、黑等颜色词。

语用与文化

人们在交际过程中需要正确使用一种语言的语音、语法、词汇,否则难免会出现各种问题,甚至使交际中断。但是,仅仅掌握语音、语法、词汇还并不能保证顺畅的交际。人们在具体使用语言时还会运用一套语用规则,有的学者称之为讲话规则。这些规则包括如何称呼对方、如何见面打招呼、如何提出一项要求、如何接受或拒绝对方的要求、如何告别、讲话谁先谁后、讲话谁多谁少等。这些方面的问题过去往往为人们所忽略,只是近二三十年来随着社会语言学、语用学的建立与发展,随着交际教学法的普及,人们才越来越感到语用规则的重要性,如礼貌原则与策略——得体准则、慷慨准则、赞扬准则、谦虚准则、一致准则、同情准则。此外还有以下语用规则。

称呼语是语言交际中最频繁出现的言语行为。

称赞语的主要功能是建立良好的社会关系,包括打招呼、感谢、表示抱歉、引出话题等。

道歉语是一种补救措施,其基本功能是对冒犯行为进行补救,从而恢复社会关系的平衡与和谐。

请求语是一种指令性的言语交际行为,说话人发出请求的意图是让听话人按照自己的意愿去做某件事。

与语言规则相比,语用规则的掌握要困难得多。首先,因为语音、语法、词汇的各种规则已经写进了语音书、语法书和各种词典,人们有章可循,有书可查。而语用规则却远远还没有总结成文字记录在书中。有的文章和书涉及某一条或某些方面的语用规则,但迄今还没有完整的对于某一语言的语用规则的总结。其次,对于语言规则人们比较自觉,而语用规则在大多数情况下人们并不自觉。你若问一个中国人,他遵循哪些讲话规则,他会很难回答。

语言交际风格与文化

(1) 直接与间接的交际风格。低语境文化的人们谈话以说话者为中心,喜欢直截了当,不喜欢拐弯抹角,直接通过语言来解读对方意图。高语境文化的人们以听话者为中心,喜欢比较委婉的表达,经常通过暗示表达真实想法,听话者间接根据语境揣摩对方心理意图。

(2) 谦虚与自信的交际风格。谦虚或自信的交际风格也是价值观的体现。个人主义文化强调人的自信和争先精神,追求与众不同,体现个人自信。集体主义文化强调个人与集体的和谐,崇尚谦虚,考虑他人感受,体现的是谦虚的美德和含蓄的表达方式。

(3) 归纳与演绎的交际风格。在谈话中亚洲人通常使用"主题—评论"的说话顺序,主要观点在充足的背景性介绍之后才提出,而西方人大多在谈话伊始就开门见山地提出主要观点,前者的会话风格称为"归纳式",后者的会话风格称为"演绎式"。例如,美国人(演绎法)认为先把自己的观点鲜明地摆出来具有说服力,而中国人(归纳法)认为先与听众建立一种和谐的关系,把材料一点一点地讲出来,最后画龙点睛才具有说服力。中国人重视和谐的人际关系,不愿意与他人形成对抗。由此可见,交际风格与深层文化密切相关。

语言交际是交际的主要方式。本单元将会介绍与跨文化交际有关的语义学和语用学的基本知识,阐述文化与语言的关系,辨析语言交际中的言语禁忌和委婉语的关系,提供一些提升语言交际能力的有用建议。

Pre-class Activity 课前活动

Verbal communication occurs when people are chatting with their friends, discussing an issue in a group, making a public speech, etc. Successful verbal communication involves cautious choice of the language that takes into account logical and emotional effects, objective and subjective factors, and the needs of the message sender and receiver, especially when they come from different cultural backgrounds. For example, if you want to be an effective communicator, you have to adapt your material and manner to the interlocutor(s). Find out what the interlocutor(s) is (are) interested in or their taboos, possibly before you meet.

Reading 课内阅读

Reading One: High-context and Low-context Language

Edward T. Hall, an American intercultural researcher, has described cultural differences in the use of language and context in communication. According to him, communication that occurs mostly through language is low-context and communication that occurs through ways other than language is high-context.

High context refers to societies or groups where people have close connections over a long period of time. Many aspects of cultural behavior are not made explicit because most members know what to do and what to think from years of interaction with each other. Your family is probably an example of a high-context environment.

Low context refers to societies where people tend to have many connections but of shorter duration or for some specific reasons. In these societies, cultural behavior and beliefs may need to be spelled out explicitly so that those coming into the cultural environment know how to behave.

High Context
- Less verbally explicit communication, less written/formal information.
- More internalized understandings of what is communicated.
- Multiple cross-cutting ties and intersections with others.
- Long-term relationships.
- Strong boundaries—who is accepted as an "insider" vs. who is considered as an "outsider".
- Knowledge is situational, relational.
- Decisions and activities focus on personal face-to-face relationships, often around a central person who has authority.

Here are some examples of high-context communication: small religious congregations, a party with friends, family gatherings, expensive gourmet restaurants, neighborhood restaurants with a regular client, undergraduate on-campus friendships, regular pick-up games, and hosting a friend in your home overnight.

Low Context
- Rule-oriented, people play by external rules.
- More knowledge is codified, public, external and accessible.
- Sequencing, separation of time, of space, of activities and of relationship.
- More interpersonal connections of shorter duration.
- Knowledge is more often transferable.
- Task-centered. Decisions and activities focus on what needs to be done, division of responsibilities.

Here are some examples of low-context communication: large US airports, a chain supermarket, a cafeteria, a convenience store, sports where rules are clearly laid out and a motel.

While these terms are sometimes useful in describing some aspects of a culture, one can never say a culture is "high" or "low" because no culture exists exclusively at one end of the scale; some are high while others are low. American culture, while not at the bottom, is toward the lower end of the scale. "High" and "low" are therefore less relevant as a description of a whole people, and more useful to describe and understand particular situations and environments. Any transaction can be characterized as high, low, or middle context.

Reading Two: Cultural Difference on Pragmatics Level

Language can be used to achieve multiple purposes: to address people, to compliment people, to make a request, to extend an invitation, to declare a man and a woman husband and wife, and even to sentence a criminal to death. Our everyday communication is filled with such pragmatic use of language, but the realization of speech act may vary across cultures and within a culture. An individual may say words clearly and use long, complex sentences with correct grammar, but still have a communication problem, if he or she has not mastered the rules for social language known as pragmatics. So a good mastery of grammar of one language does not mean that successful communication is carried out. When the speech behavior is not appropriately done, misunderstandings, even damage will be brought about between communicators.

1. Addressing People

Some terms for addressing people in Chinese and English can be equally misleading for Chinese learners of English or English learners of Chinese. For instance, in China "a comrade" was once used for all people regardless of their gender, social and marital status, which means "Mr.", "Mrs. or Ms." in English speaking countries. "师傅（master）" is another extended term of addressing frequently used to show respect and politeness for strangers, which roughly equals "Sir" or "Madam" in English. In addition, Chinese has a much more generalized system of kinship than English does. Terms such as "叔叔（uncle）" "阿姨（aunt）" "爷爷（grandpa）" "奶奶（grandma）" are used as titles for senior people or strangers, which would be puzzling to English native speakers.

2. Showing Gratitude

In English-speaking countries, people tend to verbalize their gratitude more often and accept thanks more directly and frankly than Chinese people do. As a result, there are a great many English sentences used to express thanks, such as "Many thanks" "Thanks a lot" "I appreciate your help" "Thank you for helping me" "Thank you all the same" and sentences of accepting thanks like, "You're welcome" "Don't mention it" "Not at all" "Any time", etc. However, Chinese people are quite the opposite. However grateful they are, they may not verbalize their thanks, or they will be considered to be insufferable people. In their conception, expressing or accepting thanks makes people alienated from one another.

3. Being Modest

Modesty is deeply rooted in Chinese culture. The Chinese are always modest about their achievements, or prefer a low-key statement to a display of their advantages. When you praise a Chinese person, he or she may humbly tell you how deficient he or she is. Therefore, the Chinese reply "哪里,哪里（Well, it is nothing）" to any complimentary remarks should not be interpreted as a denial of the truth. However, Americans like praising people. Receiving such a reply of refusal, Americans often wonder whether they have made a wrong judgment or not.

4. Saying "No"

It's difficult for one from a high-context culture to say "no". For example, Chinese people will accept a more indirect way to give negative answers. People prefer to say "Please don't bother" "I'll think it over" "We'll discuss it again" while people in English speaking countries would like to say "No, thank you" directly, or "I disagree with you", "You're absolutely wrong".

Reading Three: The Relationship between Language and Culture

Language is used to preserve and transmit culture and cultural relations. Different ideas are derived from different language usages within one's culture and the whole intertwining of these relationships starts at one's birth. When an infant is born, it is not unlike any other infant born; in fact, they are all quite similar. It is not until the child is exposed to his/her surroundings that he/she becomes individual in and of his/her cultural group.

This idea, which describes all people as similar at birth, has been around for thousands of years and was discussed by Confucius. From birth, the child's life, opinions, and language are shaped by what it comes in contact with. Physically and mentally everyone is the same, while the interactions between persons or groups vary widely from place to place. Patterns which emerge from these group behaviors and interactions will be approved of, or disapproved of. Behaviors which are acceptable will vary from location to location, thus forming the basis of different cultures. It is from these differences that one's view of the world is formed.

Culture is the beliefs and practices governing the life of a society for which a particular language is the vehicle of expression. Therefore, everyone's views are dependent on the culture which has developed his way of thinking, and are described with the language which has been shaped by that culture. The understanding of a culture and its people can be enhanced by the knowledge of their language. This brings us to an interesting fact that even when people are brought up under similar behavioral backgrounds or cultural situations since they speak different languages, their world views may be very different. Different thoughts are brought about by the use of different forms of language. One is limited by the language used to express one's ideas. Different languages will create different limitations and therefore people who share a culture but speak different languages will have different world views. Still, language is rooted in culture and culture is reflected and passed on by language from one generation to the next.

The relationship between language and culture is deeply rooted. Look at the metaphors below about language and culture. They may help you further understand their relationships.

Language and culture are like a living organism. Language is flesh while culture is blood. Without culture, language would be dead; without language, culture would have no shape.

Language and culture are like an iceberg. The language is the part above water while the greater part which is hidden beneath the surface is the invisible aspect of culture.

Reading Four: Why Do Words Have Meaning and Power?

Words are merely sounds in essence, but they will have meaning and power once they become associated with an object, an action or a feeling. And the way sounds come to have meaning is through repetitive exposure to spoken language in context of a relationship. An infant who hears spoken words only from a radio would never really come to understand language. But the infant with a caregiver who will say, "Here, see the dog, this is a doggy," or open up a book and say, "Find the ball, find the ball," soon learns that a unique combination of sounds signifies the dog or the ball. As soon as the infant makes the connection between the object and the sounds, then those sounds become a word. That's how meaning comes to words, by making the association between the sound and the object.

And of course, later in life, we make the further association between the sounds, the physical representation of the object (for example, a photo or a drawing) and the written word. At the beginning of our lives, however, sounds become words through repetitive opportunities of experiencing the parent, teacher, or caregiver making the connection between the sound and an object, the sound and a behavior, or the sound and a feeling. That's why it's so important that we spend time with our young children and infants teaching them language. We can't teach them language by putting them in front of a video or a TV. But we can teach children language by reading to them, talking with them, and singing to them.

However, it should be noted that sometimes words might become detached from their meaning. The important part about human communication is that it is a wonderful, complex combination of nonverbal cues and verbal language, and when those are synchronous, it can be incredibly powerful. But when someone is using words that don't match the action or don't match the emotion that's being conveyed, it's confusing. Everyone has had that feeling that "this just doesn't fit or there's more to that story". Many abusive parents say all the time words like, "I love my baby; I love my child." And this is sometimes within hours of them putting a cigarette butt out on the child, or leaving the child for 48 hours with no food, or beating the child senseless. And clearly, the meaning of the word "love" for someone who would do that to their child is different from that for most parents.

Children, as they're learning language, begin to see the power in different words. Not all words have the same power. What they find is that there are certain words that will get an adult's attention. For young children, these are typically words about physical function. As they get older, sexualized words become more popular. Or, there are some children, who when they get frustrated or overwhelmed, and don't feel they're getting the attention of their parents, will say, "I wish I were dead." They usually don't really wish they were dead. But they know that as soon as they say that, everybody stops, everybody looks and pays attention. They learn, "Wow, that's a powerful phrase." So children use words and wordplay to literally experiment, to find out what the meaning of the word really is. So when children get the attention of adults with a few words, they learn the power of specific words.

Reading Five: Taboos and Euphemisms

Language taboo is one aspect of social taboos, which is referred to as prohibitions in language behavior. It can also be collectively defined as "tabu" and translated into "taboo" or "tabu" in English, which means "sacred and untouchable".

Language taboo includes a wide spectrum of words supposed to be a kind of inconsideration and recklessness according to religion, society and culture. Taboos in every language are related to words and expressions which are not mentioned because of their negative connotations and because using them provokes embarrassment and negative reactions from society. There are words and expressions in every language which have a negative face or an unpleasant, unfavorable and impolite concept. Therefore, the members of this language society avoid using them directly and explicitly; these aspects are called language prohibitions or "taboos".

There are generally three categories of English taboos: sacred words, sly words, and insulting words.

For example, due to faith, some words such as "God, Jesus", are regarded as sacred and inviolable, and only on formal and solemn occasions, or on religious occasions can these words be used.

For defamatory words, most of them are related to sex. With the development of society, some words about aging, disease, death, poverty, obesity and other topics have naturally become taboo words to a certain extent.

The term "euphemism" refers to polite, indirect expressions that replace words and phrases considered harsh and impolite, or which suggest something unpleasant. A euphemism, used as an idiomatic expression, always loses its literal meaning and refers to something else. For example, "pass away" is a euphemism that describes the death of a person. In addition, many organizations use the term "downsizing" for the distressing act of "firing" its employees. Euphemisms depend largely on the social context of the speakers and writers, where they feel the need to replace certain words that may prove embarrassing for particular listeners or readers in a particular situation.

Euphemisms can be divided into three types: one type is closely related to taboo words. For example, the old people are often referred to as the elderly, senior citizens, venerable people, people who get on years, and so on. The second type is euphemisms related to courtesy. For example, people often use big, plump, stout or over-weight instead of fat. The third type is related to politics. For instance, a poor nation can be said to be a developing nation; poor people are replaced by low income. The last type is related to the occupation.

The relationship between taboos and euphemisms has been explained by Yang Hua (2020): "Taboos and euphemisms are two common and closely related language phenomena, and they are also a common cultural phenomenon ... Language is an inevitable outcome of the development of human society and a response to social life. The development of society promotes the evolution of language. With the development of society, in real life, people have taboos on certain things and behaviors for various reasons. Over time, they become taboos. Their expressions in language are called taboo words. The development of society and the existence of taboo words have prompted the emergence of euphemisms. Every country and every nation has its own taboos and euphemisms, which also profoundly reflect the development and changes in society".

Reading Six: 7 Tips to Improve Verbal Communication Skills

It is necessary for people to have a good command of strong verbal communication skills. They are extremely valuable in both your personal and professional life. When speaking clearly, confidently, and with poise, you are much more likely to earn the respect of others and build rapport. This is particularly important in business interactions.

The following 7 tips will help you improve your verbal communication skills so that you can better connect with your audience, earn respect, and build the relationships necessary for successful business interactions:

1. Think Before You Speak

By organizing your thoughts in advance, you can eliminate many of the awkward pauses that occur when speaking. It will also help you relay your information more concisely. While writing down your thoughts is not always possible in impromptu discussions, it is still effective to take a minute to organize your thoughts in your mind before you begin to speak.

2. Be Clear and Concise

The most effective way to get your point across is to make it in a clear and concise manner. Avoid using complex, convoluted sentences, and try to state your argument in direct language. Before speaking, ask yourself, "What is the clearest way I can make my point?"

3. Speak with Confidence

Speaking in a confident manner will help you build trust and command the respect of your audience. There are several factors which can impact your ability to speak confidently, including your command of the subject matter, your word choice, the tone of your voice, your body language, and your ability to make direct eye contact with your audience.

4. Vary Your Vocal Tone

Speaking in a monotone voice is a surefire way to bore your audience and show you're disengaged. Instead, use voice inflection to add emphasis to important points, and vary the pitch of your voice to express emotions. This will help keep your audience engaged in your message.

5. Be an Active Listener

Being a good listener is as important as being a good speaker, and it will improve the quality of your verbal interactions. Keep the 5 stages of active listening in mind:

(1) Receiving: to listen to the speaker attentively.

(2) Understanding: to interpret the messages conveyed.

(3) Remembering: to summarize the key points in the communication.

(4) Evaluating: to figure out the necessary feedback.

(5) Responding: to offer timely responses.

It shows the people you are speaking with that you genuinely care about their ideas, and it helps ensure you understand their needs. Summarize what you've heard and ask further questions. This will enable you to build trust and rapport much quicker.

6. Be Aware of Non-verbal Communication Cues

Your body language significantly impacts the way others interpret what you say and your attitude to the conversation. Pay attention to the gestures you make, your facial expressions, and your body language to ensure they align with the message you are trying to get across.

It's equally important to be able to read the body language of the people you're speaking to. Keep eye contact (while still blinking) while communicating in order to pick up on any hesitations or lack of engagement.

7. Think About the Perspective of Your Audience

The fact that you have a strong command of a topic doesn't mean the people you are speaking to have the same knowledge as you. Try to think about how someone else will understand what you are trying to communicate, particularly if they lack the technical knowledge about a subject that you possess. The best advice is to simplify your pitch.

Read to Learn More

Apologies in Different Cultures

Apologies in different cultures may vary enormously, and they are key to resolving disputes and repairing trust between negotiators. A simple apology can redirect distrustful negotiators or angry disputants back to focusing on underlying interests and the search for mutually compatible deals. However, norms for apologizing may vary greatly across different countries(Maddux W W, Kim P H, Okumura T, et al., 2011).

The US

In the US, apologies often come by way of assuming guilt. If you have done something wrong, you should apologize by expressing remorse and admitting responsibility.

The first step of acknowledging your mistake and expressing remorse often requires a simple "I'm sorry" or "I apologize". These words need to be authentic and are best received when they are followed by listing the specific actions you are sorry for. In the second step, empathize with how the other person feels about your actions. By admitting fault, you can restore trust and good will from the person you hurt. After apologizing, it is important that you correct the behavior to avoid making the same mistake. Don't offer excuses, and don't expect instant forgiveness.

China

According to the type of apology you want to convey, there are multiple ways to say sorry in China.

The phrase "yi han（遗憾）" is used to express regret or pity. An example is when you have to turn down an invitation or deliver bad news.

"bu hao yi si（不好意思）", is used to apologize for an embarrassing situation or something that isn't your fault. A case in point is that this phrase may be used if you show up late or interrupt somebody.

"dui bu qi（对不起）", or "bao qian（抱歉）" are used when you want to accept blame. This apology can be used for both big and small mistakes. It is important to know the distinction between different terminologies and when to use each.

France

If you do not speak French, you will often be expected to first apologize for your lack of fluency before engaging in further conversation. This can be done with a simple "Excusez moi" "Pardonnez moi" or "Desole".

Sophie Vignoles, the team leader for French and Scandinavian languages at Babbel, said an apology is best conveyed with little formality. Be straight and to the point, without delving too much into detailed excuses. Saying sorry for something that doesn't really require an apology, like interrupting someone, will signal a lack of sincerity.

For more serious apologies, it is advised to provide a peace offering, such as a bottle of wine or a decent cheese. If the recipient invites you to enjoy these items with them, you should always accept, as this is your opportunity to smooth things over.

Russia

In Russia, there are several ways to apologize, and it is important to know which apology is the most appropriate in the given context. The correct apology in a working environment depends on whom you are apologizing to.

If it is a senior colleague or a new business acquaintance, you would use "izvinite", which means "excuse me", while if speaking to a close colleague, you can get away with the less formal "prosti", which simply means "sorry" or "forgive me".

Japan

Apologizing is seen as a virtue in Japan and is often coupled with a bow. The more sorry you feel, the deeper you bow. When apologizing to a senior colleague or new acquaintance, you can say "moushiwake arimasen", or "sumimasen". The latter is more common and can also be used to show gratitude.

If you are apologizing to a close friend or family member, you can use the phrase "gomennasai", commonly shortened to "gomen ne" or "gomen". However, this is a casual phrase and can come across as childish, so it should never be used in a professional setting.

Britain

British people pride themselves on polite manners towards one another in public. Whether British people are apologizing for asking a question, for the bad weather or because they sneeze, they are probably the number-one nation for apologies. They often use the word "sorry" quite a lot—even when they don't really mean it! Usually, if you want to ask a stranger for the time, you would start by saying "Sorry to bother you. Do you know what time it is?" If you're five minutes late for an appointment, you would generally greet the person by saying "Sorry I'm late!" and if you're 15 minutes late, you might want to be even more apologetic and say, "I'm so sorry I'm late!" In the British culture, saying "sorry", or apologizing in general, is a way to be polite, especially to people who you don't know very well. It's also a very clever way to get what you want.

In a word, apologies are important for the smooth operation of business. Meanwhile, how apologies are given and perceived differs across the world and learning how to properly apologize according to different cultural customs is of great importance.

In-class Activity 课堂练习

I. Comprehension questions.

Go over this chapter and try to make an assessment on what you have learned with the following self-assessment questions.

1. How many terms do you know when you express thanks in Chinese?

2. Chinese people like being modest. How do you explain this phenomenon?

3. What is the relationship between language and culture? Try to offer two or three examples in your discussion.

Ⅱ. Comparative analysis.

Insert the phrase "verbal communication" into a search engine on the Internet and report to your group what you have found out about the studies of intercultural communication both at home and abroad.

Ⅲ. True or false questions.

(   ) 1. Verbal communication is the transferring of thoughts between individuals only via spoken messages.

(   ) 2. Language is a means to express and exchange thoughts, concepts, knowledge and information as well as to transmit experience and so on.

(   ) 3. Language and culture are closely related, reflecting, influencing and shaping each other.

Ⅳ. Case analysis.

1. An invitation to dinner.

A: Are you free this Sunday?

B: Yes, I'm free.

A: I would like you to come over and have a dinner together.

B: No, it is too much trouble for you to prepare dinner.

A: No trouble at all. We can just order take-out.

B: But it'll cost you too much. Don't bother.

A: It's a casual dinner. Let's just have a chat and relax a little bit. Besides, there aren't any other people.

B: But you are being too polite; you always invite me to dinner.

A: That's not true at all. OK, it's settled then. Do come, please, or I'll be offended.

B: All right.

Questions:

(1) In which cultural background does the conversation most probably take place?

(2) What are the cultural factors behind the conversation?

2. How to be a guest?

Shao Bin, a Chinese student studying in Britain, was once invited by her British classmate Brain to his house to cook a Chinese meal. Her two Chinese friends were also invited. They busied themselves in the kitchen, making dumplings while Brain did something in the garden and his wife sat on the sofa reading. Shao Bin felt a little upset for she thought that both the host and the hostess should offer to help with the kitchen work. The meal was great and everyone enjoyed themselves. The couple kept complimenting them on their cooking skills and asked for the recipe. But then after the meal, the couple just put down their chopsticks and started minding their own business, leaving the Chinese guests to clear the table and do the dishes. Shao Bin felt absolutely confused or even angry.

Background Information 背景知识

1. Lexical meaning(词汇意义)错综复杂,具体表现为其多样性、层次性和可变性。它不仅涉及词自身的含义,还涉及词与词之间的关系,也涉及词与外部世界的关系。词汇语用学研究者认为要以语境为基础动态地研究词语的语用意义。对词汇意义的解释、使用和理解不仅仅是一个语言问题,更是一个语用与认知的问题。

2. High-context culture(高语境文化)是指在传播过程中,绝大部分信息或者已经存在于传播双方的物质语境中,或者已经内化于个人内心,而极少存在于双方所运用的语言和信息之中。换言之,语言和信息模糊而不充分。高语境文化强调含蓄,重视交流双方的互动。

3. Low-context culture(低语境文化)与高语境文化正好相反,即在传播过程中,沟通交流双方主要依赖他们所运用的语言。换言之,语言和信息是清晰而充分的。举例而言,对于朝夕相处的家庭成员来说,长期共同生活使他们形成了许多默契。因此,他们在交流中,直接通过语言或动作来表达的成分较少,更多的内容存在于由双方共同生活体验形成的心灵感应。而两个初次见面的陌生人的交流,就要花费更多时间来沟通。

Cultural Kaleidoscope 文化万花筒

俗语的翻译

英语中存在大量的谚语、俚语和其他一些结构固定的短语、短句,我们称为俗语。俗语的使用往往会使文章语言更生动鲜明。

(1) 批评了这个人,那个人又犯了同样的错误,真是按下葫芦浮起瓢。
Like one who has hardly pushed one gourd under water when another gourd bobs up, he has criticized one person when another makes the same mistake.

(2) 他是初生牛犊不怕虎。
He is like a newborn calf which is not afraid of tigers.

(3) 敌人夹着尾巴逃跑了。
The enemy ran away with the tail between their legs.

(4) 管他三七二十一,吃个饱再说。
Who would care so much? The first thing to do is to eat my fill.

(5) 妈妈唱红脸,爸爸唱白脸,孩子说出了实话。
Mother coaxing and father coercing, the child spoke out the truth.

(6) 得了,我们上了人家的当了。
All right, we were cats' paws.

(7) 我的确骂了他了,但我是被逼上梁山才这么做的。
I did call him names, only because I had been driven to it.

(8) 他吓得屁滚尿流。
He wetted his pants in terror.

(9) 你这无赖,竟敢骂我!
How dare you call me names, you scoundrel!

(10) 这个混蛋,他把我骗了。
That brute! He cheated me.

(11) 我明人不做暗事。
I am open and above board.

(12) 他没有三头六臂。
He is not as strong as gigantic superman with three heads and six arms.

(13) 活到老,学到老。
Never too old to learn.

(14) 她不怕家丑外扬。
She is not afraid of fouling her own nest.

(15) 一个和尚挑水喝,两个和尚抬水喝,三个和尚没水喝。
One boy is a boy, two boys half a boy, three boys no boy.

中国传统文化 4

Business Etiquette in Belt and Road Countries
"一带一路"国家的商务礼仪

希 腊

希腊人热情好客,不喜受拘束。第一次与别人会面时,习惯别人引荐介绍,第一次见面时,用力握手是最为恰当的礼仪。对于好朋友和相识很久的人,拥抱和亲吻面颊都是可以接受的。男性朋友之间互相握手或者碰肩也很常见。

虽然餐桌礼仪整体上较为随意,但还是很重要,很多讨论会在餐桌上进行,因为进餐时间对希腊人来说是社交场合。跟在中国一样,在希腊,拒绝别人夹菜是一种不礼貌的行为。如果客人表示想要再多吃一点某道菜,主人会很高兴,因为这样等于肯定了他们的烹饪技巧。一般菜的分量都很大,而且桌子上会一直配有几道配菜。主人会把客人当作家人,并期望客人品尝桌上的每道菜。如果客人表示想要帮忙摆设餐桌,或者帮忙洗碗,主人都会很高兴,但他们不会真的让你帮忙,所以不要强行去做这些。

Greeks are known for their hospitality and laid-back attitude. When meeting someone for the first time, it is customary to either allow someone to introduce you or state your name. Shaking hands firmly is the most appropriate greeting during the first meeting. Good friends and people who have known each other for a very long time may also embrace and kiss each other on both cheeks. Shaking someone's hands while tapping their shoulder is also quite common among male friends.

Table manners are also crucial during a meal. Although table manners are almost universally casual, many discussions may happen around the dinner table because meal times are social occasions for the Greeks. Just as in China, refusing food in Greece is considered impolite. Asking for another serving will delight the hosts, as it is considered a compliment to their cooking skills. However, portions are usually big and there are often several side dishes on the table at all times. Guests are considered as a part of the family which means that they should eat or at least try whatever is on the table. Offering to help with setting the table or cleaning the dishes will be appreciated, but your help will not be accepted so do not be too pushy or insistent.

Intercultural Tips 跨文化拓展知识

交际风格与文化

交际风格可以笼统地定义为"在人们连贯地表达思想时,不仅词汇反映文化背景,表达方法、说理方式、思维模式无不表现特定文化的某些特点"。在这方面所表现的文化特点不如词汇那样易于识别。

西方的逻辑学经历了古代、中世纪、近代、现代四个时期,内容不断丰富和发展,公元前四世纪亚里士多德提出的逻辑学基本理论(如三段论)对后世影响极大,因此西方逻辑仍笼统地称为亚里士多德逻辑。由此,有的学者笼统地把逻辑分为两类:亚里士多德逻辑与非亚里士多德逻辑。

Karl Pribram 将世界上的思维模式、说理方法归纳为四类。

(1) 借助于某些普遍接受的概念说理,法国、地中海国家及罗曼语系国家(包括拉丁美洲)通常使用这种说理方法。

(2) 借助归纳和验证说理,这种模式下的人们对抽象概念抱怀疑态度。英、美、澳、新及加拿大的讲英语者采用这类说理方法。

(3) 直感式说理方法,强调整体与局部的协调,常引证权威。这类思维模式包括德语及斯拉夫语国家。

(4) 马克思主义的辩证说理方法,是基于事物本身包括对立面基本事实的一种思维模式。Pribram 未说明这一种风格属于哪个语言区,但马克思主义者认为辩证法并不以国界或语言划分,它经历了古代朴素辩证法、以黑格尔为代表的唯心辩证法和马克思主义唯物辩证法三个阶段,唯物辩证法是各国无产阶级的世界观和方法论。

Satoshi Ishii 曾把美国和日本的思维方式分别比喻成"桥式"和"垫脚石式"。在美国思维方式下,作者(讲话人)组织思想的方式是明白直接地把自己的意思传达给对方,犹如一座桥,读者(听话人)只要从桥这头走到桥另一头就把意思弄清楚了。而在日本人的思维模式下,作者(讲话人)不把自己的意思直接表示出来,而是采取迂回、隐含的方法,犹如在水中投下一块一块垫脚石,使读者(听话人)借助于"垫脚石"悟出作者的意思。美国是"低语境"(low-context)国家,一切都要用语言讲清,而日本是"高语境"(high-context)国家,许多意思都包括在语境之中,不需要每一点都明白无误地讲出来,Ishii 认为两种思维模式反映了美日的不同文化。一项统计资料也可作为佐证:夏威夷的美国成年人平均每天谈话 6 小时 43 分,而日本成年人只谈话 3 小时 31 分。这说明美国人通常需要通过谈话讲清问题,而日本人不一定非要通过谈话才能交流思想。

Movie to See 观影学文化

Please watch the movie *My Fair Lady* (《窈窕淑女》) with your classmates and discuss what intercultural elements are involved in it.

Unit 5　Nonverbal Communication

非语言交际

 Learning Objectives 学习目标

- 了解非语言交际的行为和手段的表现、含义与功能。
- 熟悉不同文化中非语言交际行为和手段的差异与冲突。
- 掌握使用非语言交际行为配合语言交际行为的正确方式。

 Lead-in 单元导读

非语言交际是人类交际的重要组成部分。当我们进行沟通、交流和表达想法时，主要依靠的是语言手段，但还有一种更古老、更方便的形式就是非语言交际。人们在传递信息、交流思想感情时，如仅使用文字或言语，有时不够生动形象，这种情况下非语言交际就起到非常重要的作用。非语言交际是指通过眼神、手势、姿态、表情、交谈者之间的距离、谈话者衣着打扮，甚至包括对时间和空间的利用来传递信息。

研究表明，在面对面交际中，我们只有大约 35％ 的信息是通过语言传递的，其他都是通过非语言行为表达和传递的。肢体语言受文化影响，不同文化群体中的身势语所表达的意思会出现一定的差异。因此，不同的国家与民族在文化上存在差异，这也使非语言交际被赋予了不同的地域文化色彩。

总体来说，影响跨文化非语言交际的因素主要有以下四类。

（1）体态语。体态语又称为身体语言，包括面部表情、眼神交流、姿势差异和身体接触等。

面部表情是人感情的自然流露。一般来说，拉美国家和西方国家人的面部表情比较丰富，而东方人相对来说比较拘谨。在西班牙、意大利，男人在公共场合哭是很正常的事情。然而在中国，男人们通常是不会在公共场合哭泣的，私下也很少哭泣。因为在中国有着"男儿有泪不轻弹"的观念,男性是阳刚的,不应该有脆弱的一面。即使有,也要隐藏起来。在集体文化中,人们时常需要考虑他人的感受,所以一般不会表达负面的感受。另外,中国人推崇"不露声色",所以中国人的表情一般比较含蓄平和。

微笑是最美丽的语言,也是世界各地情感沟通的重要手段之一。有研究表明,微笑是开启信任和沟通最有效、最直接的方式。那是因为微笑是内心情绪在面部或身体姿态上的表现。微笑可以展现出温馨、亲切,能拉近人与人之间的距离,给对方留下美好的印象,从而形成融洽的交往氛围,也可以反映出我们自身的修养及待人的真诚。

眼神交流也存在差异。眼神可以传递关注、无聊、同情、敌意、爱慕、理解、误解等各种情绪。在二语交际中,通过眼神传递信息是非常常见的方式。在日本,人们把长时间注视别人看作一种无礼和不敬的文化,而在阿拉伯国家,男性之间长时间的注视是得体的。在他们看来,注视表示对方对自己的讲话内容感兴趣。

姿势差异。在西方国家,蹲被认为是一种很不雅的姿势,所以他们对中国的蹲厕非常不理解。欧洲人列举的不文明行为,其中就包括在公共场所蹲着。中国人的蹲通常是男性的行为。如果一个中国女性在公共场所蹲着,也会被认为是不雅的行为。

身体接触。在东南亚一些佛教国家,触摸别人的头部是一种禁忌。他们认为人的头是心灵的住所,是神圣不可侵犯的。在穆斯林文化中,左手被认为是不干净的,所以与人握手或吃饭,都需要用右手。

(2) 副语言。副语言又称为伴随语言,指人们在语言交际过程中的辅助语言,比如一些没有声音和意义的伴随语言,包括沉默、非语义声音、话轮转换等。

由于文化的差异,沉默在不同的国家传达的意思不一样。比如在中国,沉默表示默许、理解,而在英美国家则是缺少自信的表现。

(3) 客体语。客体语包括衣着、化妆、颜色、气味和个人用品的交际作用等。

服饰是静止的无声语言,也是一种重要的体态信号,无时无地不在向世人展示主人的形象和风度。在社交活动中,服饰在建立"第一印象"的所有因素中占有最重要的地位。服饰也是非语言交流中的重要媒介。

西方人追求变化和突出个人价值。这一点也体现在他们的穿衣打扮上。他们习惯每天洗澡和换衣服,给人焕然一新的感觉。而中国人并不那么勤于换衣服,在冬天可能一个星期才换一次,只要衣服不脏。在服饰风格上,通常欧美人比较休闲随意,英国人比较绅士庄重。服饰体现着一个国家与民族的文化特色,在国家与国家的交往中,也代表着各国家的文化软实力。近些年来,汉服的崛起,就是典型的我国软实力逐渐强大的体现。

(4) 环境语。环境语一般包括空间信息、领地观念、时间信息、声音、颜色和标识符号等。如,中国人的龙图腾,代表着神权、尊贵、权力;但是,在西方圣经中,龙却是凶恶和罪恶的象征。

以人际距离为例,人类学家霍尔(1914—2009)认为"人际距离"可区分为 4 种:亲密距离(distance for intimate discourse)为 0～18 英寸,相当于 0～0.5 米,常见于父母与子女之间、夫妻之间;个人距离(personal space)一般为 18 英寸～4 英尺,相当于 0.45～1.2 米,常见于朋友或熟人之间;社会距离(social space)为 4～12 英尺,相当于 1.2～3.5 米,常见于公开关系而非私人关系之间;公众距离(public space)为 12～25 英尺,相当于 3.5～7.5 米,常见于正式交往的个体之间或陌生人之间。

文化不仅对语言交际影响巨大,对非语言交际也同样起着重要的支配作用。非语言交际手段十分丰富,手势、身势、面部表情、衣着服饰、体距、时间、空间等方面都是我们进行跨文化交际需要注意的地方。本单元将介绍语言交际的概念、功能、非语言交际的常见表现形式，以及不同国家非语言交际的不同特点；阐述语言交际和非语言交际的关系，并提供一些帮助学习者有效利用非语言交际提升语言交际效果的方法。

Pre-class Activity 课前活动

Successful interaction in intercultural settings requires the understanding of not only verbal messages but also nonverbal messages. Nonverbal communication refers to all intentional and unintentional stimuli between communicating parties, other than spoken words. These nonverbal processes, often account for as much as 70% of the communication. As the silent language of communication, nonverbal communication is counterculturally ambiguous. Nonverbal code systems are less precise and systematized and less consciously used and interpreted than verbal code systems; however, they sometimes exert greater effects on the results of our intercultural communication.

Reading 课内阅读

Reading One: Functions of Nonverbal Communication

Nonverbal communication is an important part of interpersonal communication. Here are some important functions of nonverbal communication in human interaction.

1. Repeating

People often use nonverbal messages to repeat a point they are trying to make. If you tell someone what they are proposing is a bad idea, you might move your head from side to side while you are uttering the word "no". You might hold up a hand in the gesture signifying that a person should stop at the same time when you actually use the word "stop". If someone asks you where the library is located, you can say something like "it is at the corner of the second block on the left" and you can use your finger to point in the direction of the library to repeat what you said.

2. Complementing

Closely related to repeating is complementing. For example, you can tell someone that you are pleased with his or her performance, but this message takes in extra meaning if you pat the person on the shoulder at the same time. Physical contact places another layer of meaning on what is being said.

3. Emphasizing

Nonverbal messages can emphasize or accent the feelings or emotions conveyed by verbal messages by adding more information to the expressions. Loudness and tone of voice can be two examples here. You can accent your anger by speaking in a voice that is much louder than the one you use in normal conversation. You can see how an apology becomes more forceful if your face, as well as your words, is saying, "I'm sorry."

4. Conveying

Nonverbal behavior conveys our emotions and our attitudes towards ourselves and towards the people we communicate with. For example, the sentence "I would love to meet you and discuss this issue in more detail" can convey different meanings and attitudes depending on the nonverbal signals accompanying the words. Nonverbal messages can be as effective as verbal messages in conveying orders.

5. Regulating

We often regulate and manage communication by using some forms of nonverbal behavior. For example, a parent might engage in "stemming" and direct eye contact with a child as a way of telling him or her to terminate the naughty behavior while guests are in the house. Hand clapping by the instructor in a classroom demands the attention of the students. Turn taking is largely governed by nonverbal signals. In short, your nonverbal behavior helps you control the situation. We use nonverbal messages to substitute for verbal messages, if it is noisy at a big meeting.

6. Replacing

The speaker may stop for a few seconds as an alternative to say, "Please calm down so that I can speak." Instead of raising your voice by shouting "bravo" after a great performance of the orchestra you may silently sit there with an awed expression. Your expression automatically indicates that the performance is excellent and that you are moved by the experience.

7. Contradicting

On some occasions, nonverbal actions send signals opposite to the literal meanings contained in our verbal messages. For example, you tell someone you are relaxed and at ease, yet your voice quavers and your hands shake. When you are sick and a friend asks you how you feel, you may say, "I'm fine" in a weak voice and with a slouchy posture. Non-verbally, you are telling your friend that you are not fine, but, verbally, you give your friend an opposite answer. People rely mostly on nonverbal messages when they receive conflicting data like these, so we need to be aware of the dangers.

Reading Two: Body Language

Body language can be defined as the nonverbal behavior related to movement, of any part of the body, or of the body as a whole, including facial expressions, postures, gestures, eye contact, etc. Body language reflects a certain cultural background. Body language is determined by customs and traditions in different cultures. As a matter of fact, there is an area of research that specially focuses on how body movement communicates, and it is called kinesics.

1. Postures

Postures refer to our body positions as a whole. The way we hold our bodies when we sit, stand or walk, can send positive or negative nonverbal messages. Since postures are subconscious in nature, if you neglect your postures in business communication, it would damage your image as a business person.

Postures are usually classified into three categories: stance, bent-knee positions (which include sitting, squatting, and kneeling) and lying.

Generally speaking, the sitting posture in America is more casual than that in China. Chinese people are accustomed to straightening clothes and sitting properly. In addition, they tend to raise themselves slightly or lean forwards for the purpose of showing respect to the communicator. Being casual and friendly is valued in America. They may often fall into chairs or slouch when they stand. Even when giving a lecture, an American teacher may sit seriously at the beginning, but lean back before long. In a college, American teachers may often sit at the desk and discuss questions with students squatting. If American people really need to take a long rest, they are more likely to sit on the floor. Shrugging one's shoulders can express that one is indifferent, powerless or has no secret to conceal. Americans often shrug their shoulders to show that they are innocent.

2. Gestures

Gestures are another aspect of body language. Actually, different gestures express different messages and some gestures seem to be known by all. One person's positive gesture may be another person's insult.

The thumbs up sign. This gesture in Britain means "good, great, well-played" and is also used for hitch-hiking, asking for a free ride. In the Persian culture, it is a sign of discontent and borders on obscenity (highly offensive).

Thumbs down. In the US and Canada, it shows disapproval or rejection of a proposal, idea, person, or a nonverbal way of saying a strong "no". In Greece, it is considered a rude sign and is often used by motorists to signal their anger over someone's crazy driving.

The "OK" sign. With the index finger and thumb held in a circle and the other three fingers extended, palm outward, the Americans are showing that they agree upon something or something is OK. However, it means anus for the Brazilians, sexual invitation for Greeks and yen for the Japanese.

The "V" sign. The "V" sign, holding two fingers upright with palm and fingers faced outward, is a sign of victory in the US and many other countries. The "V" sign signals number "two" in countries like China, Greece, Turkey and Bulgaria. It was first used by Winston Churchill during World War Two, yet quickly spread all over the world. However, palm facing inward toward the face is an obscene gesture in England.

Good luck sign. If you put your middle finger on top of your forefinger, that means you wish someone good luck. This gesture is basically peculiar in Anglo-American cultures. Germans wish others good luck by making two fists with thumbs inside and pounding them on an imaginary table. While in Portugal, people would place the thumb between the index and third finger.

3. Facial Expressions

Psychological research has told us that facial muscles can form more than 7,000 different expressions. Facial expressions are one of the most obvious and important sources of nonverbal communication. In many cases, people would be intrigued by how the looks on other people's faces have influenced their reactions.

Is there a universal language of facial expressions? One position holds that similar expressions may occur in everyone, but the meanings people attach to them differ from culture to culture. The majority believe that there are universal facial expressions for which people have similar meanings. They hold that there are a basic set of at least six facial expressions that are innate, universal and carrying the same basic meanings throughout the world. The six pan-cultural and universal facial expressions are happiness, sadness, fear, anger, disgust, and surprise.

While many facial expressions carry similar meanings in a variety of cultures, the frequency and intensity of their use may vary. That is to say, cultural norms often dictate how, when, and to whom facial expressions are displayed. Latin and Arab cultures use more intense facial expressions, whereas East Asian cultures use more subdued expressions. In the US, white males suppress the desire to show these emotions. Japanese business people even go so far as to hide expressions of anger, sorrow, or disgust by smiling or laughing. Chinese business people will control their feelings and demonstrate little emotion through their faces in public or when they are in face of strangers.

Reading Three: Personal Space

Personal space refers to the physical area surrounding an individual that is considered personal or private. In other words, we carry body bubbles with us that are like invisible walls defining our personal space. Actually, there is a research area specializing in personal space for the purpose of communication which is called Proxemics(近体学,空间关系学).

In one sense, personal space is culturally determined. For example, some cultures simply do not think of private, personal body space. Sometimes, fifty Africans can crowd into the same amount of space that holds only twenty North Americans. The reason is that the Africans' personal space suffers no sense of intrusion from crowding and touching.

In another sense, personal space results from varying relationships. In general, we establish shorter distances with people with whom we seek approval and maintain greater communication distances from those with whom we feel negatively. Also, the longer distances may refer to figures of authority. Edward Hall has suggested that people interact within four spatial zones or distance ranges: intimate (0—50cm, reserved only for intimate lovers and family members), personal (50—120cm, used only for friends), social (120—350cm, kept with acquaintances), and public (350—750cm, used for talking across a room and for public speaking).

Our difficulty in intercultural communication comes from conversing in unexpected and different zones, which happen to have cultural connotations. For example, in Middle Eastern countries, being close enough to breathe on another person is proper. In fact, for many people in such cultures, the breath is like their spirit or life, so sharing their breath in close conversation is like sharing their spirit. However, North Americans tend to prefer comparatively greater distances between themselves and others. As a result, many Middle Easterners converse in zones they perceive as personal, but viewed as intimate by North Americans. This is why some US government officials and visitors return from the Middle East, Southern Europe, or Latin America and say things like, "It's all right if you don't mind having people breathe on your face." Meanwhile, North Americans themselves may be perceived as distant and cold because of how they define their personal space.

Reading Four: Interesting Body Language in Different Cultures

There are substantial cultural differences in how people use body language to communicate. Small everyday gesticulations in Western culture may be perceived as rude and ignorant in other cultures. Similarly, certain aspects of body language in other cultures may seem overly familiar or invasive to those that are more reserved.

Kissing

Kissing in the Western world is a complex thing. A person can kiss and be kissed affectionately, platonically or passionately. There is a world of difference in appropriateness between a peck and a smooch. Kissing between the opposite sexes is widespread both privately and publicly.

In some more conservative cultures, kissing a member of the opposite sex in public is a definite faux pas, especially in deeply religious societies. In China and Japan, kissing is not usual as a greeting. Whilst countries such as the US, Australia and the UK have yet to see men kissing as a greeting, a welcoming platonic kiss on both cheeks with the same sex is a matter of course in many regions, especially around the Mediterranean, North Africa and the Middle East.

Pointing

In the Western world, we often point at things to help explain a point. Although it is sometimes considered rude to point directly, a general point with the forefinger at an inanimate object is fine. However, in many Asian countries, such as China, pointing with the forefinger in public is considered quite rude. The alternative is to gesticulate towards the point of interest with an open palm that faces upwards.

The Right Handshake

The way you meet and greet someone is perhaps one of the most diverse body language practices in the world. Where you come from will often determine the way that you greet a person.

In the Western world, handshakes between men and women are of course the most widespread form of greeting. In less formal circumstances, hugging and a kiss on the cheek is also commonly practiced. This also tends to be the case now for many Middle Eastern, African and Asian countries, particularly in business situations. But again, certain social etiquette will come into play — for instance in a strict Muslim culture, kissing a woman in public, especially if she is unmarried, would not be acceptable. A man would only shake hands with a woman if she offers him her hand first.

There is also more emphasis placed on using the correct hand in Muslim and Hindu societies. The left hand is considered unclean, so practices such as handshaking and eating are only ever performed with the right hand.

Bowing

The historic act of bowing is still very much in practice in places like Japan, and South Korea. These countries are steeped in a culture where respect for elders and those in authority is of the utmost importance, and are sometimes regarded as the most reserved cultures in the world.

However, do you know that bowing can vary among different cultures and regions? The way you bow can also depend on the social situation and the reason you are bowing. For instance, the way you bow when greeting someone can be different to a bow of apology or thanks. In the Western world, direct eye contact is seen as a sign of strength and interest. But in many Asian countries it is perceived as rude, so there is no direct eye contact when someone is bowing.

Reading Five: Celebrations of National Day

A festival can be defined as a time of celebration marked by special observances, bringing people from every religious, economic and social background together. Cultural festivals can be categorized into different types, such as national, religious and seasonal festivals, serving the purpose of bringing happiness to our lives and strengthening our sense of community.

National Day is a day with significance and usually celebrated throughout a nation, connecting citizens to important moments of a nation's history such as the founding day of a nation or independence day and solidifying patriotic spirit in the society. Every country has its own National Day celebrations.

China

In China, National Day is a holiday celebrated on October 1st to mark the foundation of the People's Republic of China. Traditionally, the festivities begin with the ceremonial raising of the Chinese national flag in Tian'anmen Square, in the capital city of Beijing. The Chinese government expands the celebrations to seven days to give its citizens a vacation period which is similar to the Golden Week holiday in Japan. Often, the Chinese spend this time staying with family or traveling. Besides, watching special television programs concerning the holiday is also a popular activity.

Norway

In Norway, the National Day is on May 17th. In Oslo, it is a red, white, and blue day. Many events involve people of all ages, especially students in traditional clothing, known as Bunad, lining the streets, and marching past the Royal Palace as the royal family waves back. High school students who will graduate, locally called RUSS, are recognized by their colored hats and uniforms. Traditionally, they board RUSS buses for RUSS parties that culminate on National Day, during which they distribute mock business cards. On this National Day, people participate in a potluck breakfast with their friends and the custom is to "eat what you like".

Indonesia

Indonesia's Independence Day is on August 17th. On this day, people most likely run into a strange kind of tree bearing prizes. Each year locals participate in Panjat Pinang, a tradition to represent how the communities learn to work together and resist the Dutch government in 1945. Tall palm tree trunks are planted in villages around the country, adorned with hoops on which baskets, toys, bicycles, and other great prizes are hung. To get the prizes, the team members have to climb up the poles that have been greasy for the challenge. In Jakarta, the capital of Indonesia, the buildings and homes fly the red and white flags with pride. While some might enjoy watching the assembly of government officials at the National Palace, others might prefer the satisfying participation of the krupuk (shrimp chip) eating contest.

France

The National Day of France is actually Bastille Day, which is celebrated on the 14th of July. It is worth remembering because it is a day when the revolted Parisians stormed the medieval prison, which is known as Bastille, and it's also a huge countrywide holiday to show national pride. Furthermore, people can see spectacular fireworks in Carcassonne where fire flows off the medieval ramparts, or watch the fireworks light up the cliffs of Etretat. Paris is nonetheless the place in which a multitude of celebrations keep people up all night.

On the 13th of July, the eve of Bastille Day, the celebrations get a head start by hitting the free dance floor at the local fire station where the firefighters organize a friendly neighborhood party. The next morning on the 14th, people wake up early to watch the parade of the French military on the Champs Elysées and catch a glimpse of the president if they are lucky enough. At night the National Day celebrations continue — fireworks take off at the Eiffel Tower, often preceded by a big concert on the Champs de Mars right in front of it.

Peru

To commemorate the day General José de San Martin proclaimed Peru's independence on July 28th, 1821, this day became the National Day of Peru. It is one of the biggest holidays of the year. To get the festivities going, in Lima, on the eve of Independence Day, people enjoy music and Marinera dancing in the Parque de la Muralla, followed by huge fireworks. On July 28th, it is recommended to observe a 21-cannon salute or other official ceremonies such as the raising of the flag, the mass showing up at the Lima Cathedral, and the president addressing to the nation. On the 29th, the celebrations are still continuing with the military parade, and people grab a Pisco drink, Peru's official liquor and toast with the locals during festivities in the Parque Kennedy.

Reading Six: Tips for Powerful Nonverbal Communication

Good communication is the foundation of successful personal and professional relationships. But we communicate with much more than words. In fact, research shows that the majority of our communication is nonverbal. Nonverbal communication, or body language, includes our facial expressions, gestures, eye contact, postures, and even the tone of our voice.

Nonverbal communication cues can be very powerful if you make good use of the following tactics.

1. Intensity

A reflection of the amount of energy you project is considered as the intensity of the communication. This has much to do with your personal preference and the consideration to make the other party feel good. It includes maintaining adequate eye contact, showing different attitudes through proper facial expressions, and avoiding distractions to show your care about the conversation you are engaged in.

2. Timing and pace

You need to be a good listener and a timely response provider, as well as the physical proximity is important. Some people need as much as three feet between themselves and the person they are talking to. But in intimate relationships, this distance could make someone feel unloved. If you don't know what's comfortable for the other person, just ask.

3. Position and posture

Leaning forward and facing your business partners unconsciously communicates receptiveness and interest. Turning away or staring off into space says you're not really there. Shaking hands can send a powerful message. For example, the two-handed shake expresses deep sincerity, a high five shows mutual approval, and a sincere grip inspires trust. What's more, pay attention to subtle gestures. They can mean different things to different people. Learn to be sensitive to how people whom you care about interpret your movements.

4. Mind other important non-verbal cues

Sounds can convey understanding. Sounds such as "ahhh, ummm, ohhh", uttered with congruent eye and facial gestures, communicate understanding and emotional connection. Smells, clothing, and color choices all send messages. Your perfume could be alluring, overpowering, or offensive. Our clothing says we're cool, we're conservative, or we're unemployed. Pay attention to how others react to your personal style and make sure you're not sending unintentional messages.

5. Reflect and learn

If you really want to get a good understanding of how you come across to other people through verbal and non-verbal communication, videotape the communicating process. If you don't like something you see, you have the power to change it.

Nonverbal communication is a rapidly flowing back-and-forth process. Successful nonverbal communication depends on emotional self-awareness and an understanding of the cues you're sending, along with the ability to accurately pick up on the cues others are sending to you. This requires your full concentration and attention. If you are planning what you're going to say next, daydreaming, or thinking about something else, you are almost certain to miss nonverbal cues and other subtleties in the conversation. You need to stay focused on the moment-to-moment experience in order to fully understand what's going on.

Read to Learn More

Color matters in Business World

Color plays an important role in corporate and marketing communication. It influences consumers' perception and preference, purchase and consumption behavior, and helps companies (re)position or differentiate from the competition. However, sometimes companies fail simply because of inappropriate choice of product or package colors. Cultures differ in their aesthetic expressions as colors represent different meanings and aesthetic appeals in different cultures, entailing careful use of color in marketing. For instance, blue is perceived as cold in East Asia, but stands for warmth in Holland, death in Iran, and purity in India. It denotes femininity in Holland but masculinity in Sweden and the US. Blue represents high quality in the US, Japan, South Korea and China, and also means sincere, trustworthy and dependable in Japan, South Korea and the US. All in all, color is much significant for products, brands and advertisements. It must be given more attention in cross-cultural business communication.

Laurence, a Japanese businessman of a multinational enterprise, remembered his terrible experience in Brazil. Several years ago, his company designed a kind of highly fashionable watch. He was assigned to Brazil to market this product. However, after a period of marketing, it didn't work out well. The sale was not good and it seemed the customers had no interest in this product. After doing some research, he found out that their watches' boxes were decorated with a band of purple ribbon which was not to Brazilians' taste. After knowing this, the company changed the color of the ribbon and the watch turned out to sell well.

The biggest reason resulting in his failure is that colors have different meanings in different cultures. In Japanese culture, purple is mostly regarded as expensive, and it becomes a status symbol among rulers and the Japanese christen it "Imperial Purple". However, in Brazilian culture, purple symbolizes unlucky and sorrow. And it is the color of mourning or death. In Japan, those watches' boxes were decorated with a band of purple ribbon to look more delicate. But people cannot accept the color because of the different culture in Brazil. Hence, in crosscultural business, you must command a better understanding of the local culture and take color into account.

In-class Activity 课堂练习

Ⅰ. Comprehension questions.

Go over this chapter and try to make an assessment on what you have learned with the following self-assessment questions.

1. What are the functions of nonverbal behavior in communication? Please give some examples to support your points.

2. How does posture convey different messages? Use specific examples to support your answer.

3. How many gestures can you name? What is the meaning of each gesture?

4. How does a culture perceive and use space to communicate messages to others?

Ⅱ. Comparative analysis.

Insert the phrase "nonverbal communication" into a search engine on the Internet and report to your group what you have found out about the studies of intercultural communication both at home and abroad.

Ⅲ. True or false questions.

(　　) 1. Nodding the head means "yes", and shaking the head means "no" in all cultures.

(　　) 2. In most Western countries, people pay more attention to their private space.

(　　) 3. Staring at people or holding a glance too long is considered to be improper in most English-speaking countries.

(   ) 4. Social distance is the longest distance among the four categories of personal space, and can often be seen in some social gatherings and impersonal business.

Ⅳ. Case analysis.

1. Share it or not?

Wang Liang worked in a Sino-German joint venture. One day, on his way to the coffee machine, he found that Wolfgang, one of his German colleagues, had seemingly gotten rather involved in a newspaper. Out of curiosity, Wang came up to Wolfgang so he could glance at the newspaper. Then he asked, "Which one are you reading? Is it interesting?" But all of a sudden, Wolfgang lost his temper, began to complain about Wang's invasion of his privacy, and demanded an apology from him. Wang felt rather upset and kept explaining that he had not realized that his behavior was rude. After this, whenever Wang stepped toward Wolfgang, he would soon cover up what he was doing, or stand up to keep a clear distance from Wang. Wang Liang got very confused, wondering why his friendly behaviors aroused such hostility in his colleague.

Questions:

(1) How would you react to Wang Liang's behavior?

(2) Why did Wolfgang get angry?

2. Eye contact.

Linda was a young Puerto Rican girl studying in a high school of New York. She was once suspected of smoking with a group of troublemakers and was punished by the principal. She was thought so because when she was interviewed by the principal, she avoided meeting his eyes and only stared down at the floor, hence being regarded as sly and dishonest.

Her mother insisted that she was a good girl while the principal firmly believed that she was not. Later a Spanish literature teacher explained some basic facts of Puerto Rican culture to the principal and he realized that he might have misunderstood the girl.

Questions:

(1) What is valued in American culture?

(2) What is valued in Puerto Rico?

Background Information 背景知识

1. Nonverbal communication(非语言交际)是指不用言语,而是通过面部表情、手势、眼神、身体的运动及对时空的态度来进行的沟通。在人际沟通中,信息的内容部分往往通过语言来表达,而非语言则通过提供解释内容的框架来表达信息的相关部分。

2. Kinesics/body language(身势语/体态语)是指传递交际信息的表情和动作。它包括身体的各部位所产生的非语言行为,如面部表情、姿势、手势、眼神交流,等等。研究结果表明,体态语具有交流思想、传达感情、昭示心理、强调指代等功能。体态语十分丰富,可以表达各种思想感情,并且不同的文化有着不同的体态语。

3. Spatial language(空间语言),就是人们利用空间表达某种思想信息的一种社会语言。美国人类学家 Edward T. Hall 把个人之间的距离分为四种:Intimate Zone(亲密距离)、Personal Zone(个人距离)、Social Zone(社会距离)、Public Zone(公共距离)。亲密距离,从没有距离到18英寸,表现出接触者的亲密。这种距离通常发生在关系亲密的人之间,如夫妻之间、情人之间,或父母与子女之间。个人距离,从18英寸到4英尺,朋友之间、熟人之间,或者亲戚之间交流时通常保持这个距离。社会距离,从4英尺到12英尺,同事之间、业务伙伴之间,或者社交场合的人们通常保持这个距离。公共距离,从12英尺到25英尺,通常在公众场合演讲或对一群人讲话时保持这个距离。

Cultural Kaleidoscope 文化万花筒

How to Improve Nonverbal Competence?

Rule number one is to bear in mind to decode nonverbal communication is to realize that there is no such a thing as a nonverbal dictionary. Although some books may contain many valid "rules" of nonverbal communication, those rules are always relative to the individual, social, and cultural contexts in which an interaction takes place.

The second guideline for decoding nonverbal signals is to acknowledge that certain nonverbal signals are related. Nonverbal rule books are not effective because they typically view nonverbal signals in isolation, similar to how dictionaries separately list denotative definitions of words.

Therefore, the third guideline is that rather than using a list of specific rules, it is more advised to develop more general tools that are useful and adaptable to interpret nonverbal cues under various specific contexts.

While it is important to recognize that we send nonverbal signals through multiple channels simultaneously, we can also increase our nonverbal communication competence by becoming more aware of how it operates in specific channels. Although no one can truly offer you a rule book on how to send and receive every type of nonverbal signal effectively, applying the right tactics may help you to communicate better with specific nonverbal messages from a less academic perspective.

中国传统文化5

Business Etiquette in Belt and Road Countries
"一带一路"国家的商务礼仪

蒙 古

蒙古和东南亚国家在问候、商务洽谈和礼物赠送等方面的商务礼俗都带有东方国家的特点,其商业文化不如西方文化那么直接。商务问候时,除非受对方邀请,否则不直呼其名而只是称姓或在姓前加上"先生"或"女士"等。商务名片尤其重要,通常见面问候之后就要互赠名片,要用双手递送名片并微微鞠躬。商务会晤通常需要提前数周预约,然后提前一至两天再确认,会谈十分讲究守时,会谈前通常是一些闲聊。如果受邀去家里做客则一般赠送包装好的礼物,客人未离开前主人一般不会打开礼物。

Mongolia and Southeast Asian countries share certain oriental features in such business etiquette as greetings, business meetings and gift-giving. Business culture in Mongolia and Southeast Asia is nowhere near as direct as it is in the west. In greeting, it is better to address people by their family names or with suitable honorific titles such as "Sir" or "Madam", unless invited by them to use a given name. Business cards are incredibly important; normally you will meet someone and conduct the appropriate greeting and then exchange business cards. Asians give their business cards with both hands and bow their heads slightly. Business appointments are set up several weeks in advance and confirmed as a courtesy a day or two before. Punctuality is extremely important even though meetings often start out with small talk. It is customary to bring a wrapped gift if you are invited home for dinner and be aware that your host will not open the gift before you leave.

Intercultural Tips 跨文化拓展知识

时间观念

不同的民族对于时间有不同的概念和态度。阿拉斯加州原住民按涨潮退潮来安排自己的工作。澳洲土著人在他们自己人中间使用的不是钟表时间而是"库里时间"(Koori time),所谓库里时间,是指完成一件任务或走一段路程所需的时间。即使在同一民族同一国家,由于社会阶层的不同、生活方式的差异,人们对于时间仍持有迥然不同的看法。例如,在我国的乡村和城市,时间具有不同的意义。农村长期的自然经济下,农民通常不需要精确计算时间,但是,在工厂里,从厂长到工人,时间概念都很强。

在今天的世界,人们的一切活动都脱离不开时间的控制,什么时候起床,什么时候吃早饭,什么时候上班,什么时候下班,什么时候回家吃晚饭,等等,都有严格的时间控制。如果打乱一切时间安排,不仅社会上会出现无政府状态,人的生理机制也无法适应。这说明具有精确的时间观念已成为现代化生活方式的一个特征。

人类学家 Hall 根据他的观察把人们大致分为两类:一类是遵守单时制(Monochronic

time，M-time)的人们；另一类是遵守多时制（Polychronic time，P-time)的人们。遵守单时制的人们（如北美、北欧、西欧等国家的人）强调时间表，强调事先安排；遵守多时制的人们（如拉丁美洲、中东等国家的人）习惯同时处理几件事情，而不强调一切都按照时间表。中国人基本上遵守单时制，在大城市中生活速度日益加快，人们越来越重视时间的安排，但在乡村情况则大不相同。

不同文化背景的人们不仅在单时制、多时制方面表现出明显的区别，他们对于一项活动的筹划、开始、延续及结束也都有不同的观念。提前计划是现代社会生活的一个显著特点，举办会议、约会、社交活动等，都需要事先通知，以便对方能早作安排。临时通知对方参加某项活动会被认为是不礼貌的。

"准时"是另一个普遍适用的概念，但不同文化对什么是"准时"却有不同的理解。即使在同一文化中，由于活动内容不同，理解也有所变化。在英国和北美，正式的约会必须准时到达，最多不能超过预定时间 5 分钟，而在阿拉伯国家迟到 15 分钟仍属正常。如果是家庭宴请活动，在美国比规定时间晚到五分钟或七八分钟是合乎礼仪的，在英国可以晚到 5~15 分钟，在意大利可以晚到一两小时，在埃塞俄比亚甚至可以更晚。在英语国家晚间宴请虽然可以允许客人迟到十分钟左右，但绝对不能提前到达，否则会被认为是不礼貌的。有一些聚会（party）并没有严格的开始时间，客人可以在规定时间之后半小时（甚至更长的时间）到达。

简单来讲，不同文化之间，同种文化之内的时间观念都有可能出现较大差异，在人们进行跨文化交际的过程中也需要关注时间这个非语言交际的重要信息。

Movie to See 观影学文化

Please watch the movie *Mulan*（《花木兰》）with your classmates and discuss what intercultural elements are involved in it.

Unit 6　Cross-cultural Business Communication Etiquette

跨文化商务交际礼仪

 Learning Objectives 学习目标

- 熟悉交换名片和电话沟通的礼仪。
- 熟悉商务会餐的礼仪。
- 了解文化因素对商务谈判的影响。
- 掌握通过得体的会面礼仪给对方留下良好的第一印象。

 Lead-in 单元导读

　　跨文化商务交际礼仪是跨文化交际能力的重要组成部分,张颖和唐娇(2019)将它定义为"商务人员在商务活动中,为了塑造个人和企业的良好形象而应当遵循的,对交往对象表示尊敬与友好的规范或程序"。商务礼仪是一般礼仪在商务活动中的运用和体现,是在商务交往中应该遵守的交往艺术,也是对人们进行商务活动时的仪容仪表和言谈举止的普遍要求,用来约束人们在日常商务活动的方方面面。不少教材和专著都对商务交际礼仪的特征、原则、社会作用及其与传统礼仪的关系做出了系统的总结。

　　(1) 跨文化商务交际礼仪的特征。在各种商业活动中,商务礼仪具有以下基本特征。

　　① 规定性。从礼仪的范围看,商务礼仪具有规定性。通过礼仪可以协调和组织人们之间的行为,而商务礼仪不同于一般的人际交往礼仪,商务礼仪的适用范围是涉及商务的组织活动和人际交往活动。

　　② 信用性。从礼仪的内涵看,商务礼仪具有信用性。商务活动要同时满足双方的利益需求,因此,诚信在商务活动中非常重要,也成为商务礼仪的要求之一。

　　③ 时机性。从礼仪的行为看,商务礼仪具有时机性。时机性是指在商务活动中要及时

抓住机遇，在合适的时候说话做事，以免失去商机。

④ 文化性。从礼仪的性质看，商务礼仪具有文化性。商务礼仪包含"商务"和"礼仪"两个方面，也就是包含了经济和文化两个层面的内容。

(2) 跨文化商务交际礼仪的原则。

① 尊重和宽容的原则。即人们在社会交往中，要敬人之心常存，处处不可失敬于人，不可伤害他人的尊严，更不能侮辱对方的人格。与人沟通时，要注意做到把握分寸，认真、得体的同时，也要能乐于听取他人的意见，表现出虚怀若谷的胸襟。

② 真诚的原则。运用礼仪时，务必诚信无欺，言行一致，表里如一。

③ 自律的原则。这是礼仪的基础和出发点。学习和应用礼仪最重要的就是要实现自我约束、自我对照和自我反省。

(3) 跨文化商务交际礼仪的社会作用。

① 有助于塑造良好的公众形象。商务活动中，企业和个人形象都非常重要，形象主要通过礼仪来展现，并且直接影响着交往双方的沟通与合作。

② 有助于培养良好的道德品质，提升个人素养。商务人员的个人素养是个人修养的表现。商务礼仪的应用可以提升员工的个人素养和素质。

③ 有助于对外开放，加强国际交流。国际经济多元化格局的形成，使得各国经济的发展面临着日益激烈的国际竞争。在这种情况下，涉外礼仪的得体应用成了对商务和外事活动参与者的基本要求。

(4) 跨文化商务交际礼仪与传统礼仪的关系。跨文化商务交际礼仪与传统礼仪既相互关联又有所区别。跨文化商务交际礼仪与传统礼仪的相通之处在于：①行为性，两者都是与人交往的艺术；②作用性，两者都有助于个人或者企业树立良好的形象；③目的性，两者的应用都是为了获得对方的尊重与信任。

跨文化商务交际礼仪与传统礼仪的不同之处在于：①规范性，商务礼仪比传统礼仪更为规范；②接受度，商务礼仪的性质和具体功能更被现代社会的商务人员认可；③适用性，相比传统礼仪，商务礼仪对行为模式的划分更加细致和规范，以便适用于不同的商务场合。

跨文化商务交际中非常重要的一点就是通过礼仪的形式体现出对对方的尊重。我们可以从以下三个方面做起。

(1) 与人交往时，热情而真诚。真诚是人与人沟通的基础，是双方在业务上长期互助协作的基本要求。

(2) 关切对方的自尊。维护自尊，得到他人的尊重是人的基本需求之一，因此，在与人交往中，一定要避免可能伤害他人自尊的行为。

(3) 保持宽容的心态。现代社会的一个基本特征就是丰富的个性色彩与多元化思维的共存。尊重交际对象，就是要做到对对方思想观点和个性的宽容。

本单元将介绍跨文化商务交际礼仪中涉及的常见问题，给出了应对这些问题的相关策略与技巧。熟悉本单元内容有助于学习者在跨文化商务交际中以合乎礼仪规范的方式应对相互介绍、电话沟通、商务会餐、商务谈判等事务。

Pre-class Activity 课前活动

Below are a few tips on western table settings. Can you figure out an easy way to remember them?

(1) The salad fork will be on the outside of your plate (for the main dish), and it'll be smaller than the forks for main courses.

(2) Forks usually go on the left, but if you ever see a small fork on your right, it's an oyster fork.

(3) Your water glass will always be on the left-hand side of your wine glass.

 Reading 课内阅读

Reading One: What Is Business Etiquette?

The etiquette of business can refer to the set of written and unwritten rules of conduct that make social interactions run more smoothly. Proper social behavior involves learning cultural variations in making introductions, exchanging business cards, recognizing position and status, dining practices, giving gifts, etc.

In today's fast-paced, high-tech world, people tend to forget the importance of simple human contact and kindness — remembering people's names, trying to make a good first impression, and greeting people with a firm handshake.

Being able to introduce people and explain who they are makes everyone feel comfortable in a new situation and is one of the most useful skills you can acquire in the business world. The ability to introduce yourself or others confidently demonstrates that you are at ease and in control — and by extension, you set others at ease too.

1. How to Make a Great First Impression

The power of the first impression might just be one of the most studied phenomena in psychology. The latest research by a team of psychologists from Canada, the US and Belgium proves that "as long as the first impression is challenged only within the same context, it will dominate regardless of how often it is contradicted by new experiences". The lead author of this study Bertam Gawronski (2010) is convinced that although you might see a person from different angles after meeting him several times, your conclusions about the person will be heavily influenced by your essential impression of him.

Let's find out what these findings mean for the business world and what are the steps you could take to make people instantly like you.

It is said that you have less than a second to make a great first impression. But don't get anxious yet. In spite of such limited time to amaze, there are ways to lead your new acquaintance to like you:

Look neat and professional. Just before an important meeting make sure your clothes are ironed and stain-free, and your shoes are polished. Spend extra time to fix your hair and make certain your nails are natty and clean.

Follow the proper dress code. Outfit can help you to fit in instantly. For example, if you are planning to meet with a start-up owner and you know he's not a fan of conventional business dress code, you might want to wear something more casual. In case you have no clue about the way people will dress, stick to conservative business outfit.

Mind the odor. It might seem basic, but sometimes we forget about the importance of odor. Don't overuse perfume, but be sure you smell nice.

Be punctual. Being late can easily ruin your reputation even before the introduction happens. Plan your trip to the destination in advance and arrive at least 5 minutes before the meeting starts.

Arrange your handbag. Make sure you take all necessary documents and your business cards with you. The papers have to be well-organized, so when you need to use some pages you don't spend precious time in searching for a right report or presentation. Take a pen and a notebook with you. Use gadgets like smartphone or laptop only if you are certain you can work on them fast and efficiently.

Remember the name of the person you are planning to meet. Sometimes you might want to go further and make a quick research on the place of his origin, or occupation.

Smile! A warm and natural smile on your face will sway people over to your side.

Be a good listener. If you are looking for a safe way to gain someone's favor, apart from the above guidelines, you also need to be a good listener. After the first greetings and necessary small talk to direct the attention from you to the other person, express your deep interest in the person's opinion. Such an approach will help you to lead any conversation and get key insights about the prospective business partner while giving an impression of you being a pleasant person to talk with.

When meeting someone, remember to shake hands. Give the person a firm and confident handshake. Maintain eye contact while engaging in shaking hands; this gesture is a great way to communicate with sincerity and confidence.

Eye contact matters. In fact, eye contact is your pillar not just while handshaking. The more you meet the eyes of the other person, the better. It gives an impression of engagement and interest in the communication. Keep good eye contact, but don't stare deep into his eyes. You don't want to be considered aggressive or dominant.

Talk clearly. If people don't comprehend what you are saying they will disregard you and the company you represent. Avoid slang and practice proper grammar while speaking at a moderate pace with a friendly and confident voice.

Use the person's name often. This shows to your companion that you are paying attention from the very beginning and that you give him enough importance to memorize his name.

Be open, friendly and very attentive. Ask relevant questions and carefully listen to what one has to say. When having a conversation let your partner know that you are paying attention. Use phrases like "I understand", "Interesting", "Tell me more", "I agree" and nod your head from time to time.

Stay away from sarcastic remarks and off-color jokes. Avoiding jokes at the first encounter is probably the safest choice, but if you can't help yourself, choose your jokes wisely, and give preference to something short and neutral.

Don't challenge your partner's statements during the first meeting. If you disagree with the person but count on the future rapport, try to "give up on the need to be right".

Exercise positive body language to support your words. One of the vital things people will notice is how you carry yourself. Always stand with confidence, with your stomach in, shoulders back and chest out. Don't fold your arms, for this posture displays aggression or disapproval. If you want to manifest confidence and composure, lose the lip biting and stop wringing hands while talking.

There is a chance that you might forget about some of these tips while meeting an important person for the first time. But the more you exercise these first impression principles the smoother your next meeting will go. Don't give up if you think you are not able to engage and impress a person, and remember, "practice is the best of all instructors".

Handshakes play such an important role in leaving a great first impression that a separate elaboration is necessary to be added here. Below are some important tips on making perfect business handshakes.

2. How to Perfect Your Business Handshakes

"I can feel the twinkle of his eye in his handshake." Helen Keller (1880—1968)

Did you know that every time John F. Kennedy needed to shake hands with someone in public he made a practice of standing on the left-hand side of photographers? This trick makes the one to the left of the image appear to be in control. The experts who studied the gestures of J.F.K. were convinced that his persuasive body language was precisely what won him the Presidency.

If you are interested in progressing your career too, you might want to check whether your handshake is as perfect as it gets:

When to Shake Hands?

Handshakes are the traditional part of greetings and partings in business. Shake hands with a client, partner or colleague every time you meet them and before the goodbyes.

The exceptions are co-workers that you see every day in your office. You don't need to shake hands with them, unless there is a special reason. If you are congratulating someone or a person was away for a week and you're really glad to see him, a handshake is totally appropriate.

Never leave a person you are greeting with his hand extended in mid-air as you refuse to shake it. If you refrain from the traditional greeting it will be close to impossible to reestablish a good relationship. Unless you explain yourself, your partner will be stuck at thinking about what he did that made you angry.

You can decline a handshake only if you have a very good reason, for example, when you are having the flu or a case of arthritis. In such situations you should always explain yourself by saying something like: "Mr. Johnson, I am very happy to meet you. I apologize for not shaking hands, but I caught a cold and I don't want to pass it on."

If someone refuses your handshake and doesn't rush to explain, to minimize the blunder, you can simply say, "Forgive me, I didn't realize shaking hands is not part of your culture."

Who Initiates Handshakes?

In the past, a man couldn't offer a handshake to a woman unless she initiated it. Nowadays, at least in the business environment, this custom has changed and it is absolutely acceptable for a man to reach out first.

At the same time, hierarchy and rank do matter. Let's say, you work in a big firm and you incidentally meet the CEO of your company in the lobby. As a senior executive of the company, he or she should initiate shaking hands with the person in lower management.

If you are a visitor in an office, for example, when you walk in to sell something, you should wait for the company representatives to initiate the handshake.

On the same principle, you should always initiate the handshake with a client who come to see you and make him or her feel welcome in your organization.

How to Shake Hands?

According to Phyllis Davis (1999), the president of EMCI, the classic American business handshake is:

You reach your hand out and you go all out until your web touches his or hers. Your palm should completely touch his/her palm. Firmly pump your hand 3 times. While shaking hands use the person's name: "Hello Amanda, it is a pleasure to see you!" Remember to look the person in the eye.

Phyllis also advises to slightly raise your eyebrows for a sixth of a second when saluting the person. This is almost unnoticeable, but gives your partner a sense that you trust him.

The handshake should be brief and shouldn't take more than four seconds.

While a limp "dead fish" type of handshake is a bad idea, a forceful grip is not a good one either. The ideal business handshake is a respectful and friendly gesture. When shaking hands, use about the same level of grip you would use for opening a door handle.

Always stand for a handshake. There are only two exceptions to the rule. First is if you have a physical disability and cannot stand. Second is if you are in a booth where it is not possible to stand. In such cases, do a kind of courtesy bow. Put one hand on your chest, raise yourself a little, and reach across to initiate the greeting.

Greetings in Different Countries

A firm handshake is a traditional form of greeting in North America and Europe.

In Japan the bow is the equivalent of shaking hands.

Though the handshake starts to be more popular in India and Thailand, still the traditional approach in these countries is placing the hands together at chest-level, prayer-like, and bowing.

When visiting Asia or the Middle East, keep in mind that the customary grip is gentler; too firm handshakes can be defined as aggressive. Also, keep in mind that women do not shake hands in some Muslim countries. Because the customs vary from religion to religion, it is better to wait until the woman initiates a handshake.

In many Latin American countries and in South Europe, a handshake can be accompanied by a touch on the forearm or elbow.

In general, if you visit a country for the first time it might be a good idea to find out what is the expected way of greeting there.

Reading Two: Ordering Food Properly During a Business Dinner

Once you are at a business dinner, numerous guidelines on table manners may come to your mind which will make you even more nervous, especially when you are a typical Asian and are dealing with a Western business dinner. The following basic guidelines may come in handy in such situations.

1. Be Familiar with the Food Items Offered on Most Menus.

Appetizers. Appetizers are finger foods usually served prior to a meal, or in the mealtimes, and are also called starters, and may range from the very simple to the very complex, depending on the occasion and the time devoted to making them.

Main courses. The entrée is the main dish, and it is usually chosen first. Main dishes generally fall into these categories: meat, poultry, fish, seafood, eggs, and pasta.

Salads. Salad is any of a wide variety of dishes, including vegetable salads, mixed salads incorporating meat, poultry, or seafood, and fruit salads.

Desserts. Common Western desserts include cakes, cookies, pastries, ice cream, pies, and candies. Fruit may also be eaten with or as a dessert.

Beverages. A beverage is a drink other than tap water. In many restaurants, the beverages available include coffee, tea, milk, cocoa, soft drinks, bottled water, and alcoholic beverages, as well as fruit and vegetable juices.

2. Take Note of What Your Host Orders.

Pay attention to what your host orders to eat, as it will give you an idea of what you should order. If they order an appetizer, you may want to order one, too. If the host is not the first person to order, you might ask for his or her recommendations.

3. Be Ready to Place Your Order.

Order simply, and don't make a scene. You can ask your server a question or two, but don't ask them to explain everything on the menu or substitute ingredients—unless you have a food allergy. Not only is it annoying, but you will also appear indecisive.

4. Don't Order the Most Expensive Item.

It's rude to order the most expensive item on the menu. Save the lobster or the decadent red meat dishes for another time.

5. Don't Order "Trouble" Foods.

Some foods can be a little difficult to eat. Save yourself the trouble—and the embarrassment—by just not ordering those foods.

Reading Three: Exchanging Business Cards

The exchanging of business cards is an important aspect of etiquette in today's world. Business cards are an internationally recognized means of presenting personal contact details, so ensure you have a plentiful supply. They are generally exchanged at the beginning of or at the end of an initial meeting.

Use both hands to receive the card and read it immediately. Be sure to offer yours in return. The biggest mistake you can make when you receive someone's business card is to glance at it and then slide it into a pocket. This treatment shows little respect for the other person, regardless of their position and rank. When you're handed a business card, read it thoroughly. You may want to repeat the person's name for pronunciation and acknowledge the person's company as being well respected, or ask something about the company or his position. Finally, express your gratitude for being given this information.

Unlike in North America or Europe, where the business card has little meaning other than a convenient form of capturing essential personal details, in other parts of the world the business card has very different meanings.

For example, in Japan the business card is viewed as a representation of the owner. Therefore, proper business etiquette demands one to treat the business card with respect and honor.

1. Business Card Etiquette in China

Have one side of your business card translated into Chinese using simplified Chinese characters that are printed in gold ink since gold is an auspicious color.

Your business card should include your title. If your company is the oldest or largest in your country, that fact should be highlighted on your card.

Hold the card in both hands when offering it.

Never write on someone's card unless so directed.

2. Business Card Etiquette in Japan

Business cards are exchanged with great ceremony.

Invest in quality cards.

Always keep your business cards in pristine condition.

Treat the business card you receive as you would do to the person.

Make sure your business card includes your title. The Japanese place emphasis on status and hierarchy.

Business cards are always received with two hands but can be given with only one.

During a meeting, place the business cards on the table in front of you in the order people are seated.

When the meeting is over, put the business cards in a business card case or a portfolio.

3. Business Card Etiquette in India

If you have a university degree or any honor, put it on your business card.

Always use the right hand to give and receive business cards.

Business cards need not be translated into Hindi as English is widely spoken within the business community.

4. Business Card Etiquette in the UK

Business card etiquette is relaxed in the UK and involves little ceremony.

It is not considered bad etiquette to keep cards in a pocket.

Business cards should be kept clean and presentable.

Do not feel obliged to hand out a business card to everyone you meet as it is not expected.

Reading Four: Making Phone Calls

Businesses communicate through various means, including emails or distributed memos, but when only a two-person conversation will do, you can't beat the telephone. During a telephone call, both parties have the benefit of live interaction and can immediately exchange ideas. Since time is important in a small business, maximize each phone call for optimum effectiveness. Prepare yourself before you pick up the phone to help you organize your thoughts and achieve your goal without an unnecessary second call.

1. Inbound Calls

(1) Pick up the phone within three rings to show the caller you are available and willing to answer questions. Use the appropriate greeting when picking up the phone. Say "Good morning" when answering the phone before noon and "Good afternoon" when answering after 12 p.m. If you work in the evening after 6 p.m., say "Good evening". State your name, and ask, "How may I help you?" This is a professional way to begin a call.

(2) Allow the caller to give his or her name and what company, if any, he or she represents. If he or she fails to do so, prompt him or her with, "May I ask who's calling?" Then say "From what company are you calling?" or "How may I help you today?" While the caller is talking, computer files can be accessed to search for the needed information.

(3) Ask for his or her account number if he or she has a billing question. Tell the caller he or she will be placed on hold if you need a minute to research his or her account.

Promise to return quickly. Find the information needed and pick up the call. Thank the customer for his or her patience and give the answer to the question.

(4) Finalize the phone call by asking the customer or associate if he or she has any other questions. Answer the additional questions as before and give one final thank you before hanging up. Say "Thank you for calling the Widget Store. Have a nice day/evening".

2. Outbound Calls

(1) Gather the necessary information before making the call. Place any script, call list or data before you and review the information. Have ready a pen and notebook for note-taking. These will help you stay on point when making the call and collecting information.

(2) Wait for the other party to pick up the call. Identify yourself politely by saying, "Good morning. My name is Lisa Jones from XYZ Corporation. May I speak to Mrs. White?" This method is the most effective because it gives the caller all the information he needs up front.

(3) Explain why you are calling when the proper party gets on the line. Give short bursts of information and don't talk too quickly or slowly. Let the speed of the other person dictate your speed. Allow the other caller to respond appropriately to questions and don't interrupt.

(4) Solicit answers by using open-ended questions that encourage conversation. Share information about your product or service but don't be too pushy. Ask the other party if he has questions you can answer.

(5) Conclude the phone call by finalizing an appointment or sale or by verifying the information you have gathered is correct and up to date. Remind the customer or associate when you will call again and what you will discuss next. Say "Thank you", and use the person's name. For example, say "Thank you, Mr. Jones".

Reading Five: Some Culture Factors in Business Negotiation

Language includes both the spoken words and the nonverbal actions and behaviors that reveal hidden clues to culture. In the negotiation process, interpersonal communication is the key activity that takes place at the verbal, nonverbal, situational and contextual level, and a total communication system can assist the negotiator to bridge the gap between utterance and felt meaning. Three key topics—time, space, body language—offer a starting point from which negotiators can begin to acquire the understanding necessary to do business in foreign countries.

1. Time

There are two different orientations to time across the world: monochronic and polychronic. Monochronic approaches to time are linear, sequential and involve focusing on one thing at a time. These approaches are most common in the European-influenced cultures of the US, Germany, Switzerland, and Scandinavia. Japanese people also tend toward this end of the time continuum. Polychronic orientations to time involve working on several activities simultaneously. The time it takes to complete an interaction is elastic, and more important than any schedule. This orientation is most common in Mediterranean and Latin cultures including France, Italy, Greece, and Mexico, as well as some Eastern and African cultures.

2. Space

Space orientations differ across cultures. They have to do with territory, divisions between private and public, comfortable personal distance, comfort or lack of comfort with physical touch and contact, and expectations about where and how contact will take place. For example, an American etiquette manual advises this about personal space: "When you meet someone, don't stand too close. An uncomfortable closeness is very annoying to the other person, so keep your physical distance, or he'll have to keep backing off from you. A minimum of two feet away from the other person will do."

There are large differences in spatial preferences according to gender, age, generation, socioeconomic class, and context. These differences vary by group, but should be considered in any exploration of space as a variable in negotiations.

3. Body Language

Body Language can be telling as it can help one determine the exact meaning of what the other side is saying and can also help you get your own message across. Likes and dislikes, tensions, and assessing an argument are shown by numerous signs such as blushing, contraction of facial muscles, giggling, strained laughter or simply silence. Wherever a party negotiates, the negotiator must watch and observe the other party. People, when seated, lean forward if they like what you are saying or are interested in listening. They sit back with crossed arms if they do not like the message. Nervousness can manifest itself through nonverbal behavior, and blinking can be related to feeling of guilt or fear.

Reading Six: How Cultural Differences Impact International Business

It is more common to see multinational and cross-cultural teams nowadays, which means businesses can benefit from an increasingly diverse knowledge base and new, insightful (富有洞察力的, 见解深刻的) approaches to business problems. However, along with the benefits of insight and expertise, global organizations also face potential stumbling blocks when it comes to culture and international business.

While there are a number of ways to define culture, put simply, it is a set of common and accepted norms shared by a society. But in an international business context, what is common in one country could be very different for a colleague from another. Recognizing and understanding how culture affects international business in these three core areas, including communication, workplace etiquette, and organizational hierarchy, can help you to avoid misunderstandings with colleagues and clients from abroad and excel in a globalized business environment.

Communication

Effective communication is essential to the success of any business venture, but it is particularly critical when there is a real risk of your message getting "lost in translation". In many international companies, English is the most widely-used international language of business. But more than just the language you speak, it's how you convey your message that's important. For instance, while the Finns may value directness and brevity, professionals from India can be more indirect and nuanced(有细微差别的) in their communication. Moreover, while fluent English might give you a professional boost globally, understanding the importance of subtle non-verbal communication between cultures can be equally crucial in international business.

Workplace Etiquette

Different approaches to professional communication are just one of the innumerable differences in workplace norms around the world. For instance, the formality of address is a big consideration when someone is dealing with colleagues and business partners from different countries. Do they prefer titles and surnames or is being on the first name basis acceptable? It can vary across organizations. Asian countries such as South Korea, China, and Singapore tend to use formal "surnames and job titles" while Americans and Canadians tend to use first names. When in doubt, being in compliance with the formality is generally the safest.

The concept of punctuality can also differ between cultures in an international business environment. Different ideas of what constitutes being "on time" can often lead to misunderstandings or negative cultural perceptions. For example, while an American may arrive at a meeting a few minutes early, an Italian or Mexican colleague may arrive several minutes — or more — after the scheduled start-time (and still be considered "on time").

Organizational Hierarchy(等级制度)

Organizational hierarchy and attitudes towards management roles can also vary widely between cultures. For example, whether or not those in junior or middle-management positions feel comfortable speaking up in meetings, questioning senior decisions, or expressing a differing opinion, which can be dictated by cultural norms. Often these attitudes can be a reflection of a country's societal values or level of social equality. For instance, a country such as Japan, which traditionally values social hierarchy, relative status, and respect for seniority, brings these values into the workplace. This hierarchy helps to define roles and responsibilities across the organization. It means that those in senior management positions command respect and expect a certain level of formality and deference from junior team members.

However, Scandinavian countries, such as Norway, which emphasize societal equality, tend to have a comparatively flat organizational hierarchy. In turn, this can mean relatively informal communication and an emphasis on cooperation across the organization. When defining roles in multinational teams with diverse attitudes and expectations of organizational hierarchy, it can be easy to see why these cultural differences can present a challenge.

International business is playing a more and more important role in our economic lives in modern society. That's why it's important to be mindful of cross-cultural communication in business. Therefore, understanding these three core areas is the key to avoiding cultural misunderstandings and training yourself with more skills to be a global citizen.

Read to Learn More

Five Tips for Doing Business in China

As Western countries remain mired in financial turmoil, business people are looking to get a foothold in China, hoping to tap its growth and expanding middle class.

But despite China's increasing influence, challenges remain for those looking to do business in the country. Intense competition, local customs and laws, business etiquette and language are some of the barriers that can be faced.

Here are five things you should know before doing business in China.

A Mosaic of Markets

China is the world's most populous nation, with its sprawling 1.4 billion people making up a highly diverse market.

"There is no such thing as the Chinese market," says Martin Roll, a business and brand strategist who provides advice to global and Asian brands in China. "You have to look at China more like a mosaic of cultures," he adds.

There is no single consumer profile, and analysts suggest companies remain flexible and innovative, while understanding how their company would fit in each specific market.

"You need people who've been in the market, you talk to trade associations, you talk to trade promotion bodies, you talk to people and bit by bit you get to understand the dynamics," says Stephen Perry, president of the 48 Group Club, an independent business network promoting business relations between China and the UK.

"There's no simple answer in China — it depends so much upon the specific market and upon the specific characteristic of your own company," he adds.

Business Culture and Etiquette

Operating in a country with a history of thousands of years — it is valuable to develop insight into China's business culture and social etiquette to avoid misunderstandings that could scuttle deals and harm working relationships.

One key aspect of Chinese culture is the concept of "face". In *China Uncovered: What You Need to Know to Do Business in China*, professor Jonathan Story describes face as a mix of public perception, social role and self-esteem that has the potential to either destroy or help build relationships.

A foreign CEO can show his/her respect for "face" by attending meetings, accepting invitations, providing suitable expensive gifts and showing sensitivity to Chinese culture.

Business outsiders can impress their Chinese counterparts with their knowledge of local customs, familiarity with local laws, and preference for local food. Such awareness of cultural nuances illustrates respect and sincere interest, says Roll.

On the flip side, Chinese business people generally respect cultural differences and won't expect Westerners to be fully customized to their tradition, analysts say.

"At the end of the day, the Chinese are very pragmatic," says Perry. "If you have something they want, they'll do business with you no matter whether you can hold chopsticks or not."

Jack Perkowski, a Wall Street veteran who's often referred to as "Mr. China" for his entrepreneurship in the Asian country since 1993, says developing mutual trust is the key to success in doing business in China. "The most important thing is, whoever you're meeting with or whoever you're dealing with, to treat them with respect." he says.

Take a Market-based Approach

Western businesses looking to tap the Chinese market should be aware of local preferences, and adapt accordingly. For example, Starbucks started serving green tea lattes in a bid to get a traditionally tea-drinking nation hooked on coffee; McDonald's adapted its menu to include items like spicy chicken wings and chicken burgers in an effort to appeal to local tastes.

"No matter how good you think your product is, no matter how well it sells in the UK, the US or anywhere else, you need to really look at that product in the context of China and ask yourself: Is that the right product? Is it too high-priced? Do we need to do something different? Do we need to adapt?" says Perkowski.

Procedures in China Take Time and Energy

Western companies looking to tap China also need to show a long-term approach that will prove that they're in the country to stay, analysts say. "It's very important when a Western company tries to go to China to realize that success in China takes time, it requires resources…" says Roll.

Build a Strong Local Team

Newcomers wanting to crack China will need to get someone from their organization to relocate or find an experienced group to represent them, says Perkowski, who's also the author of a book on doing business in China.

"When you're just starting, you've got to recognize there's going to be a limit to what you can do travelling back and forth to China," he adds. "You're never going to get a deal done [without basing yourself there]."

Surrounding yourself with local talents can help you make deals, understand the culture and the complexities of the market as well as compensate for the language barrier for those who don't speak Mandarin, analysts say.

"The only way you are going to ultimately be successful is by putting together a good team," says Perkowski.

In a word, to do business in China, overseas businessmen need to do some preparation work and be ready to adapt to and comply with local values and customs.

In-class Activity 课堂练习

Ⅰ. Comprehension questions.

Go over this chapter and try to make an assessment on what you have learned with the following self-assessment questions.

1. What does cross-cultural business etiquette mean? Please give some tips on making a great first impression in business settings?
2. What are the rules for ordering food during a business dinner?
3. In business negotiations, what are the major cultural factors?

Ⅱ. Comparative analysis.

Insert the phrase "intercultural/cross-cultural communication business etiquette" into a search engine on the Internet and report to your group what you have found out about the studies of intercultural communication both at home and abroad.

Ⅲ. True or false questions.

The executive of a Chinese township enterprise, after entertaining his American guest, offered his partnership in a business venture. The American businessman is very keen to enter into an agreement with the Chinese. He then suggested that they meet again the next day with their respective lawyers to fill in the details. The Chinese executive's tone suddenly became hesitant. Later that day the American was informed that the Chinese side "needs more consideration on their cooperation."

(　　) 1. In this case, the perceived meaning of inviting lawyers was different for the American and the Chinese.

(　　) 2. The American saw the lawyer's presence as facilitating the successful completion of the negotiation.

(　　) 3. The Chinese interpreted the lawyer's presence as a signal of mistrust of his commitment.

Ⅳ. Case study.

1. How is Jan supposed to behave there?

Jan graduated from a leading Polish business school. He had learned a lot about economics, finance, and marketing strategy and his grades were excellent. Everything indicated that he was well prepared for his starting career. Very soon he found a job he was dreaming of and started applying what he had learned in real business environment. He has been advancing his career rather quickly and taking over new areas of responsibility. Recently, his boss has asked him to identify a company potentially interested in cooperation, especially in the area of research and development. Since his company was operating in a niche market manufacturing very specialized products, very early Jan realized that for a potential partner he would have to look in Japan, Korea, and possibly in China. Not without difficulty he came up with a short list of potential partners and scheduled the first meetings with them. Today, his secretary gave him the tickets. Next week Jan and his boss are flying to Asia. Suddenly, he realized that all he knows about Asian culture actually come from TV and movies. The same was true for his boss. So, how should Jan behave when he arrives in the destination countries?

2. Why did the Chinese delegation leave the deal?

In 1992, a Chinese delegation, consisting of business negotiators and other 12 experts of different specialties, went to the US with 30 million US dollars to purchase chemical equipment and technology. The US part naturally thought about some ways to satisfy them. One of them was that each of the delegation was presented a small souvenir after the first round of negotiations; the souvenir was very particular in the packaging, which was a beautiful red box. When the members of the delegation were pleased to open the boxes face to face in accordance with the habit of the Americans, everyone's face looked unnatural. The souvenir was a golf cap, but the color was green. After that, the Chinese delegation didn't have further negotiations with them.

Background Information 背景知识

1. Group serving(合餐制),我国是一个美食大国,又是热情好客的礼仪之邦。逢年过节、婚丧嫁娶,免不了围桌合餐以共享食味、叙旧话新。合餐制是我国传统的饮食方式。中国家庭聚餐多用混餐式——主食和菜肴置于公用的碗盘内,用餐者根据自己偏好,使用自己的餐具,直接取食。随着时代发展,中国人开始使用公筷、公勺,在维系感情的同时,也更加有利于健康的维护。

2. Individual serving(分餐制),顾名思义就是将各自用餐的器具分开,每人一份自己的食物;或是在进餐时,使用公筷、公勺盛菜。西方国家不论家庭聚餐还是正式宴会均采用分餐制——餐具和食物一人一份。

Cultural Kaleidoscope 文化万花筒

商务谈判是经济合作双方为实现某种交易,或为了解决某种争端,而进行的协商洽谈活动(左显兰,2014)。除了谈判双方的说话方式与言谈技巧,跨文化商务协商中双方的形象打造、见面、接待、拜访、送礼、宴请、通信、洽谈、签约等关键环节都需遵循适宜的交际礼仪规范,这些对于谈判的进程与结果都起着举足轻重的作用(吕维霞、刘彦波,2016)。

Intercultural Negotiation Styles

It is difficult to track the myriad starting points used by negotiators from different national settings, especially as cultures are in constant flux, and context influences behavior in multiple ways. Another complication is that much of the cross-cultural negotiation literature comes from the organizational area. While it cannot be applied wholesale to the realm of intractable conflicts, this literature may provide some hints about approaches to negotiation in various national settings. Dr. Nancy Adler (1992) compares key indicators of success as reported by negotiators from four national backgrounds. Her table is reproduced here, ranking characteristics of negotiators in order of importance as reported by managers in each national setting:

AMERICAN NEGOTIATORS	JAPANESE NEGOTIATORS	CHINESE NEGOTIATORS	BRAZILIAN NEGOTIATORS
preparation and planning skill	dedication to job	persistence and determination	preparation and planning skill
think under pressure	perceive and exploit power	win respect and confidence	think under pressure
judgment and intelligence	win respect and confidence	preparation and planning skill	judgment and intelligence
verbal expressiveness	integrity	product knowledge	verbal expressiveness
product knowledge	demonstrate listening skill	interesting	product knowledge
perceive and exploit power	broad perspective	judgment and intelligence	perceive and exploit power
integrity	verbal expressiveness	competitiveness	integrity

 Business Etiquette in Belt and Road Countries
"一带一路"国家的商务礼仪

中国传统文化6

伊 朗

商务会议礼仪

- 会晤前最好提前四到六周预约。
- 提前一周确认一次会议预约信息,抵达该国时再次确认会议预约相关信息。
- 避免在斋月期间安排会议,因为斋戒期间,伊朗的生意伙伴很可能无法接待你。
- 准时参加会议。在伊朗,守时被视为一种美德。

- 与伊朗生意伙伴第一次会面通常不以商业业务为重点。他们会花些时间,通过一起吃吃喝喝和闲聊来了解你。
- 保持耐心。你与伊朗生意伙伴的会议可能经常会被打断。
- 书面材料应同时提供波斯语和英语两个版本。
- 未经允许,请勿脱掉西装外套。
- 不要看表或表现出你赶时间。如果你对会议所花费的时间过于在意,可能会失去你的伊朗生意伙伴的信任。

Iran

Business Meeting Etiquette

- Appointments are necessary and should be made 4 to 6 weeks in advance.
- Confirm the meeting one week in advance and when you arrive in the country.
- It is a good idea to avoid scheduling meetings during Ramazan (Ramadan) as the need to be fast would preclude your business colleagues from offering you hospitality.
- Arrive at meetings on time, since punctuality is seen as a virtue.
- The first meeting with an Iranian company is generally not business-focused. Expect your colleagues to spend time getting to know you as a person over tea and snacks.
- Be patient—meetings are frequently interrupted.
- Written materials should be available in both Farsi and English.
- Do not remove your suit jacket without permission.
- Do not look at your watch or try to rush the meeting. If you appear fixated on the amount of time the meeting is taking, you will not be trusted.

 Intercultural Tips 跨文化拓展知识

中西方宴请招待

  宴请的规格,与被宴请客人的身份有关,这一点在西方或者东方都是一样的。对于高贵的客人,宴请时规格要高一些。对于一般的客人,宴请的方式可以随意一些。

  对于什么是丰盛的宴会,中西方有十分不同的理解。丰盛的西餐,一般有四五道菜,分量以能吃完或稍有剩余为最佳。如果是家宴,客人把菜全部吃完,主人会很高兴,认为大家非常喜欢自己做的菜。宴会前、宴会当中及宴会之后,一般准备各种酒及饮料,主要是葡萄酒,而喝哪一种葡萄酒又有很多讲究。例如,如果主菜是鱼、火鸡,应该上白葡萄酒;如果主菜是牛肉或羊肉,应该上红葡萄酒。夏季和冬季喝的酒,又有不同。宴会结束客人离开餐桌以后,主人会拿出各种甜的烈性酒,由客人挑选。在我国一般都是在餐桌上饮酒,在饭后没有饮酒的习惯。

  在英美等国家,朋友之间宴请,一般来说一道汤、一盆沙拉、一道主菜再加上一道甜食就可以招待客人了。但是饮料和酒必须充分供应,他们把吃饭看成一个聚会和交流的机会,因此沟通交流比吃饭更重要。

在美国,朋友聚餐有两种常见的方式。一种是采取大家都作贡献的做法,他们称为"potluck",每人或者每家都带一样菜,在其中一家聚会,这家主人准备一些饮料,也可以请来客中的一位专门带饮料。这种聚餐方式,主人显得不那么突兀,大家不分主人与客人,重心主要放在闲谈沟通上。另一种聚餐他们称为"party"。这类聚餐准确一些应该称为松散的聚会,以见面聊天和结识新朋友为主要目的,主人一般只提供饮料、酒和一些简单的吃食,如奶酪、炸薯条、三明治等,并不提供饭菜。客人到达和离去的时间也比较灵活。

相对而言,中国人的宴席要丰盛得多。一般中国宴席至少要准备八道菜,即四冷四热。如果是正式的高规格的宴会,菜式会更多,而且宴席的主人会提供名贵、奇特的菜式力图表达自己的热情和对客人的重视。除此之外,中国宴席上提供的饭菜的量一般都要超过主人和客人所能消耗的量,否则就不足以表示主人的热情好客。席间,主人还应不断向客人劝酒,使就餐的气氛热烈而友好。这类宴席提供的酒以酒精含量比较高的白酒居多,啤酒和果酒近年来也开始流行。在中国人的宴席上,沟通和感情交流非常重要,但美食也同样占有至关重要的地位。如果主人家提供的饭菜不丰盛,或者烹饪技术不佳,会使主客双方都感到扫兴。

总的来说,西方人到中国人家里做客,常常会觉得过于丰盛,而中国人到西方人家里做客,往往觉得饭菜比较简单。

中国宴席上菜的一般程序

中国宴席为一席多菜,上菜有相对固定的程序。了解这个程序不但可以帮助我们体会到中国宴席菜点品尝中的节奏,还可以使我们做好赴宴的心理准备,做到对宴席过程心中有数。

当然,中国宴席的上菜程序并不是固定不变的,这里仅介绍一般的程序。

第一道程序是品尝冷菜。这一阶段,宾客们可以边喝酒吃菜边聊天交流情感,大型宴会可以安排主人和客人致辞。

第二道程序是品尝炒菜(热菜)。热菜要趁热吃,所以品尝速度加快,口味上逐渐转向浓重。这时,宴会进入第一个高潮。

第三道程序是品尝烧菜(热菜)。口味更浓重,节奏也更快了。宴会进入第二个高潮。吃过烧菜,宾客们可以用餐巾擦擦脸、擦擦手,稍微休息一下,为进入最后的高潮做好准备。

第四道程序是品尝主菜。主菜是一场宴席中最主要的菜,如烤鸭、火锅等。这时宴席上气氛活跃,宾客们往往互相敬酒,或拍照留念,或唱歌,或表演小节目等。如果是婚礼,新婚夫妇要在这个时候向来宾行礼,全场往往一片欢腾。人们欢快地品尝佳肴,宴席达到最高潮。

第五道程序是品尝素菜、清汤、点心、水果,口味甜淡,余味无穷。此时,宾客们酒足饭饱,心满意足,宴席进入尾声。

Movie to See 观影学文化

Please watch the movie *Wall Street* (《华尔街》) with your classmates and discuss what intercultural elements are involved in it.

Unit 7 Culture Shock

文 化 冲 击

Learning Objectives 学习目标

- 熟悉与文化冲击相关的基本概念。
- 了解文化冲击产生的原因。
- 熟悉文化冲击的阶段和表现。
- 掌握应对文化冲击、提升跨文化适应能力的相关策略。

Lead-in 单元导读

当我们从母语文化进入目的语文化时,会经历很多由于文化差异带来的诸多不适应感,甚至焦虑感,即所谓的"文化冲击"或者"文化休克"现象,并由此产生不同的交际结果。

文化冲击的内涵及表现。"文化冲击"原意是指一个人从其原有的文化环境中移居到一个新的文化环境中所产生的文化上的不适应。"二战"后,随着人口的大量流动,产生了大批移民,他们从一个国家移居到一个新的国家,从一种文化背景移居到新的文化背景,等待他们的是诸多跨文化的社会心理问题,"文化冲击"这个词就应运而生了。文化冲击可以是多方面的,从气候、饮食、语言、服饰,直至行为举止、人口密度、政治经济环境,等等;有身体的因素,但更多的是精神因素。在一个崭新的文化环境中,文化冲击使得受冲击者无所适从,甚至整个心理平衡和价值判断标准完全丧失,具体可能表现为沮丧、抑郁、困惑、焦虑、孤独。

文化冲击的阶段及表现形式。第一阶段:"蜜月期"。在这一阶段,新老文化差异处在一个浪漫的相识氛围中。比如,你会因生活在一个不同国度里而兴奋,喜欢那里的食物、生活方式及当地习惯。在最初几周,每一样东西看上去都妙不可言。你什么都喜欢,而且好像每个人都对你很好。另外,新文化中的生活乐趣好像无穷无尽。但正如大多数蜜月期一样,这个阶段最终也会结束。语言障碍、公共安全、交通安全、食品质量也会加重你与周边环境的隔离感。第二阶段:"危机阶段"。一段时间后(一般是3个月左右,当然每个人具体长短不一),你会发现新旧文化差异变得很明显,以至于你开始为之变得焦虑不安。最初的兴奋感让步于沮丧和愤怒的感觉。你会持续遇到一些令你不快的事情。在这个阶段最大的变化是交流困难,人们在适应新文化中常常会因为尚未适应新环境且天天跟陌生人打交道而变得想家和孤独。交友的最大障碍是语言交流困难,你必须特别注意交流中的文化差异,如其他人的肢体语言信号、谈话语气、语言的细微差别和习惯。第三阶段:"恢复/调整期"。一段时间后(通常6~12个月),你开始习惯新文化,也养成了固定习惯。在大多数情况下你知道了要干什么,你的生活再次回到"正常",事情也回到正轨。你开始能够解决文化冲突中遇到的问题,也试着积极地接受新文化中的处事方法。新文化也变得容易理解了,针对新文化的逆反心理也逐渐减少了。第四阶段:"适应阶段"。在这个阶段里你达到了真正感觉良好的境界,你感到很舒服,已经适应了新的文化。最后一个阶段为"逆向文化冲击阶段"。当一个人在异国不同文化环境里生活了一段时间、经历了文化冲击、适应了异国文化后,再次回到祖国,出现对本国文化不适应的症状,这就是"逆向文化冲击"。

　　文化冲击的应对策略。首先,学习目标语言。有大量研究显示,语言技能不足可能导致"人际交往"的失误。学习主流文化的语言能产生积极的效果。只有在有交流的情况下才有可能与他人达成理解,而学习语言对于有效的交流是必不可少的。其次,了解目标国的相关文化。提前查阅目标国的基本概况,了解目标国的日常礼仪、禁忌等。最后,提前做好准备是对抗文化冲击最好的防御机制。出国之前,最好先了解一下所去国家的情况,并与最近去过的人交流。如果你对不同的文化有很好的了解,就可以很容易地对抗文化冲击。因此,你必须了解你的旅行目的地的食物、服装模式、信仰和习俗、喜好和厌恶。阅读旅游指南、旅行小贴士,并尝试找出一些社会生存技巧,如如何称呼不同社会群体中的人,性别角色如何影响社会关系,日常有哪些不同于自己国家的行为,又有哪些手势和肢体语言是可接受的。当然,从自身角度,调整好心态,以积极的态度面对新的环境也是十分必要的。

　　踏入异域文化,我们难以避免文化冲击。为了更好地应对文化冲击,学习者应认真学习文化冲击的相关知识,以便更好地进行跨文化交际。本单元主要介绍文化冲击的定义、文化冲击产生的原因、文化冲击的几个阶段,以及应对文化冲击的策略,帮助学习者了解人们适应新文化的过程,更好地处理跨文化交际障碍,顺利适应新的文化环境。

Pre-class Activity 课前活动

Work in small groups to discuss the following questions:

(1) What will you feel when you enter a completely new culture for the first time? And how will you react?

(2) What may be the differences in a new culture? Try to list as many as possible, and explain the reasons.

Reading 课内阅读

Reading One: Definitions & Causes of Culture Shock

1. Definitions of Culture Shock

The term culture shock can be defined in various ways. It can be described as a common experience for people who have been transplanted abroad. It arises from cross-cultural miscommunication and happens when different cultures clash with each other. Culture shock can also refer to phenomena ranging from mild irritability to deep psychological panic and crisis. It is associated with feelings in the person of estrangement (being unfriendly or hostile to others), anger, hostility, indecision, frustration, unhappiness, sadness, loneliness, homesickness, and even physical illness. The term, culture shock, was first introduced by Kalvero Oberg in 1958. He found that all human beings experience the same feelings when they travel to or live in a different country or culture. He found that culture shock is almost like a disease: it has a cause, symptoms and a cure. Culture shock describes the anxiety produced when a person moves to a completely new environment. This term expresses the lack of direction, the feeling of not knowing what to do or how to do things in a new environment, and not knowing what is appropriate or inappropriate. The onset can vary from a few weeks to months after coming to a new place. In Robert L. Kohl's book—*Survival Kit for Overseas Living* (1996), culture shock is described as "the physical and emotional discomfort one suffers when coming to live in another country or a place different from the place of origin. The person undergoing culture shock views his new world out of resentment, and alternates between being angry at others for not understanding him and being filled with self-pity".

Culture shock concerns the impact of moving from a familiar culture to one which is unfamiliar. People's response to culture shock varies greatly. The following are some people's feelings and experiences when they went abroad.

Case 1

Hattie, an overseas student, describes his own experience abroad:

In Denmark, the entire city is divided into zones and you have to buy a travel card each month. You should know what zones you are going to travel through. That is not the news, but the point is that after zone 2 you may find zone 31(in my case). I couldn't get it in a month and was absolutely sure that zone 2 would logically be followed by zone 3. Every day I went from zone 3 where I lived to zone 1 where I studied, having zones 1, 2 and 3 on my travel card. You should have seen the faces of the subway conductors, who were about to fine me when I said that I had been using that very card for that very route for a month. They were really puzzled to know that I knew nothing about the illogical zone ordering.

Case 2

Xu Xiaoli, a Chinese student who studied in America:

Here, you often come across another way of thinking, doing, reacting and valuing. In the States, I had a boyfriend. Once he invited me to have a drink with him. It was on campus and I was going to the dormitory from the computer lab. I accepted the invitation. When it was time to pay the bill, I was surprised to find that tax charge was specially listed as part of the bill which is quite different from the practice in China. After some time abroad, you may get used to the new environment, but still feel homesick now and then.

Culture shock can be described as the feeling of confusion and disorientation that one experiences when faced with a large number of new and unfamiliar people and situations (Kalvero Oberg, 1958). Many things contribute to it—smells, sounds, flavors, even the very feeling of the air one is breathing. Of course, the unfamiliar language and behavior contribute to it, too.

The notion of culture shock calls two useful points to mind. First, most people experience some degree of culture shock when they go to a new country. Culture shock is more a product of the situation of being in a new culture than it is of the traveler's personal character. Second, culture shock, like other kinds of "shock", is normally transitory. It passes with time.

Academic analysts of culture shock point out that the experience of culture shock need not be negative. While there may be some unhappiness and unpleasantness along with confusion and disorientation, these are necessary steps in learning about a new culture. If everything in the new place is just like home, no learning will come from being there.

2. Causes of Culture Shock

Generally speaking, culture shock is caused by the history of human being's development. Geography and climate lead to different ways of living and thinking, which lead to different cultural backgrounds and social values. Thus, specific cultures are products of historical development. Each country has its own distinctive cultural characteristics in languages, diet, institutions, economic systems, educational systems, customs, etc.

Narrowly speaking, there are mainly three causes which can lead to culture shock. Losing all the familiar signs and symbols of social intercourse is the first main cause. When people enter a strange culture, all or most of these familiar cues are removed, and he or she is like a fish out of water. Obviously, climate and food have direct relations with people's life and mood. When people are accustomed to the climate and food in their home countries, they might experience physical and mental culture shock after arriving in a new environment. Meanwhile, when living overseas in a place where the other people speak a different language, people will suffer a lot even in a relatively simple but important part of life such as walking around and shopping. It can be frustrating trying to ask for help, to pay for the bill, or to tell the taxi driver where to go. It is always not enough for the language learners to catch the sound, the words, and the grammar. The most important thing is to care culture elements like idioms, slang, facial expressions, body language, and so on. Moreover, the changes in lifestyle, transportation, mode of economy and politics, even the skin's color of the strangers around these people may make them feel panic and not know what to do or how to react. The most important aspect is the change in family relations and friendships that they used to rely on. Families and friends are important because they are the ones who will see you through your happy and sad moments, and help you overcome the difficulties.

Secondly, customs and etiquette are also essential factors which influence the consequences of intercultural communication. The key to the cause of culture shock is being unfamiliar with local customs and etiquette. As for religion, the status of women, individualism, collectivism, attitudes toward authority, forms of government, the legal system, and attitudes to the environment and so on, all these the local citizens may be sensitive about. People may offend the local citizens unconsciously.

Lastly, culture shock is caused by the lack of necessary cultural knowledge and corresponding social skills. Visitors or sojourners in unfamiliar settings who lack culturally relevant social skills and knowledge will have difficulty in initiating and sustaining harmonious relations with their hosts. Their culturally inappropriate behavior will lead to misunderstandings and may cause offence. It is also likely to make them less effective in both their professional and personal lives. In other words, culturally unskilled persons are less likely to achieve their goals, whatever they might be.

Reading Two: Symptoms and Stages of Culture Shock

1. Symptoms of Culture Shock

Culture shock can be understood as the physical and emotional discomfort one suffers when going to live in another country or a place different from the place of origin. Often, the way that we lived before is not accepted as or considered as normal in the new place. Thus, people might suffer a lot physiologically, psychologically as well as behaviorally. However, there are many different effects, time spans, and degrees of severity of culture shock. Some people may just experience little of it, while some others are handicapped by its presence. Considered comprehensively, the symptoms of culture shock consist of physical, psychological and behavioral symptoms.

Physical Symptoms (生理症状) of Culture Shock

Physical symptoms of culture shock are mainly caused by the differences in climate, food, water and even the differences in the plants in the surroundings. They are a kind of naturally physical reactions towards the change of the environment. The physical symptoms of culture shock are headaches, allergies, fatigue, diarrhea, nausea, sweating, overeating or loss of appetite, frequent minor illnesses, a need for excessive sleep or insomnia, dry mouth, difficulty in swallowing, abdominal pain (especially in children), etc.

Psychological Symptoms（心理症状）of Culture Shock

Psychological symptoms of culture shock are psychological reactions to unfamiliar environments. When familiar signs and symbols are lost, the life style is changed, the language and behavior of people in the surroundings are different, people will feel frustrated, angry or anxious because of the changes in the situation or thinking pattern. Culture shock is more than a feeling of homesickness or jet lag. It can lead to quite severe symptoms like helplessness, boredom, loneliness, vulnerability, disorientation, dissatisfaction, heightened irritability, hostility towards the host culture, unwillingness to interact with others, feelings of inadequacy or insecurity, a sense of being overwhelmed or frustrated, feelings of being unimportant and overlooked, extreme homesickness, desire for home or old friends, sudden intense feeling of loyalty to one's own culture and Utopian ideas towards it.

Behavioral Symptoms（行为症状）of Culture Shock

Behavioral symptoms of culture shock are the combination of physical symptoms and psychological symptoms of culture shock. The conditions of physiology and psychology determine human's behavior to a large extent. Thus, people in culture shock behave unusually. The behavioral symptoms of culture shock are staring blankly, unexplainable crying, loss of sense of humor, difficulty in concentration, lack of self-belief or confidence, rebellion against rules and authority, constant complaints about everything, loss of ability to work or study effectively, unable to solve simple problems during daily life, refusal to learn the language and the important cues of the host culture, developing obsessions such as over-cleanliness, excessive concern over heath, security, withdrawal from people who are different from them and spending too much time alone in their room (only socializing with people from their home country), etc.

To summarize, individuals differ greatly in the degree to which culture shock affects them. Thus, not everyone will experience all of these symptoms, and each person's reaction may be different. There are no fixed symptoms ascribed to culture shock. Meanwhile, people are sometimes unaware of the fact that they are experiencing culture shock when these symptoms occur since the symptoms of cultural shock can appear at different times.

Although people experience real pain from culture shock, it is also an opportunity for redefining one' life objectives. It is a great opportunity for learning and acquiring new perspectives. It can also make people develop a better understanding of themselves and stimulate personal creativity. Those who have gone through culture shock can see steps in the process.

2. Stages of Culture Shock

The feeling of culture shock generally sets in after the first few weeks of getting to a new place. Culture shock is frequently described as a series of stages that a person goes through. People will experience these stages when they are in a new country which enjoys a different culture from their own. There are five main stages of culture shock and sufferers do not necessarily pass through all of them.

The Honeymoon Stage

The honeymoon stage is usually the first stage of culture shock. As you can already guess from the name, people in this stage consider the differences between the new environment and the old one as wonderful and romantic. They view their new surroundings as a welcome and pleasant change and enjoy the differences in fashion, food, social customs, music, clothing, pace of life, people's habits, buildings and the fresh appeal of the new experience that keeps them feeling interested. Besides, they usually have an initial reaction of enchantment, fascination, enthusiasm, admiration and cordial, friendly, superficial relationships with hosts. Overall, they embrace with open arms the lifestyle, environment and practically everything about their new environment; thus, most people feel energetic and enthusiastic during this stage. Yet, this kind of feeling will not accompany you all the time during your stay in other cultures. The honeymoon stage usually lasts from several weeks to half a year depending on circumstances.

If you are on honeymoon, vacations, or brief business trips, you probably do not stay long enough for this stage to wear off but go on to the next new location or back to your hometown. There are people who frequently change jobs, majors, romantic partners, travel plans, clothing styles, food or diet so that they never get very far away from the honeymoon stage of culture shock. It is very pleasant to travel and explore whatever is new.

However, for those people who set out to study, live or work in a new country, they will invariably experience difficulties with language, housing, friends, schoolwork, and understanding the idiosyncrasies（习性、癖好）of the local culture, which often result in frustration. Afterwards, the next stage will present itself.

The Crisis Stage

When people stay in a new environment for a period of time, they move to stage two, that is, the crisis stage, in which the shine wears off and day-to-day realities sink in. People may encounter some difficult times with many aspects of daily life, school and work. They begin to become confused and do not know what to do, such as how to solve all the relevant problems when renting an apartment, how to register in school and make sure everything about one's studies has been settled in, how to greet others and what to say when different people meet, when and how to give tips, how to give orders to the servant, how to make purchases, when to accept and when to refuse invitation, when to take statements seriously and when not, how to make oneself understood and so on.

People have to pay a great deal of conscious energy that is not required in the old environment to confront the new environment. And the role that people play in the native culture may be dramatically different in the new culture.

At this stage, initial differences in language, concepts, values, familiar signs and symbols lead to the changes of many different feelings and emotions from confusion, anxiety, homesickness, and loneliness, to being unsure of oneself, feeling less competent than in one's home country, feeling overwhelmed, and feeling angry for being in this situation. Furthermore, because the high expectations set during the honeymoon period appear much farther out of reach, the individual feels disillusioned.

Hence, the second stage is always characterized by a hostile and aggressive attitude towards the host country. This hostility evidently grows out of the genuine difficulty which the visitor experiences in the process of adjustment.

The Recovery Stage

People who survive the second stage successfully move into the third stage of culture shock called the "recovery stage". In this stage, people start to accept that they have a problem and that they have to work on it. Both recovery and the final adaptation stages usually involve a compromise between the feeling and thinking of the honeymoon stage and the crisis stage. This compromise is between one's exaggerated expectations and reality.

In recovery, people determine to seek out the boundary lines and see what differences surround them. They begin to see and compare the home culture to the new culture and gain some understanding of the new environment. At the same time, they try to put themselves into this new culture but do not know how to approach it correctly. This is when confusion and mixed feelings start to hit a person.

As people become more comfortable with the language, nonverbal signs, food, customs and surroundings of the host country, they realize that the new culture has not only disadvantages but also merits. No country is that much better than another—it is just different lifestyles, different ways to deal with the problems of life. And the problems associated with the host culture are due not to deliberate attempts by the natives, but to a real difference in values, beliefs, and behaviors. Without any notice, the host culture begins to make sense in those people's mind, and pessimistic reactions and responses are lessened. They begin to actively seek effective problem-solving and conflict-resolution strategies.

The Adaptation Stage

The adaptation stage occurs when people feel that they not only accept the foods, drinks, habits and customs but also begin to enjoy them. They no longer need to make mental conversions before they start to say something. They get to know where the services or goods that they are looking for are located and how to use them. They understand some of the customs that accompany their daily life. And they find that it is relatively easy for them to adjust to the culture. As we all know, the environment does not change. What has changed is people's attitude towards it. When people feel at ease with what they meet and where they are, they have successfully adapted to the new culture. At this time people may regain some of the initial positive regard they had in the honeymoon stage.

People in this stage have already developed a level of competency in communicating with the natives. As a result of their success, people also require psychological well-being, take on an intercultural identity, and foster a sense of integration with their host environment.

The Reverse Culture Shock

When people in the adaptation stage return to their homeland, they are entering the fifth stage of culture shock. This is called "reverse culture shock". Similar to culture shock, reverse culture shock refers to the phenomenon that when a person who studied and lived abroad for a period of time returns to his or her motherland, he or she may fail to adapt well to the life and culture of his or her home country, and he or she may even experience a similar, yet unexpected readjustment process (Thompson & Christofi, 2006).

Different people will experience differently in the reverse stage. It may take several days to readapt, depending on the length of time they were away. However, since people are in a place where they grew up, their culture shock wears off faster than the culture shock that they experienced in the new culture.

Studies have shown that the phenomenon of reverse culture shock is widespread among returnees, and some theories have also suggested that reverse culture shock is inevitable. In reality, people may encounter different degrees of reverse culture shock. Some people may hardly feel reverse culture shock, while others may be plagued by various problems for months or even longer (Sun Zhige, 2019).

Reading Three: Strategies for Dealing with Culture Shock

Culture shock can be alleviated, or minimized with good preparation. Culture shock is an unfortunate side effect of going abroad, but people need to know that it will pass. If they have prepared themselves by learning about potential problems and differences, developing their language skills, and making a plan to get involved, they will be able to deal with the challenges effectively, and alleviate or minimize culture shock. Actually, there are many ways for people to reduce cultural clashes. What follows are some suggestions that may be useful in alleviating culture shock.

1. Learning the Target Language

An understanding with someone is only possible when there is communication and learning language is essential for effective communication. It is also clear that learning the language of the host culture produces positive results. There is ample research that supports the notion that insufficient language skills may result in negative consequences in "interpersonal interactions".

2. Acquiring the Cultural Knowledge of Host Country

We often have this experience: When we are listening to something familiar to us, no matter what is concerned, usually it is easier to understand. Even if there are some new words in the material, we are able to guess the meaning according to its context. However, when we encounter some unfamiliar material or something closely related to cultural background, we may feel it is rather difficult to understand. Even if the material is easy, we only know the literal meaning, but cannot understand the connotation, because we lack knowledge of the cultural background(Li Jianfeng, 2020).

Here is a sentence from a report: "The path to November is uphill all the way." "November" literally means "the eleventh month of year". But here it refers to "the presidential election held in November". Another example is "blue Monday", which is a simple phrase and is easy to hear, meaning unhappy Monday, but non-native speakers are often unable to understand them without other's explanation.

3. Preparing Ahead

Good preparation ahead of time is the best defense mechanism against culture shock. Prior to traveling to a foreign land, it is advisable to read about the country and talk to others who have traveled there recently. If you are well aware of the different cultures, you can easily combat culture shock. Thus, you must know about the food, dress patterns, beliefs and practices, likes and dislikes of the people of the proposed destination of your travel. Read travel guides, travel tips, and try to find out some social survival skills, such as how to address people in different social groups, how gender roles affect social relationships, what constitutes acceptable behavior in a range of everyday situations, and how gestures and body language differ from your own country. Go through any challenges that travelers may face while in a specific destination.

In a word, do ample research before going abroad and educate yourself on the place you are going to visit through whatever means possible.

4. Mastering Simple Tasks

Within the first several days of arrival, work on familiarizing yourself with some of the basic, everyday survival skills that local people take for granted. These include such capacities as using the local currency, using the public transportation system, buying stamps, using the telephone system, and ordering from a menu in a restaurant. By mastering these simple tasks, you will minimize frustrations and embarrassment quickly, and gain the self-confidence to master some of the more subtle aspects of the host culture.

5. Building up Appropriate Attitudes to Cross-cultural Communication

Besides language and cultural knowledge of host country, personal attitudes towards cross-cultural communication are also very important. People who build intercultural awareness with a right perspective can lessen the conflicts in the cross-cultural context. Two suggestions on building up appropriate attitudes toward cross-cultural communication are to be flexible and to improve empathy.

Here are some tips that are helpful in fighting culture shock:

(1) Recognize that you are experiencing culture shock, and your reactions are not from some other sources. Remember that many others have had the same thing. Understand that your feelings are part of a response to learning about the other culture and

consider it a positive sign.

(2) Find others from your home culture and spend time together talking about home, eating and sharing experiences.

(3) Help others who have recently arrived from your home culture. You will be surprised at how much you've learned.

(4) Communicate with family and friends. Remember that those at home might not realize that culture shock is a normal experience. Let them know it is a temporary phase of adjusting to a different culture.

(5) Keep busy. Get to know the area where you live by walking around and observing. Say hello to a neighbor in the place you live, which perhaps can start a friendship.

(6) Do something you enjoy. Contact a relative or acquaintance nearby, browse through department stores, visit a museum, etc.

Generally speaking, we should learn to respect and understand different cultures. As the saying goes, "If you want others to respect yourself, you should respect others first." This sentence is also applicable to cross-cultural communication. Only by respecting different cultures can we reduce the negative transfer of mother culture to a large extent (Zhao Fenyan, 2021).

Read to Learn More

Two Views on Culture Shock

People mostly feel culture shock when they stay abroad where all the expected, familiar hints and help are stripped away from them. Suddenly they do not know what to do, how to act, or what in the world to think. There are two major views on culture shock: the disease view and the self-awareness view (Peter S. Adler, 1975).

One perspective on culture shock is the disease view. The culture-shocked person experiences a breakdown in communication, is unable to cope, and feels isolated and lost. He thus develops a number of defensive (and sometimes offensive) attitudes and behaviors to protect the mind from the confusion of an entirely new situation. In this view, he is a helpless victim. The only thing this victim can do to "get well" is to adjust to the new culture somehow, or else to leave the culture quickly.

In this disease view, people can experience many different emotional and mental difficulties. They can become extremely frustrated, angry, and antagonistic to the new culture. They consider the host country bad, ridiculous, stupid, or hopeless—precisely because they themselves feel bad, ridiculous, stupid, or hopeless. Culture-shocked person may start to glorify the home country. Suddenly everything about the native land is wonderful compared to this terrible new place! Some culture-shocked people fear physical contact with anyone or anything from the new culture, no matter how safe or clean they are. Feeling helpless about delays and confusions can turn rapidly into resentment. People in culture shock may feel harmed, tricked, deceived, injured, or ignored—or all of these.

People can become physically ill from the stress of culture shock. Ulcers, headaches, stomach aches, backaches, the flu—these and hundreds of other physical symptoms can often be traced back to an underlying culture shock condition.

The disease view of culture, in which the person is an unwilling victim, is not the only view of culture shock. There is another, much more positive concept of culture shock. This is called the self-awareness view of culture shock. Culture shock can be part of a positive learning experience. Culture shock, if handled well, can lead to profound self-awareness and growth.

Day-to-day living in another culture is undoubtedly an educational experience. While traveling or living abroad, people learn a second language, observe different customs, and encounter new values. Many people who have lived in other countries feel that exposure to foreign culture enables them to gain insight into their own society. When facing different values, beliefs, and behaviors, they develop a deeper understanding of themselves and the society that helps to shape their characters. The striking contrasts of a second culture provide a mirror in which one's own culture is reflected.

Peter Adler (1975), a well-known expert on culture shock, says that positive cross-cultural learning experiences typically:

- involve change and movement from one cultural frame of reference to another.
- are personally and uniquely important to the individual.
- force the person into some form of self-examination.
- involve severe frustration, anxiety, and personal pain, at least for a while.
- cause the person to deal with relationships and processes related to his or her role as an outsider.
- encourage the person to try new attitudes and behaviors.
- allow the person to compare and contrast constantly.

The strong, creative person can deal with culture shock positively, instead of sinking into steady complaints about the culture, wallowing in very real physical ailments, or running away at the first opportunity. Culture shock can become an opportunity for growth.

In-class Activity 课堂练习

Ⅰ. Comprehension questions.

1. Could you describe the characteristics of each stage of culture shock? Make a form and list them briefly and clearly.

2. What do you think is the most effective strategy for dealing with culture shock?

And do you have any more strategies to add?

II. Case analysis.

1. What's the major problem between Li Hongzhang and the restaurant owner in this case?

Li Hongzhang, one of the top officials in the Qing Dynasty, was invited to visit the US. He was warmly welcomed. One day, Li was hosting a banquet for the American officials in a popular restaurant. As the banquet started, according to Chinese custom, Li stood up and said, "I am very happy to have all of you here today. Although these dishes are coarse and not delicious and good enough to show my respect for you, I hope you will enjoy them.（今天承蒙各位光临，不胜荣幸。我们略备粗馔，聊表寸心，没有什么可口的东西，不成敬意，请大家多多包涵。）"

The next day, the English version of his words was shown in the local newspaper. To his shock, the restaurant owner flew into a rage. He thought it was an insult to his restaurant and insisted that Li Hongzhang should show him the evidence of which dish was not well-made and which dish was not delicious. Otherwise, it meant Li Hongzhang intentionally damaged the reputation of the restaurant, and he should apologize. All the fuss made Li rather embarrassed.

2. What's the major problem in the case? And what can we learn from this case?

In 1997, a Danish woman left her 14-month-old baby girl in a stroller outside a Manhattan restaurant while she was inside. Other diners at the restaurant became concerned and called the New York Police. The woman was charged with endangering a child and was jailed for two nights. Her child was placed in foster care. The woman and the Danish consulate explained that leaving children unattended outside cafes is common in Denmark.

III. Word naming exercises.

The following are some excerpts from the e-mails of international students studying in Hangzhou. Please identify their stages of culture shock and explain their typical symptoms.

Dear Ben,

This is a fantastic place! So many interesting things to see, such as the West Lake and Lingyin Temple. Even wandering the street is a delight with all the bustle and hordes of cyclists. I am really happy to be here. The food here is so delicious!

Best regards,
Madeline

Dear Helen,

　　Thanks for your letter. It was so nice to hear from you. I've been thinking about your questions about what I find strangest about living in China, but the trouble is that I've been here so long and have settled into the way of life so much that everything seems perfectly ordinary! So, if you want to find out, you'll have to come out to see for yourself with a fresh pair of eyes. I can be your guide.

Warmest regards,
Paul

Dear Brake,

　　I am really feeling fed up with my life here and longing for home. Getting anything done over here is a nightmare. I always feel an upset stomach, severe headache, and lower back pain. And on top of all that I feel down and sleepy all the time, I seem to have lost all my zest and the school doctor is of little help. I wish I could be back home right now.

Affectionately,
Kent

Background Information 背景知识

　　1. Culture Shock(文化冲击、文化休克或文化震撼)主要是因两种不同文化的差异而引起。当一个人到达一个全新的地方,接触一种全新的文化,突然发现一切都与过去熟悉的事物截然不同,以往的生活经验不管用了,不知道该怎样表现才恰当,不知道自己的角色是什么,觉得很不舒服、很不自在、很是困惑时,就是遇到了文化冲击或文化震撼。很多时候,文化冲击会引起身体上的一些症状,如头痛、胃口不好、睡眠失调或者心理上的焦虑、沮丧。实际上,文化震撼并不是指突发一次即结束的"shock"的感觉,而是在一段时间内发生的密集式的有强有弱的震惊、仓皇和被冲击到的感觉。过去的文化背景和新文化的差异越大时,震撼的感觉会越强且越密集。文化震撼从开始到结束,其实就是一个适应新文化的过程。

　　2. The Honeymoon Stage(蜜月阶段)是指人们刚到一个新的环境,由于有新鲜感,心理上兴奋、情绪上亢奋和高涨的阶段。这个阶段一般持续几星期到半年的时间。人们经常在到其他国家前对异邦生活、工作充满美好的憧憬。来到异国文化环境中后,刚开始,对所见所闻都感到新鲜,对看到的人、景色、食物都感到满足,处于乐观的、兴奋的"蜜月"阶段。

3. The Crisis Stage(危机阶段)是指人们真正感受文化冲击在学习和生活中给他们带来种种不便的阶段。在其他国家的生活正如结婚一样,蜜月不会永久存在。几周或者几个月后,人们就会发现,这里的工作和生活并不像想象的那么顺利,甚至一些小的问题也成了不可逾越的障碍,从而真正感受到了文化冲击。

4. The Recovery Stage(恢复阶段)是指在经历了一段时间的沮丧和迷惑之后,"外乡人"逐渐适应新的生活,找到了对付新文化环境的办法,解开了一些疑团,熟悉了本地人的语言,以及食物、味道、声音等非言语信息,了解了当地的风俗习惯,理解到异国文化中不仅有缺点,也有优点。他们于是与当地人的接触多了起来,与一些当地人建立了友谊。他们心理上的混乱、沮丧、孤独感、失落感渐渐减少,慢慢地适应了异国文化的环境。

5. The Adaptation Stage(适应阶段)是指"外乡人"的沮丧、烦恼和焦虑消失了的阶段。他们基本上适应了新的文化环境,适应了当地的风俗习惯,能与当地人和平相处。这个阶段里他们达到了真正感觉良好的境界,感到自在舒服,已经适应了新的文化。

6. The Reverse Culture Shock(逆向文化冲击阶段)是指归国者归国初期表现出对自己祖国环境的种种不适应状况。他们几乎像是最初在新文化中调整时受伤一样,尤其是长期生活在国外,当他们返回自己的祖国时,也会像最早进入别的国家那样重复以上几个阶段。

Cultural Kaleidoscope 文化万花筒

对于朋友之间的友谊,中西方人在理解和态度上有着很大的差异。多数中国人很难理解西方人所谓好朋友的概念。尽管随着我国的对外开放,越来越多的西方文化涌入中国,更多的人渐渐懂得了哪些该问,哪些不该说,以尊重朋友的隐私,但是由于长期受到文化传统的浸透,双方对于保持友谊在做法上差异很大。

在西方,人们更喜欢独立而不是依赖,所以在一种一方付出更多而另一方依赖于对方付出的关系中,他们会感到不舒服。对西方人来说,友谊主要提供情感支持和共度时光。另一方面,中国人友谊的责任和义务实际上是无限的。一个人对自己的朋友负有巨大的责任。中国朋友给予对方的帮助比西方朋友多得多。在困难时刻,西方和中国的朋友都会给予对方情感上的支持,但方式不同。当朋友遇到麻烦时,西方人会问:"你想做什么?"这个想法是帮助朋友思考问题,发现他或她真正喜欢的解决方案,然后支持这个解决方案。中国朋友更有可能给朋友具体的建议或提供具体的帮助。美国人愿意在家接待外国人,分享他们的假期和家庭生活。中国人作为他们的朋友,不必担心之后要承担一项持久的义务,也无须因为无法回报而犹豫是否接受他们的款待。美国人不会指望我们这样做,因为他们知道我们远离家乡。如果我们能轻松地接受他们的款待,他们会很高兴地欢迎我们。

另外,在我们国家,我们可能会非常慷慨地把时间花在朋友身上。有时候,作为主人,我们会在半夜出现在机场接朋友。我们可以请几天假给朋友当向导。然而,美国人通常在家里欢迎客人,但在日常生活之外,他们不会花太多时间陪客人做很多事情。对于美国人来说,邀请朋友到家里做客通常被认为比去餐馆更友好,除非是纯粹的商务关系。

American and Chinese Views on Friendship

America is a mobile society. Friendships between Americans can be close, constant, strong, generous and real, yet fade away in a short time if circumstances change. Neither side feels hurt by this. Both may exchange Christmas greetings for a year or two, perhaps a few letters for a while — then no more. If the same two people meet again by chance, even years later, they pick up the friendship where it left off and are delighted. This can be quite difficult for us Chinese to understand, because friendships between us here in our country flower more slowly but then may become lifelong ties, with mutual obligations, extending sometimes deeply into both families.

In the West, people prefer to be independent rather than dependent, so they do not feel comfortable in a relationship in which one person is giving more and the other person is dependent on what is being given. For Westerners, a friendship is mostly a matter of providing emotional support and spending time together. On the other hand, the duties and obligations of Chinese friendship are virtually unlimited for all practical purposes. One has enormous responsibility for one's friends. Chinese friends give each other much more concrete help and assistance than Western friends do.

In times of trouble, both American and Chinese friends give each other emotional support, but they do it differently. A Westerner will respond to a friend's trouble by asking, "What do you want to do?" The idea is to help the friend think out the problem and discover the solution he or she really prefers and then to support that solution. A Chinese friend is more likely to give specific advice to a friend.

Americans are ready to receive foreigners at their homes, share their holidays and their home life. We need not fear that we are taking on a lasting obligation and we should not hesitate to accept their hospitality because we cannot reciprocate. Americans will not expect us to do so for they know we are far from home. They will enjoy welcoming us and be pleased if we accept their hospitality easily.

Another difficult point for us Chinese to understand Americans is that although they include us warmly in their personal everyday lives, they don't demonstrate a high degree of courtesy if it requires a great deal of time. This is usually the opposite of the practice here in our country where we may be extremely generous with our time. Sometimes we, as hosts, will appear at airport even in the middle of the night to meet a friend. We may take days off to act as a guide to our foreign friends. The Americans, however, extend their welcome usually at their homes, but truly cannot manage the time to do a great deal with a visitor outside their daily routine. They will probably expect us to get ourselves from the airport to our own hotel by public transport, and they assume that we will phone them from there. Once we arrive at their homes, the welcome will be full, warm and real. We will find ourselves treated hospitably. For Americans, it is often considered friendlier to invite a friend to their homes than to go to restaurants, except in purely business relationships. So accept their home and hospitality at home for what it is, a warm and friendly gesture.

Business Etiquette in Belt and Road Countries
"一带一路"国家的商务礼仪

俄 罗 斯

俄罗斯商人有着俄罗斯人特有的冷漠与热情两重性。商人们初次交往时,往往非常认真、客气,见面或道别时,一般要握手或拥抱以示友好。俄罗斯商人非常看重自己的名片,一般不轻易散发自己的名片,除非确信对方的身份值得信赖或确认是自己的业务伙伴时才会递上名片。

在进行商业谈判时,俄罗斯商人对合作方的举止细节很在意。站立时,身体不能靠在别的东西上,而且最好是挺胸收腹;坐下时,两腿不能不停抖动。在谈判前,最好不要吃散发异味的食物。在谈判休息时可以稍微放松,但不能做一些有失庄重的小动作,比如伸懒腰、掏耳朵、挖鼻孔或修指甲等,更不能乱丢果皮、烟蒂和随地吐痰。

许多俄罗斯商人的思维方式比较古板,固执而不易变通。所以,在谈判时要保持平和宁静,不要轻易下最后通牒,不要只想着速战速决。大多数俄罗斯商人做生意的节奏缓慢,讲究优柔尔雅。

在商业交往时宜穿庄重、保守的西服。俄罗斯人较偏爱灰色、青色。衣着服饰考究与否,在俄罗斯商人眼里不仅是身份的体现,而且还是此次生意是否重要的主要判断标志之一。

俄罗斯商人认为礼物不在贵重而在于别致,太贵重的礼物反而使受礼方过意不去,常会误认为送礼者另有企图。俄罗斯商人对喝酒吃饭也不拒绝,但他们并不在意排场是否大、菜肴是否珍贵,而主要看是否能尽兴。

俄罗斯商人十分注重建立长期关系,尤其是私人关系,在酒桌上,这种关系最容易建立。千万要记住,女士在俄罗斯礼仪上是获得优先照顾的。俄罗斯人特别忌讳"13"这个数字,认为它是凶险和死亡的象征。相反,认为"7"意味着幸福和成功。

俄罗斯人不喜欢黑猫,认为不会带来好运气。他们认为镜子是神圣的物品,打碎镜子意味着灵魂的毁灭。但是如果打碎杯、碟、盘则意味着富贵和幸福,因此在喜筵、寿筵和其他隆重的场合,他们还特意打碎一些碟盘,表示庆贺。俄罗斯人通常认为马能驱邪,会给人带来好运气,尤其相信马掌是表示祥瑞的物体,认为马掌既代表威力,又具有降妖的魔力。

在社交场合与客人见面时,俄罗斯人一般惯施握手礼。拥抱礼也是他们常施的一种礼节。他们还有施吻礼的习惯,但对不同人员,在不同场合,所施的吻礼也有一定的区别:一般对朋友之间,或长辈对晚辈之间,以吻面颊为多,不过长辈对晚辈以吻额更为亲切和慈爱;男子对特别尊敬的已婚女子,一般多施吻手礼,以示谦恭和崇敬之意。吻唇礼一般在夫妇和情侣间常见。

Russia

Russians show both indifference and enthusiasm on business occasions. When businessmen first meet, they are often very serious and polite. When they meet or say goodbye, they usually shake hands or hug each other to show friendship. They attach great importance to their business cards and generally do not distribute their business cards unless they are convinced that the identity of the other party is trustworthy or they are their business partners.

In business negotiations, Russians are very concerned about the details of the behavior of their partners. It's not advisable to lean on other things while standing, and not appropriate either to shake legs constantly. It is best not to eat smelly food before negotiation. During the negotiation break, you can relax a little, but do not do such things as stretching yourself, picking your ears or nostrils, manicuring your nails, spitting, etc.

Many Russian businessmen tend to be rigid, stubborn and inflexible. Therefore, in the negotiation, try to keep calm and peaceful. Do not give an ultimatum easily, and do not just think of a quick decision from them. Most Russians do business slowly.

In business contacts, it is appropriate to wear solemn and conservative suits. Russians prefer gray and cyan. Whether the clothes are exquisite or not is not only the embodiment of identity, but also one of the main reasons to judge whether this business is important.

When exchanging gifts, they prefer those which are quite unique. Gifts that are too expensive make the recipient feel sorry and uneasy, and they often mistakenly believe that the giver has some other intention. Russian businessmen don't refuse to drink or eat outside. They don't care where to drink or eat, but mainly whether they can enjoy themselves.

Russian businessmen attach great importance to establishing long-term relationships, especially personal relationships, which are easiest to establish during meals. Remember that women enjoy a priority in Russian social etiquette. To Russians, the number "13" is their taboo, which is regarded as a symbol of danger and death. On the contrary, the number "7" means happiness and success.

Russians don't like black cats and think it won't bring good luck. The Russians believe that mirrors are sacred objects, and breaking them means the ruin of the soul. However, breaking cups, dishes or plates means wealth and happiness. Therefore, on such important occasions as a wedding or birthday banquet, they even break some dishes on purpose to express their congratulations.

Russians generally believe that horses can expel evil spirits and bring good luck to people. They regard horseshoes as auspicious objects. They believe that horseshoes represent power and have magic power to subdue demons.

When Russian people meet guests on social occasions, they usually shake hands.

Hugging is also quite common. In addition, they also have the habit of kissing, but there are certain differences between different people and different occasions. Generally speaking, between friends or between the elder and their younger generation, most of them kiss on the cheek, but the elder often tend to kiss the forehead to show more affection and love to the younger ones. Men generally kiss the hand of married women to show their humility and respect. Lip kissing is generally popular between couples and sweethearts.

 Intercultural Tips 跨文化拓展知识

跨文化交际的障碍

第一类障碍源自认识上的误区。不同文化背景的人们在交际过程中最易犯的一个错误是误以为对方与自己没有什么两样。一旦发现对方的行为与自己的预期相差很远，就会困惑、失望，从而造成跨文化交际的失败。

第二类障碍是刻板印象。刻板印象在英语中是 stereotype，也可以称作定型，是指在没有接触某种文化前，我们已经拥有一种先入为主的印象，或者说，刻板印象是人们对于某些个人或群体属性的一套信念。这些属性可能是正面的，也可能是负面的。刻板印象使人们不能客观地观察另一种文化，失去应有的敏感。在观察异国文化时只注意那些与自己的刻板印象吻合的现象，而忽略其他。它妨碍我们与具有不同文化背景的人们相处，不利于顺利开展跨文化交际。

第三类可能出现的障碍是民族中心主义。民族中心主义在英语中是 ethnocentrism。民族中心主义可以定义为按照本族文化的观念和标准去理解和衡量他族文化中的一切，包括人们的行为举止、交际方式、社会习俗、管理模式及价值观念等。尽管我们努力去克服自己的民族中心主义，但是，人们很难完全避免民族中心主义。这是因为我们每个人都是在一定文化中成长起来的，要完全摆脱我们在社会化过程中获得的各种思想观念是不可能的。民族中心主义的表现很多，比如：各个国家的地图都是把本国放在中心；谈到对世界文明的贡献，一般总是突出自己国家的成就，而对于其他国家的成就展示得较少；各国的新闻报道也习惯从各个国家自己的角度选择和报道所发生的事情，在报道同一事件时的观点和材料也可能不同。

跨文化交际过程中出现的诸多障碍很多时候都是因为人们想当然地以为别人跟自己总是一样的，习惯于从自己的文化角度去理解其他文化背景中的人和事。刻板印象和民族中心主义也容易使我们以自己的认知和标准去衡量其他文化从而引起跨文化交际的障碍。

 Movie to See 观影学文化

Please watch the movie *Pushing Hands* (《推手》) with your classmates and discuss the different cultural views involved in it.

Unit 8　Improving Intercultural Competence

跨文化交际能力提升

Learning Objectives 学习目标

- 了解跨文化交际能力的内涵。
- 熟悉跨文化交际能力的构成要素。
- 掌握提高跨文化交际能力的策略和技能。

Lead-in 单元导读

　　跨文化交际能力的内涵。Spitzberg(2000)认为,跨文化交际能力仅仅是"在特定环境下适当有效的行为"。Kim(1991)从更具体的层面,指出跨文化交际能力是个体所具有的内在能力,能够处理跨文化交际中的关键性问题,如文化差异、文化陌生感、本文化群体内部的态度,以及随之而来的心理压力等。

　　事实上,跨文化交际能力是一个可以被不同的人出于不同的原因而使用的术语。本质上,跨文化交际能力可以概括为跨文化工作的能力。因此,我们将跨文化交际能力理解为"在特定环境中,有效、适当地执行沟通行为以获得所需响应的能力"。这一定义表明,有能力的人不仅必须知道如何与人和环境进行有效和适当的互动,还必须知道如何利用这种能力实现自己的沟通目标。

　　跨文化交际能力的构成要素。沟通能力领域的大多数研究认为,要实现有效沟通,至少应该具备以下几个条件:有动机;有足够的知识;拥有一定的沟通技能;具有良好的性格。这些都是跨文化交际顺利实现的重要保障。

　　提高跨文化交际能力的策略。第一,要试着多了解你自己。包括了解你的文化、个人态度、沟通方式,并在此过程中学会自我监控和管理,控制自己的情绪反应,创造良好的印象,还能在不同情况下相应地改变自己的行为。第二,考虑物理和人文环境。开始任何形式的交流前,都应该关注周围的环境,因为交流不是在真空中进行的,而是在特定的物理环境和特定的社会因素下与他人的互动。因为所有的交流都发生在一个被称为语境的环境或情境中。另外,对不同文化习俗的适应能力也决定了你的跨文化交流能否成功。第三,培养同理心,学会移情。移情行为包括读懂他人的语言表述和非语言信息。需要注意的是,同理心并不意味着"设身处地为他人着想"。这在生理和心理上都是不可能做到的。然而,我们可以对他人的情况表示关注和兴趣,并让对方感到我们想要设身处地地为他们着想。第四,鼓励反馈。反馈是由接收消息的人生成的信息,即"反馈"给发送原始消息的人的信息。这些信息可能是一个微笑,甚至是完全的沉默,没有任何外在的表达。无论是何种形式,都会帮助我们做出一定的判断。第五,学会容忍歧义。另一个成功的跨文化交际的好方法是培养对歧义的容忍度。由于许多跨文化接触是不可预测的,而且往往涉及处理一套新的价值观和习俗,因此混淆和模棱两可的现象时有发生。处理歧义是提高跨文化交际能力的一个关键因素。第六,学会管理冲突。随着人们相互接触,冲突在所难免。为了改进处理冲突的方式,我们需要确定冲突的一些常见原因,以便采用适当的方法来处理冲突。

跨文化交际能力是交际者进行文化交流时所需的一种必要的综合能力,是指与其他文化背景的人进行成功交际的能力。本单元主要介绍跨文化交际能力的定义,以及构成跨文化交际能力的各个要素,并给出了提高跨文化交际能力的策略,有助于学习者对跨文化交际能力的内涵有较为深刻的认识;对跨文化交际能力的构成与发展模式有清晰的理解;对跨文化交际能力和策略的培养与提高有比较全面的认识。

Pre-class Activity 课前活动

Some years ago, several international businessmen were on a conference cruise when the ship began to sink. "Go tell those fellows to put on life jacket and jump overboard," the captain directed his first mate.

A few minutes later, the first mate returned. "Those guys won't jump," he reported.

"Take over," the captain ordered, "and I will see what I can do."

Returning moments later, he announced, "They are gone."

"How did you do it?" asked the first mate.

"I told different things to different people. I told the Englishman it was a sporting thing to do, and he jumped. I told the Frenchman it was chic; the German it was a command; the Italian that it was forbidden; the Russian that it was revolutionary; so they all jumped overboard."

"And how did you get the American to jump?"

"No problem," said the captain, "I told him he was insured."

Question:

If there had been a Chinese businessman on board, what should the captain say in order to make him jump overboard?

Reading 课内阅读

Reading One: Definition of Intercultural Communication Competence

The increase of globalization and worldwide contacts between companies, organizations and individuals call for successful intercultural communication, which makes intercultural communication competence become more and more important during recent years.

Basic needs are sensitivity and self-consciousness: the understanding of other behaviors and ways of thinking as well as the ability to express one's own point of view in a transparent way with the aim to be understood and respected by staying flexible where this is possible, and being clear and transparent where this is necessary.

Intercultural communication competence is the ability to successfully communicate with people of other cultures. This ability can exist in someone at a young age, or may be developed and improved due to willpower and competence. The basis for successful intercultural communication is emotional competence, together with intercultural sensitivity.

In its most unadorned form, we agree with Spitzberg (2000) when he suggests that intercultural communication competence is simply "a behavior that is appropriate and effective in a given context". Kim (1991) offers a more detailed definition when she notes that intercultural communication competence is "the overall internal capability of an individual to manage key challenging features of intercultural communication: namely, cultural differences and unfamiliarity, inter-group posture, and the accompanying experience of stress". What these two definitions, one general and one specific, are saying is that being a competent communicator means analyzing the situation and selecting the correct mode of behavior.

In fact, intercultural communication competence is a term that can be applied by many different people for many different reasons. In essence, intercultural competence can be summed up as the ability to work well across cultures. Thus, we conceive of intercultural communication competence as "the ability to effectively and appropriately execute communication behaviors to elicit a desired response in a specific environment". This definition shows that competent persons must not only know how to interact effectively and appropriately with people and environments, but also know how to fulfill their own communication goals using this ability.

Reading Two: Components of Intercultural Competence

The research on communication competence mainly holds that in selecting the most appropriate course of action, effective communicators are those who (1) *are motivated*,

(2) *have a fund of knowledge to draw upon*, and (3) *possess certain communication skills and* (4) *are of good character*. Let us look at these four components one by one in detail.

1. Motivation

Motivation as it relates to competence means that as a communicator you want to do a good job. Simply put, you have a positive attitude toward the communication event and put forth the effort to bring about constructive results. For now the message is basic — be motivated to improve your communication behavior and you will increase the chances that you will be successful in your efforts.

Motivation includes the overall set of emotional associations that people have as they anticipate and actually communicate inter-culturally. Human emotional reactions include both feelings and intentions. *Feelings* refer to the emotional or affective states that you experience when communicating with someone from a different culture. Feelings of happiness, sadness, eagerness, anger, tension, surprise, confusion, relaxation and joy are among the many emotions that can accompany the intercultural communication. Feelings involve your general sensitivity to other cultures and your attitudes toward the specific culture and individual with whom you must interact. *Intentions* are what guide your choices in a particular intercultural interaction. Your intentions are the goals, plans, objectives, and desires that focus and direct your behavior. Intentions are often affected by the stereotypes（模式化的思想）you have of people from other cultures because stereotypes reduce the number of choices and interpretations you are willing to consider.

2. Knowledge

Knowledge refers to the cognitive information you need to have about the people, the context, and the norms of appropriateness that operate in a specific culture. Without such knowledge, it is unlikely that you will interpret correctly the meanings of other people's messages, nor will you be able to select behaviors that are appropriate and that allow you to achieve your objectives. Consequently, you will not be able to determine what the appropriate and effective behaviors are in a particular context. The kind of knowledge that is important includes culture-general and culture-specific information. The former provides insights into the intercultural communication process abstractly and can therefore be a very powerful tool in making sense of cultural practices, regardless of the cultures involved. For example, the knowledge that cultures differ widely in their preferred patterns (or rules) of interaction should help to sensitize you to the need to be aware of these important differences. Knowledge about interpersonal communication and the many ways in which culture influences the communication process is very useful in understanding actual intercultural interactions.

Intercultural competence also depends on culture-specific information, which is used to understand a particular culture. Such knowledge should include information about the forces that maintain the culture's uniqueness（独特性）and facts about the cultural patterns that predominate (主导). The type of intercultural encounter will also suggest other kinds of culture-specific information that might be useful. Exchange students might want to seek out information about the educational system in the host country. Business people may need essential information about the cultural dynamics of doing business in a specific country or with people from their own country who are members of different cultural groups. Tourists would benefit from guidebooks that provide information about obtaining lodging, transportation, food, shopping, and entertainment.

3. Skills

Skills refer to the actual performance of the behaviors felt to be effective and appropriate in the communication context. For Spitzberg (2000), skills must be repeatable and goal-oriented. If a person accidentally produces a behavior that is perceived as competent, this would not be adequate, because the person may not be able to replicate the same behavior with the same effect. The person needs to be able to perform the script fluently and with cause (i.e. an appropriate rationale for its performance). This brings us to the notion that skills must be goal-oriented. There must be some teleological basis for the performance, or else it is just a behavior, not a skilled behavior. These goals may be personal, dyadic, social, or contextual.

Skills can be divided into two categories. The first is the "ability to interpret a document or event and relate it to documents from one's own" (Byram, 1997). The second is the "ability to acquire new knowledge of a culture and cultural practices and the ability to operate knowledge, attitudes and skills under the constraints of real-time communication and interaction." Both sets of skills obviously require the development of language competence. In addition, though, skills of analysis and interpretation are necessary, as are skills of relating between different cultures, and the ability to put all this knowledge and skill into practice in real situations.

4. Character

While most of the literature dealing with communication competency includes only the three components mentioned above, it is our belief that one more feature needs to be added to the profile of a competent communicator. This attribute is *character*. The idea behind including character is simple — if you are not perceived by your communication partner as a person of good character, your chances for success will be diminished. In many ways your character is composed of both your personal history and how you exhibit that history. As the American philosopher and teacher P. B. Fitzwater said, "Character is the sum and total of a person's choices." The key, of course, is how you act out those choices when you interact with someone from another culture. Perhaps the single most important trait associated with people of character is their *trustworthiness*. Characteristics often associated with the trustworthy person are integrity, honor, altruism (利他主义), sincerity, and goodwill.

Reading Three: Strategies of Improving Intercultural Competence

To improve intercultural competence is our primary goal for learning knowledge on intercultural communication. This passage will offer you some direct recommendations on promoting your intercultural competence. And more importantly, all of the suggestions for improvement enable you to exercise your ability to make choices. Our propositions place you in the center of the activity. Whether we are asking you to learn more about a culture's view toward the elderly or appealing to you to develop some new skills, the power is all yours. What is being said here should be quite clear — you must act on what you have learned about other cultures. The Persian poet Sa'di said much the same thing over seven thousand years ago: "Whoever acquires knowledge and does not practice it resembles him who ploughs his island and leaves it unsown."（凡得知识而不去实践的人,就像那开垦自己的岛屿而不耕种的人一样。）

Before we offer our first bit of advice, we want to acknowledge a major danger in offering anyone personal advice. Whenever you tell another individual how to think or act you run the risk—particularly if he or she listens to you—of making matters worse. The person may have been better off without your advice. For example, we believe that many of you already know a great deal about intercultural communication and, in fact, are very good practitioners of the art. In these cases, we run the risk of spoiling what has taken you years to develop. What we are saying is somewhat analogous to an old Chinese fable. In this fable, a monkey and a fish were very good friends. One day, however, a dreadful flood separated them. Because the monkey could limb trees, he was able to scramble up a limb and escape the rising waters. As he glanced into the raging river, he saw his friend the fish swimming past. With the best of intentions, he scooped his paw into the water, snatched his friend from the river, and lifted him into the tree. The result was obvious. From this modest story, you can see the dilemma we face. So please remember as we offer advice that, like the monkey, we have the best of intentions.

1. Know Yourself

It seems only fitting that we ask you to begin with yourself, for as simplistic as it sounds, what you bring to the communication event greatly influences the success or failure of that event — and what you bring is you. Although the idea of knowing yourself seems obvious, it is nevertheless a crucial element in becoming a competent intercultural communicator. As with many of the suggestions we offer in this section, it is easier to state the advice than to practice it, and it will take a great deal of effort to translate this assignment into practice.

(1) Know Your Culture

Each of us is a product of our cultural background, including gender, ethnicity, family, age, religion, profession, and other life experiences. Our cultural inventory provides us with valuable insights for understanding our beliefs and attitudes, our values and assumptions. Thus, it is critical that we reflect on the various aspects of our own cultural identity and examine their positive and negative impacts on our personal and professional development. In short, you are a "cultural being" and therefore must be ever vigilant as to the impact of your cultural "membership" on perception and communication.

(2) Know Your Personal Attitudes

By exhorting you to examine your attitudes and perceptions, we are not referring to any mystical notions involving another reality, nor are we suggesting you engage in any deep psychological soul searching. Rather, we are asking you to identify those attitudes, prejudices and opinions that you carry around and that bias the way the world appears to you. If you hold a certain attitude toward gay men, and a man who is gay talks to you, your pre-communication attitude will color your responses to what he says. Knowing your likes, dislikes and degrees of personal ethnocentrism enables you to place them out in the open so that you can detect the ways in which these attitudes influence communication.

(3) Know Your Communication Style

The third step in knowing yourself is somewhat more difficult than simply identifying your prejudices and predispositions. That is, you need to learn to recognize your communication style — the manner in which you present yourself to others. Good communication skills require a high level of self-awareness. Understanding your personal style of communication will go a long way toward helping you to create a good and lasting impression on others.

(4) Monitor Yourself

Remember that all of you have unique ways of interacting. Discovering how you communicate is not always an easy task. It is awkward and highly irregular for you to walk around asking people if they think you are relaxed, argumentative, friendly, animated, and the like. You must, therefore, be sensitive to the feedback you receive and frank in the reading of that feedback. The process of self-observation and analysis is often called "self-monitoring". Some of the advantages of self-monitoring are discovering appropriate behaviors in each situation, having control of your emotional reactions, creating good impressions, and modifying your behavior as you move from situation to situation.

2. Consider the Physical and Human Settings

To begin any communication, you should be aware of your surroundings, because communication does not take place in a vacuum. We interact with other people within specific physical surroundings and under a set of specific social factors.

Your ability to adapt to the physical and human settings and the conventions of each culture will, to a large extent, determine the success of your intercultural communication. The ability enables you to avoid serious communication problems, because you have free choice to make necessary concessions.

For example, at many parties, strangers may get to know each other. If they are from the East, they will very respectfully present calling cards to the stranger before any conversation starts. However, if they are from the West, only when they find they like each other and hope to further their relationship, will they exchange cards. That is to say, when you are attending a cocktail party in Western countries, on such an occasion, it is better not to present cards before any real conversation gets underway. And in an Eastern country, please remember, it is a required courtesy to exchange cards.

Being aware of timing is another important element. It often makes the difference between a successful engagement and one that produces ill feelings and misunderstandings. In this part, we hold that even settings carry meanings. Three attributes of this setting that can influence the encounter are timing, physical setting, and customs.

(1) Timing

The effective communicator knows the importance of timing and has developed the skill to determine the appropriate time to talk about a subject, or ask a question. You know from your own experiences that there are right and wrong times to ask your parents for a loan or to ask an acquaintance for a date. Few professors will sympathize with the student who waits until the last week of the semester to announce, "I would like to come to your office and talk about the midterm examination I missed a few months ago." This is poor timing!

Your use of timing is also influenced by culture. For example, students may use different views of timing when they are asked to respond to questions from the teacher. And we point out that considering the "correct time" is a crucial aspect of doing business with other cultures. In the US, people learn to "get down to business" quickly. Even the overused phrase "just give me the bottom line" is a reflection of North Americans' desire to get things done quickly. However, in Japan, other Asian countries, and Mexico, the most fitting time to talk about business matters is not at the start of a business session. Business contracts are often made during the two or three-hour lunch break. These are social meetings for the most part, with business being conducted in the last few minutes. Notice the words "the last few minutes". This is a vivid example of what we mean by the phrase "consider the timing".

(2) Physical Setting

All communication takes place within a setting or situation called a context. By context, we mean the place where people meet, the social purpose for being together, and the nature of the relationship. The physical context includes the actual location of the communicators: indoors or outdoors, crowded or quiet, public or private, close together or far apart, warm or cold, bright or dark. The physical context influences the communication process in many obvious ways. An afternoon conversation at a crowded sidewalk café or an evening of candle-light dining in a private salon will differ in the kinds of topics that are covered and in the interpretations that are made about the meanings of certain phrases or glances. Knowledge of the physical context often provides important information about the meanings that are intended and the kinds of communication that are possible.

(3) Customs

Your ability to adapt to the customs of each culture will, to a large extent, determine the success of your intercultural encounters. Your experience will not be fruitful if the custom calls for you to remain standing when you enter a room but you take a seat. When, if at all, do you bow? And what is the appropriate bow? When, if at all, do you touch members of the opposite sex? And where do you touch them? What are the customs that prevail with regard to age? These and other questions need to be asked and answered so that you can fashion your behavior to meet the needs of each culture.

3. Develop Empathy

Those individuals who are able to communicate with an awareness of another person's thoughts, feelings, and experiences are regarded as more competent in intercultural interactions. Empathetic behaviors include verbal statements that identify the experiences of others and nonverbal codes that are complementary to the moods and thoughts of others.

It is necessary to make an important distinction here. Empathy does not mean "putting yourself in the shoes of another". It is both physically and psychologically impossible to do so. However, it is possible for people to be sufficiently interested and aware of others so that they appear to be putting themselves in others' shoes. The skill we are describing here is the capacity to behave as if one understands the world as others do. Of course, empathy is not just responding to the tears and smiles of others, which may mean something very different than your cultural interpretations would suggest. Although empathy does involve responding to the emotional context of another person's experiences, tears, and smiles are often poor indicators of emotional states.

4. Encourage Feedback

Feedback is the information generated by the person who receives the message — information that is "fed back" to the person who sends the original message. This information may be a smile, the words "No, thank you", or even complete silence void of any outward expression. Feedback may be verbal, nonverbal, or both, and it may be intentional or unintentional. Regardless of the form of the feedback, it allows you the opportunity to make qualitative judgments about the communication event while it is taking place. These judgments offer useful data that enable you to correct and adjust your next message.

5. Learn to Tolerate Ambiguity

Another good way to communicate successfully across cultures is to develop tolerance for ambiguity. Because many intercultural encounters are unpredictable and often involve dealing with a new set of values and customs, confusion and ambiguity can often proliferate. For example, if your culture values competition and aggressive action, and you are around someone from a culture that values cooperation and interpersonal harmony, you might find his or her behavior ambiguous and confusing; yet coping with ambiguity is a key element in intercultural competence.

6. Learn to Manage Conflict

It is not an exaggeration to say that as people have been coming into contact with one another there has been conflict. In an intercultural setting, conflict may be defined as "the perceived and /or actual incompatibility of values, expectations, processes, or outcomes between two or more parties from different cultures". To improve the manner in which you deal with conflict we need to identify some common causes of conflict, and prepare ourselves with some proper approaches to the conflict.

Read to Learn More

The Future of International Communication

As Shakespeare wrote in *Hamlet*, "We know what we are, but know not what we may be." The same, of course, can be said for intercultural communication. You know what you have been, but what of the future? You can, however, use the past and present as a predictor and speculate about the future of intercultural communication. If you use the past as a guide, the most apparent notion of the future is that your intercultural relationships and interactions will grow in both number and intensity. The growth will impact the future of intercultural communication in four dimensions: (1) cultural diversity, (2) international problems, (3) global culture, and (4) ethnic and cultural identity.

1. Cultural Diversity

We start with a statement *"Cultural diversity has become a fact of life"*. We have used statistics and demographic studies to document the fact that on a variety of levels and in a multitude of settings, people from different cultures will come together. Whether or not the people of the world accept this reality is not the issue. In one way or another people must recognize that for the first time in history, cultural groups throughout the world are increasingly in contact with one another. In the US, diversity will pick up the pace because of increasing immigration. Even now nearly one in ten "Americans" were born outside of the country. In addition, the immigrant population is growing six and one-half times faster than the native-born population. Increasing diversity is forcing Americans to think about intercultural communication in new terms.

Apart from China, it's safe to say that most other countries are also experiencing a coming together of ethnic and cultural groups. Fueled both by a worldwide flood of refugees (some 16 million now seeking asylum), and a need to be part of the "global marketplace", no nation may remain immune to diversity.

2. International Problems

We have mentioned the issue of cultural diversity will be a major concern in the future. If you peruse the daily newspaper, or switch from news channel to news channel, you will encounter a long list of problems requiring your attention in the next decade. These problems will require that people learn to "talk" to each other.

(1) Increased Violence

Once again you can use the past and present as a partial guide to the future. Long before the tragic events of September 11, 2001, conflicts between ideologies and neighbors were going on in places such as Israel, India, and Africa. But when those three planes struck the Twin Towers and the Pentagon, people were jolted into the realization that cultural or religious discord can lead to violence anywhere in the world. While the September 11 attack is a most striking example of the dangers of cultural ethnocentrism, it may only be a prelude to what the future might bring. For example, the National Defense Council Foundation noted that at the start of 2002 fifty-nine countries were experiencing serious violence that was related to ethnic, religious, and/or cultural conflicts. These clashes are, of course, only part of the problems that face the world as cultures collide.

(2) World Hunger

As we all know, world hunger is a major problem facing mankind, yet, despite massive efforts by food-producing nations, world hunger continues to accelerate. "Millions of people at the start of the 21st century continue to face malnutrition and starvation." This problem reveals that people from different cultures must interact with each other in the next decade. "The immediate cause of world hunger has less to do with food production than with warfare and food distribution." In short, both these causes have their roots in a lack of communication.

(3) Pollution

Worldwide pollution is yet another reason that makes it necessary for cultures to interact. Global warming, deforestation, soil erosion, chemicals poisoning water and soil, acid rain, water scarcity, and the like know no boundaries. Pollution is indeed one of those topics that reflect the truism that notes, "What happens in one part of the world happens in all parts of the world." While people know the causes of pollution and the dangers of pollution, most have refused to make any significant advances in dealing with this crisis.

3. Global Culture

Since Marshall McLuhan (1962) first proposed his notion of a "Global Village", there has been a belief that the world would evolve into one massive homogeneous culture. The voices behind such a hypothesis are abundant. You can find superficial examples such as people from Australia to Zambia eating a Big Mac and holding a Coca-Cola, to the wide spread of people wearing jeans. On a less superficial level, those who advance the single-culture argument make note of the rapid demise of many of the world's languages and the replacement of these icons such as people "reading the same kind of newspapers, watching the same kind of television programs, communicating directly with one another via the Internet, satellites, and World Wide Web, and so on". There were even predictions that the world would see a single political system by the 23rd century. Regardless of the merit of such arguments, it is nevertheless true that the future of intercultural interaction will have to confront the issues associated with the idea of a homogeneous, single, unified culture.

4. Ethnic and Cultural Identity

There is a second trend moving throughout the world that would seem to contradict those who predict a single global culture. This counter hypothesis has its roots in the belief that people and cultures, for a host of reasons, are refusing to accept globalization and a universal ideology. In fact, scholars who give voice to this position see a world where nations, cultures, and individuals are turning inward. This "turning inward" movement seems to be gaining strength as the world becomes more unpredictable, complex, and stressful. Cleveland (1995) makes the same point when he writes, "Many millions of people believe that their best haven of certainty and security is a group based on ethnic similarity, common faith, economic interests, or political like-mindedness." Many Americans believe everyone wants to be just like them and often have a difficult time accepting the view that other people are retreating to the sanctuary of their own ethnic and cultural identity. The real dilemma we will face in the future is how the world balances ethnic and cultural identity with the inter-connective nature of the world and its cultures. Often the cost of cultural isolationism, comfort, and security is conflict. Cleveland voices the same fear when he says, "Ethnic and religious diversity is creating painful conflicts around the world." Ethnic discords are not confined to distant locations. There are "disturbing signs of rising racial and ethnic tension at home". This, of course, makes the need for cultural understanding even more demanding. Cleveland (1995) notes, "Finding ways to become unified despite diversity may be the world's most urgent problems in the years ahead." We must all begin to realize that diversity can be rich without being threatening, for in the end, people of all cultures long for the same things: a place to raise their children, ply their trades, and express themselves aesthetically and socially. When those forms of expression differ from our own, we must respect the rights of people from other cultures.

Now, we live in a world that can easily destroy itself with powerful bombs, toxic gases, or global pollution; we do not consider it romantic or idealistic to issue an appeal that we strive to develop a greater understanding of people who may not be like us; the task is not simple. We do not quite know how to create "wholeness incorporating diversity" (包含多样性的整体性), but we owe it to the world, as well as ourselves, to keep trying.

 In-class Activity 课堂练习

Ⅰ. **Comprehension questions.**

Discuss the following questions with your partner:

1. How can we improve intercultural competence? Besides the strategies from the

reading passage, what other suggestions can you give?

2. What should be our attitude towards people who act and think differently from ourselves?

Ⅱ. Case analysis.

1. How do you explain what happened?

An American invited a group of Japanese students to his house. He and his wife had spent a great deal of time preparing food and getting the house ready. They were looking forward to the party and hoped that the Japanese would enjoy themselves. They came at about 8:00 at night and right away seemed to be enjoying themselves. There was a lot of dancing, singing and good conversation. Then, almost suddenly, one of the students said "Thank you" to the hosts and said that it was time to go. After that, all of the Japanese began to get ready to leave. The American and his wife couldn't understand why this happened. They felt insulted because everyone left so early at the same time.

2. Why did Mr. Zheng and Mr. Wang feel unhappy when they opened the envelope and saw the 100 dollars?

Mr. Wang and Mr. Zheng met Dr. Huang, a Chinese Australian while doing their MA course in TESOL at the former Canberra College of Advanced Education. Every other weekend, Dr. Huang would ask Mr. Wang and Mr. Zheng, together with one or two other students, to come to her home for dinner. Everyone seemed to be at home with each other and got on very nicely. During one conversation, Dr. Huang found out that Mr. Wang and Mr. Zheng were good carpenters, so she asked if they could help her tear down the old fence and erect a new one around her house. Feeling grateful to her for all the wonderful things she had done for them, and all the efforts she had made in helping them adjust to the new culture, the two Chinese students instantly agreed and promised to make her a Chinese-style fence that would add a home feeling to her typical Australian house. During the semester break, the two students arrived at Dr. Huang's place, where they looked around and enjoyed some drinks. Just as they were to start to work on the fence, Dr. Huang asked how much money they wanted for the whole "project". Mr. Zheng smiled and said, "You don't have to pay. We are happy to be able to do something for you." At Dr. Huang's insistence, Mr. Wang shyly asked if one hundred dollars would be all right. Dr. Huang smiled and agreed, and the two Chinese students started their work. Within three days, the old fence was gone and a new Chinese-style fence was erected to the pleasure of Dr. Huang. As they were about to leave, Dr. Huang handed them an envelope with 100 Australian dollars enclosed. Seeing that Mr. Zheng did not open the envelope, Dr. Huang insisted that they confirm there was $100 enclosed. A bit embarrassed, Mr. Zheng opened it and assured her that there was no mistake. They thanked each other, and Mr. Wang and Mr. Zheng left her place, with Dr. Huang feeling confused about their uneasy feeling. When Mr. Wang and Mr. Zheng returned to their residence, they complained about her being stingy (小气).

Ⅲ. Finish the following cultural activities.

Activity 1：Please interview someone who comes from another culture and let the interviewee introduce his/her own culture and his/her deep understanding of how to improve intercultural communication competence.

Activity 2：You are about to send a young staff member to host a group of Western guests，and you want to make sure that he/she will be a good host. Make a list of tips you would give this young person on how to be a good host. State each one as a complete sentence. Be ready to explain why each tip is important.

Background Information 背景知识

1. Intercultural communication competence(跨文化交际能力)是指不同文化背景的人们(people from different cultures)之间进行有效交际的能力。具有跨文化交际能力的人，能够无障碍地理解另一种文化，进而恰当而高效地与人沟通。

2. Component of intercultural competence(跨文化交际能力的构成因素)，跨文化交际能力由知识、动机、技巧三个因素构成，三者相互影响、相互依存。跨文化交际能力需要足够的跨文化知识、积极的动机和有效的交际技巧，三个因素应同时具备，任何一个因素都不能单独构成跨文化交际能力。

3. Develop empathy(培养同理心)，即设身处地从对方的情况入手，考虑问题，争取达到"将心比心，感同身受"。

Cultural Kaleidoscope 文化万花筒

"多元文化"的起源

多元文化是指在一个社会或国家内存在多种不同的文化背景和价值观念，并且这些文化之间相互交流、融合、共存的现象。多元文化不仅是单一文化的存在，而且是一种多元共生、相互影响的文化现象。其中，不同的民族、宗教、语言、习俗等都可以被视为不同的文化元素(王宏伟，2019)①。陈世杰(2019)②认为多元文化是人类社会发展的必然产物，是不同文化之间相互交流、融合、共存的结果。在教育领域，多元文化的存在意味着需要重视和尊重不同文化背景的学生，提供多元化的教育资源和教学策略，促进学生的全面发展。刘立峰(2018)③则认为多元文化是国际商务沟通中必须面对的现实。在跨国商务活动中，不同的国

---

① 王宏伟.多元文化视阈下的中国文化自信[J].文化研究，2019(6)：1-9.
② 陈世杰.多元文化的概念、内涵及其在教育中的意义[J].教育教学论坛，2019(20)：38-39.
③ 刘立峰.多元文化视角下的国际商务沟通策略[J].国际商务，2018(11)：45-47.

家和地区存在着不同的文化背景和价值观念，因此需要采取不同的沟通策略。多元文化视角下的国际商务沟通策略包括了解不同文化背景和价值观念、避免语言和文化障碍、尊重对方文化习俗等。

Origin of "Multiculturalism"

Multiculturalism refers to the phenomenon of multiple cultural backgrounds and values coexisting and interacting with each other within a society or country. It is not just the existence of a single culture, but a multicultural symbiosis and mutual influence. Different cultural elements, such as ethnicity, religion, language, and customs, can be viewed as different cultural components. According to Chen Shijie, multiculturalism is an inevitable product of human social development, resulting from the exchange, fusion, and coexistence of different cultures. In the field of education, the existence of multiculturalism means the need to value and respect students with different cultural backgrounds, provide diversified educational resources and teaching strategies, and promote students' comprehensive development. Liu Lifeng argues that multiculturalism is a reality that must be faced in international business communication. In cross-border business activities, different countries and regions have different cultural backgrounds and values, thus requiring different communication strategies. International business communication strategies from a multicultural perspective include understanding different cultural backgrounds and values, avoiding language and cultural barriers, and respecting each other's cultural customs.

In the US, multiculturalism led a quiet life until it became a keyword in the "culture wars" of the 1980s and 1990s. Liberals began voicing their dream of the US as a multicultural country, one with diverse peoples and cultures drawn from all over the world, sharing a common belief in freedom and democracy. Instead of seeing the country as a melting pot cooking up a single American way of life, they celebrated diversity.

They also began to expand the definition of culture beyond ethnicity, race, and religion to include gender and lifestyle, so that multiculturalism could mean "respect for different ages, sexes, physical or mental capabilities, and sexual orientation". At an extreme, respect might even be demanded for the distinct "cultures" of vegetarians, animal rights activists,

中国传统文化 8

millenarians, and transvestites. For some conservatives, this was too much. They saw multiculturalism as undermining respect for the unique American ideals and way of life, for the Western Civilization from which these ideals sprang, and for "family values". The debate continued inconclusively as the century drew to an end.

Business Etiquette in Belt and Road Countries
"一带一路"国家的商务礼仪

泰 国

泰国是君主立宪制国家。国王和王室有很高的地位。泰国人民对王室很尊敬,身为游客也应入乡随俗,对他们的国王、王后、太子、公主等表示敬意,电影院内播放国歌或国王的肖像时,也应起立。凡遇盛大集会、宴会,乃至影剧院开始演出之前,都要先演奏或播放赞颂国王的"颂圣歌",全场肃立,不得走动和说话,路上行人须就地站立,军人、警察还要立正行军礼,否则就会被认为对国王不敬。

泰国人见面时要各自在胸前合十相互致意,双掌连合,放在胸额之间,这是见面礼,相当于西方的握手,双掌举得越高,表示尊敬程度越深。平民百姓见国王双手要举过头顶,小辈见长辈要双手举至前额,平辈相见举到鼻子以下。长辈对小辈还礼举到胸前,手部不应高过前胸。地位较低或年纪较轻者应先合十致意。别人向你合十,你必须还礼,否则就是失礼。合十时要稍稍低头,口说"萨瓦迪卡"(即"您好")。双方合十致礼后就不必再握手,男女之间见面时不握手,俗人不能与僧侣握手。

在泰国进行商务活动,必须尊重当地的教规。如果你对泰国的寺庙、佛像、和尚等做出轻视的行为,就被视为是有罪的,拍摄佛像尤其要小心,比如依偎在佛像旁或骑在佛像上面,就会惹出轩然大波。进入寺庙必须赤脚而行。到当地人家做客,如果发现室内设有佛坛,要马上脱掉鞋袜和帽子。

泰国是一个很注重着装礼仪的国家,在正式的商务会谈里都会穿正式的西装、衬衣、皮鞋,即使不是一整套正式的西装,也会穿着有领子、袖子的商务 T 恤和非牛仔裤的长裤。

泰国人非常重视人的头部,他们认为头是神圣不可侵犯的,因此,千万不要轻易抚摸别人的头部,即使是喜爱的小朋友,也绝不可以用手去摸他们的头,否则将被视为是对此小孩所带的神不尊重。如长辈在座,晚辈必须坐在地上或者蹲跪,以免高于长辈的头部,否则就是极大的不尊敬。人坐着的时候,忌讳他人拿着东西从头上面经过。在泰国人面前盘腿而坐是不礼貌的,如进行商务谈判坐下时,千万别把鞋底露出来,这样也被认为是极不友好的表示。用脚踢门会受到当地人的唾弃,更不能用脚给别人指东西,这是泰国人最忌讳的动作。

因此,在和泰国朋友打交道时,提前了解他们的文化禁忌就显得十分重要。

Thailand

Thailand is a constitutional monarchy country. The king and the Royal Family enjoy high status. Thai people pay great respect to the royal family. Tourists should also follow their ways to pay homage to their king, queen, prince and princess. When the National Anthem or the portrait of the king appears on the screen of the cinema, people should stand up to show their respect. In the event of a grand assembly, banquet, or even before the performance of a theater, the "hymn" praising the king should be played first. The whole audience stand in awe without walking or speaking. Pedestrians must stand on the spot, and soldiers and police should also stand upright and salute. Otherwise, they will be regarded as disrespectful to the king.

When Thai people meet, they greet each other by closing their palms on their chests. They put their palms together and put them between their chests and foreheads. This is the meeting etiquette which is equivalent to a Western handshake. The higher the hands are held, the deeper the degree of respect they show. When the common people see the king, their both hands should be raised above the head; when the younger see the elder, their hands should be raised to the forehead; and when they meet their peers, they hold their hands below the nose. The elder often return the courtesy to the younger by raising their hands to the chest. Those of lower status or younger age should salute first. If someone else salutes you, you must return the courtesy; otherwise, it will be impolite. When you close the palms, you should bow your head a little and say, "savadika" (i.e. "hello"). After that, they do not need to shake hands. Thai people don't shake hands between men and women, and the average people can't shake hands with monks.

Business activities in Thailand are conducted in accordance with local religious rules. If you despise the temples, Buddha statues and monks in Thailand, you will be considered guilty. You should be especially careful when photographing Buddhist statues. For example, if you lean close to or ride on the Buddha statues, you will cause a great disturbance. When entering the temple, you must walk barefoot. If you are invited to local people's home and find a Buddhist altar in the house, you'd better take off your shoes, socks and hat immediately.

Thailand is a country that attaches great importance to dressing etiquette. In formal business talks, they will wear formal suits, shirts and shoes. Even if it is not a full set of formal suits, they will also wear business T-shirts with collars and sleeves and trousers (not jeans).

Thai people attach great importance to the head, and think that the head is sacred and inviolable. Therefore, do not touch other people's heads carelessly. Even to the beloved children, do not touch their heads. Otherwise, it will be regarded as disrespectful to the God brought by this child. If the elder is present, the younger must sit on the ground or kneel down, so as not to be higher than the head of the elder to show their respect. When people are sitting, passing something over the head is not allowed. It is also impolite to sit cross-legged in front of Thai people. Furthermore, when sitting down in business negotiations, do not show the bottom of your shoes, which is considered to be extremely unfriendly. Kicking the door with one's feet will be rejected by local people, and it is not allowed to point things to others with feet, which is the biggest taboo of Thai people.

Therefore, when dealing with Thai people, it's very important to understand their "dos and don'ts" in advance.

Intercultural Tips 跨文化拓展知识

跨文化训练的方式

胡文仲（2005）引用 Brislin 的总结，对六类跨文化训练的方式做了如下介绍。

第一类跨文化训练以信息介绍为主。比如，介绍某个国家的历史和文化习俗等情况，可以通过作演讲、播放录像、提供阅读材料、组织讨论等方式。这种训练方式较传统，也是相对比较容易的一类方式。

第二类跨文化训练以原因分析为主。常见的做法是提供一件发生在对象国的反映文化冲突的事件（通常是真实发生的事情，而非杜撰），然后，被训练者需要从训练者提供的几种不同的解释中选出他认为合理的那一种解释，然后与正确的答案作比较并据此与训练者展开讨论。这是一种比较受欢迎的训练方式。

第三类是提高文化敏感度的训练。这是提高一般文化敏感度的训练方式。受训者通过活动对自己的文化有所了解，从而举一反三，了解文化的特性，并进而了解其他的文化。

第四类是改变认知行为的训练。这种方式使用较少。这种方式的要领是提高受训者的认知水平，并进而改变他们的行为模式。

第五类是体验型的训练。体验型的训练又可以分为两种方法：一种是使用角色扮演，通过角色扮演使学习者体会在跨文化交际中的困难和问题；另一种是组织受训者参加田野作业（field trip），人为地制造另一种文化环境，让受训者在这种环境中学会解决各种问题的能力。

第六类是互动式的训练。在训练中，受训者与请来的客人——另一种文化的代表或专家——进行交往，在交往中学习对方的文化习俗，学会各种交际的技巧。

值得注意的是，以上方式可以交叉使用，互为补充，它们之间没有互斥性。

 Movie to See 观影学文化

Please watch the movie *Babel*（《通天塔》）with your classmates and discuss what intercultural elements are involved in it.

参考文献

[1] 班固.汉书(第06册)[M].颜师古,注.北京:中华书局,2000.
[2] 冯友兰.中国哲学简史[M].北京:北京大学出版社,2013.
[3] 国务院侨务办公室.中国文化常识[M].北京:高等教育出版社,2007.
[4] 郭素红.20世纪中国《论语》文献学研究回顾与展望[J].东疆学刊,2007(1):23-26.
[5] 韩鉴堂.中国文化[M].北京:北京语言文化大学出版社,2000.
[6] 河北省文物研究所定州汉墓竹简整理小组.定州汉墓竹简《论语》[M].北京:文物出版社,1997.
[7] 姜亚洲,黄志成.作为核心素养的跨文化素养:欧盟的经验与启示[J].比较教育研究,2018(11):52-57.
[8] 靳晓燕.研究报告指出:未来公民七大素养最受重视[N].光明日报,2016-06-06(8).
[9] 世界文化多样性宣言[OL].联合国教科文组织官网,2012[2021-06-05].http://unesdoc.unesco.org/images/0012/001246/124687c.pdf#page=84.html.
[10] 梁启超.梁启超全集(卷17):古书真伪及其年代(1926—1928)[M].北京:北京出版社,1999.
[11] 李盈,王健.跨文化视角下的北美与中国文化[M].北京:高等教育出版社,2014.
[12] 司马迁.史记(上卷)[M].银川:宁夏人民出版社,1994.
[13] 唐明贵.论语学史[M].北京:中国社会科学出版社,2009.
[14] 汤勤福.《论语》选评[M].上海:上海古籍出版社,2006.
[15] 王晖.中国文化与跨文化交际[M].北京:商务印书馆,2017.
[16] 王燕.跨文化商务交际[M].武汉:武汉理工大学出版社,2011.
[17] 王晓毅.王弼《论语释疑》研究[J].齐鲁学刊,1993(5):94-96.
[18] 王催春.跨文化交际[M].4版.大连:大连理工大学出版社,2020.
[19] 杨筱霞.跨文化商务交际[M].大连:大连理工大学出版社,2012.
[20] 詹作琼.跨文化商务英语交际[M].重庆:重庆大学出版社,2016.
[21] 祖晓梅.跨文化交际[M].北京:外语教学与研究出版社,2015.
[22] 张智远.跨文化管理案例[M].北京:经济科学出版社,2015.
[23] 张力群.翻译与跨文化交际[M].北京:对外经济贸易大学出版社,2013.
[24] 朱熹.四书章句集注(上)[M].金良年,译.上海:上海古籍出版社,2006.
[25] 张岱年.孔子大辞典[M].上海:上海辞书出版社,1993.
[26] 周小微.跨文化商务交际[M].北京:对外经济贸易大学出版社,2011.
[27] 庄恩平.跨文化商务沟通教程:阅读与案例[M].上海:上海外语教育出版社,2018.
[28] 贝剑铭.茶在中国:一部宗教和文化史[M].北京:中国工人出版社,2019.
[29] 陈金海.中国传统文化[M].2版.北京:北京出版社,2019.
[30] 陈荣,庄军平.咖啡学概论[M].广州:华南理工大学出版社,2020.
[31] 窦卫霖.跨文化商务交流案例分析[M].北京:对外经济贸易大学出版社,2012.
[32] 冯雪燕,杨汉瑜.中国传统文化[M].济南:山东大学出版社,2018.
[33] 弗朗索瓦·艾蒂安.咖啡实用指南[M].南京:江苏凤凰科学技术出版社,2021.

[34] 胡文仲.英美文化辞典[M].北京:外语教学与研究出版社,1995.
[35] 李常磊.英美文化博览[M].上海:上海世界图书出版公司,2000.
[36] 林晓欣,曹丽敏.中国传统文化[M].南昌:江西高校出版社,2020.
[37] 乔丹·米歇尔曼.咖啡新规则[M].黄俊豪,译.北京:中信出版集团,2021.
[38] 钱放.商务礼仪[M].2版.武汉:武汉理工大学出版社,2013.
[39] 汤忠钢.传统文化与人文精神[M].北京:光明日报出版社,2020.
[40] 王琦,舒卷,朱凤梅."一带一路"沿线国家商务礼俗一本通(汉英对照)[M].成都:西南交通大学出版社,2017.
[41] 王霁.中国传统文化[M].北京:清华大学出版社,2014.
[42] 王淑花.英美文化博览[M].北京:科学出版社,2013.
[43] 肖坤学.美国文化知识一本通[M].广州:暨南大学出版社,2016.
[44] 西东社编辑部.咖啡事典[M].郑寒,译.沈阳:辽宁科学技术出版社,2020.
[45] 杨奎武.英美概况[M].3版.长春:吉林科学技术出版社,2001.
[46] 叶朗,朱良志.中国文化读本:普及本[M].北京:外语教学与研究出版社,2016.
[47] 张斌.中国传统文化概论[M].长春:吉林出版集团股份有限公司,2020.
[48] 郑晓泉.跨文化交际[M].杭州:浙江大学出版社,2010.
[49] 蔡卫,游飞.美国电影艺术史[M].北京:中国传媒大学出版社,2009.
[50] 恒宽.盐铁论注译[M].合肥:安徽大学出版社,2012.
[51] 江康宁.美国概况:美国社会、历史和文化[M].南京:东南大学出版社,2011.
[52] 李盈,王健.跨文化视角下的北美与中国文化[M].北京:高等教育出版社,2014.
[53] 梁漱溟.中国文化要义[M].上海:学林出版社,1987.
[54] 林晓欣,曹丽敏.中国传统文化[M].南昌:江西高校出版社,2020.
[55] 刘沛.美国音乐教育概况[M].上海:上海教育出版社,1998.
[56] 裘姬新,王海表.走进美国[M].杭州:浙江大学出版社,2014.
[57] 袁娟,潘山.中国传统文化选讲[M].镇江:江苏大学出版社,2020.
[58] 袁明.美国文化与社会十五讲[M].北京:北京大学出版社,2015.
[59] 朱世达.当代美国文化[M].北京:社会科学文献出版社,2011.
[60] 安小可.跨文化交际[M].重庆:重庆大学出版社,2019.
[61] 蔡青.跨文化交流[M].2版.北京:北京交通大学出版社,清华大学出版社,2018.
[62] 蔡仲林,周之华.武术[M].3版.北京:高等教育出版社,2015.
[63] 杜瑞清,田德新,李本现.跨文化交际学[M].西安:西安交通大学出版社,2004.
[64] 高校公共体育选项可教材编写组.武术[M].2版.北京:北京体育大学出版社,2007.
[65] 胡文仲.跨文化交际学概论[M].北京:外语教学与研究出版社,2005.
[66] 林友标,章瞬娇.醒狮[M].广州:暨南大学出版社,2013.
[67] 刘凤霞.跨文化交际教程[M].北京:北京大学出版社,2016.
[68] 莫爱屏,莫凡.跨文化交际教程[M].北京:北京大学出版社,2016.
[69] 瞿明安.中国婚礼通志[M].北京:商务印书馆,2020.
[70] 闻度.中华民族婚礼(大陆篇)[M].北京:文化发展出版社,2021.
[71] 余卫华,谌莉.跨文化交际教程[M].杭州:浙江大学出版社,2019.
[72] 张永刚.太极运动[M].北京:北京体育大学出版社,2008.
[73] 于群.跨文化能力:学习与实训[M].南京:南京大学出版社,2020.
[74] 朱建新,刘玉君.跨文化交际与礼仪[M].南京:东南大学出版社,2019.
[75] 隋虹.跨文化交际:理论与实践[M].武汉:武汉大学出版社,2018.

[76] 王海华,徐瑾,许琳. 跨文化商务交际[M]. 大连:大连理工大学出版社,2020.

[77] 刘从梅. 民俗体育与民俗体育文化[M]. 南昌:江西高校出版社,2019.

[78] 张桂萍. 跨文化交际:中英文化对比[M]. 北京:外语教学与研究出版社,2019.

[79] 陆宇榕,王印,陈永浩. 体育文化与健康教育探究[M]. 北京:新华出版社,2018.

[80] 任晓霏,刘锋,余红艳.跨文化交际与国际中文教育[M]. 南京:东南大学出版社,2019.

[81] 杨文秀.英汉语中的隐性礼貌策略研究[M]. 南京:南京大学出版社,2018.

[82] 陈新仁.语用身份论[M]. 北京:北京师范大学出版社,2017.

[83] 林友标,章瞬娇.醒狮[M]. 广州:暨南大学出版社,2013.

[84] 钮力书.近代以来粤侨与广东体育发展研究[M]. 广州:暨南大学出版社,2020.

[85] 安素红,吴雷波. 中医护理学[M]. 上海:上海交通大学出版社,2018.

[86] 柯威. 跨文化商务英语交际[M]. 重庆:重庆大学出版社,2017.

[87] 李晓红. 酒店英语[M]. 北京:中国人民大学出版社,2021.

[88] 吕维霞,刘彦波. 现代商务礼仪[M]. 3 版.北京:对外经济贸易大学出版社,2016.

[89] 冯修文.文秘英语[M]. 北京:中国人民大学出版社,2018.

[90] 金焕. 现代商务礼仪[M]. 3 版.北京:电子工业出版社,2020.

[91] 金正昆. 现代商务礼仪[M]. 3 版.北京:中国人民大学出版社,2021.

[92] 景韵.酒店应用英语[M]. 上海:复旦大学出版社,2015.

[93] 秦伯未. 中医入门[M]. 北京:人民卫生出版社,2020.

[94] 简亚平,沈小平.中医护理学[M]. 2 版. 大连:大连理工大学出版社,2018.

[95] 孙秋华. 中医护理学[M]. 4 版.北京:人民卫生出版社,2017.

[96] 文旭. 跨文化交际教程[M]. 北京:中国人民大学出版社,2015.

[97] 王君华,韩福乐.点击职业英语职业英语模块酒店英语学生频道[M]. 2 版.大连:大连理工大学出版社,2014.

[98] 王茹,胡燕. 秘书英语实务[M]. 2 版.北京:中国人民大学出版社,2019.

[99] 张颖,唐娇. 商务与社交礼仪[M]. 北京:北京理工大学出版社,2019.

[100] DAVIS L. 中西文化之鉴——跨文化交际教程[M]. 北京:外语教学与研究出版社,1999.

[101] 左显兰. 商务谈判与礼仪[M]. 北京:机械工业出版社,2014.

[102] 李建峰,骆云梅.跨文化交际理论与实践研究[M]. 长春:吉林大学出版社,2020.

[103] 仝慧. 探索与解读——独具特色的俄罗斯文化探析[M]. 北京:新华出版社,2020.

[104] 梁悦,李莹.商务礼仪实务英语[M]. 2 版.北京:对外经济贸易大学出版社,2020.

[105] 陈宝翠,李东伟. 跨文化交际案例阅读[M]. 成都:西南交通大学出版社, 2017.

[106] 房玉靖,姚颖.跨文化交际实训[M]. 2 版.北京:对外经济贸易大学出版社,2014.

[107] 熊丽君,刘学华. 跨文化交际学[M]. 上海:上海交通大学出版社,2010.

[108] 廖华英. 跨文化交际案例分析[M]. 北京:北京理工大学出版社,2010.

[109] 杜瑞清,田德新,等.跨文化交际学选读[M]. 西安:西安交通大学出版社,2004.

[110] 胡文仲.英美文化辞典[M]. 北京:外语教学与研究出版社,1995.

[111] 张海英.中国传统节日与文化[M]. 太原:书海出版社,2006.

[112] 徐亮. 知道点中国文化[M]. 南昌:二十一世纪出版社,2006.

[113] 王奕飞. 你不可不知的中国文化精华[M]. 北京:新世界出版社,2007.

[114] 刘珊. 苏州园林[M]. 南京:江苏凤凰美术出版社,2019.

[115] 舒静庐. 亚洲国家礼仪[M]. 上海:上海三联书店,2014.

[116] 戚盛中. 泰国民俗与文化[M]. 北京:北京大学出版社,2017.